# PALE GREEN ROOM

A novel by

ELIZABETH WILDE McCORMICK

**Brigand**
London

Copyright © Elizabeth Wilde McCormick

The moral right of the author has been asserted.
All rights reserved. No part of the publication
may be reproduced or transmitted in any form
or by any means, without permission.

Brigand Press,
All contact: info@brigand.london

British Library Cataloguing-in-Publication Data
A catalogue record for this book is
available from the British Library
Printed and Bound in Great Britain by
Datum Creative Media Limited

ISBN: 978-1-912978-40-3

Also by Elizabeth Wilde McCormick
Non-fiction
*The Heart Attack Recovery Book* 1984, 1989 Optima
*Surviving Breakdown* 1989, 1990, 1997 Vermillion
*Change For The Better* 1990, 2002, 2008, 2012, 2017 Sage
*Healing The Heart* 1994 Optima
*Living On The Edge* 1997, 2007 Sage
*Your Heart And You* (with Dr. Leisa Freeman) 2002 Piatkus
With Nigel Wellings
*Transpersonal Psychotherapy, Theory And Practice 2000* Sage
*Nothing To Lose* 2004, 2012 Woodyard Publications
*Present With Suffering* 2022 Karnac Books
Fiction
*The Ruthless Furnace* 2019 Brigand
*Wordless Threads* 2023 Brigand

# Acknowledgements

The first draft of this novel was completed in 2009, but it took me until 2011 to feel able to complete the project fully and the first publication, which I undertook myself, was that year. I owe a debt of gratitude to several people who always believed in it, in particular my sister Dr Jane Buckle, my thanks for keeping me going and for your faith in the story.

My friends Annalee Curran, Rosemary Cook, the late Susan Needham, and my daughter Nicky Wilde all read early drafts and made helpful suggestions and comments. My friend and colleague Margaret Landale helped me to make the decision to take time from professional work to commit to it, and my children, Simon, Kate and Nicky Wilde frequently chided me to return to work with the imagination, with narrative and story. Thank you, everyone.

It is not easy to write a novel one is satisfied with, and the shift between writing non-fiction and fiction has been complex. I would like to thank all the people who have supported me in many ways, my Suffolk sangha, my close colleagues and friends, throughout these recent years of writing.

In 2011 my husband Keith Maunder meticulously prepared the manuscript for the original printing and electronic publication. Elaine Leek, copy editor on my works of non-fiction, worked on the manuscript over Christmas. My friend and co-author of three non-fiction titles Nigel Wellings helped me to settle on the title. And in recent years I have been most fortunate that The Pale Green Room has been taken on by the publishers, Brigand London, who now publish the entire Dr Max trilogy. *The Pale Green Room*, the first of the trilogy has been followed by *The Ruthless Furnace* and *Wordless Threads*.

I am most grateful to Peter Holland and Scott Pearce for their interest and support for my fictional work.

## Author's declaration

This is a work of fiction. Any similarities with persons, living or dead, is purely coincidental. No characters, life events, psychological material, images, dreams, have been drawn from my professional work as a psychotherapist.

# 1

SHE had to drive south over Hammersmith Bridge to get to his rooms. "Dr Max Maxwell. Psychotherapist." His appointment card was like hers, plain white with black lettering: "5pm Wednesday September 14th 2005."

The collective damp of continual rain made the fallen sycamore leaves cling to the soles of her shoes as she walked across the hospital car park. Limpets. "Get on with it," she wanted to say to the wet laden branches. "Get it over with; just die so we can clean you up."

She had forced her eyes to glance to left and right, checking to see if her suspicions of a mystery follower might be confirmed. No movement. Perhaps she had thrown him off. Perhaps it was her imagination. She shook her head. *Too much, too much.*

London rush hour traffic was already filling the roads and she found herself waiting on the bridge, suspended. She lit a cigarette and stared down river through the autumn haze towards Westminster. Evening lights blurred and smeared the landscape in the way of a Monet or Turner. She thought of the river bending around the Palace of Westminster, the heart of political power, flowing on to the new glass towers built in worship to another kind of power. Money and The City of London.

*Not unlike the conglomeration in Hong Kong Harbour.*
"No! I won't go there."

Feeling a slight nausea, she turned her gaze to the right, where the Thames flowed by the leafy gardens of Kew and Richmond, and small boats could be moored alongside. She swallowed hard, her breathing shallow, coming from the flat upper part of her chest. That familiar grip in the sides of her neck nagged as it had all day. "Hell." Whatever she did, or told herself, she was cornered. She tried to twist her head from side to side to relieve the iron grip that went from her neck down the length of her spine and spun up into her head. She raised her shoulders then dropped them, trying to relax, as she, Dr Saxon Pierce, advised her cardiac patients.

She had been forced to agree to a professional assessment as to her state of mind; to actually go and see a shrink, and one on the wrong side of London at that!

Underneath her coursed the hidden currents of those murky Thames waters.

*That swell of water. The boat heaving. The heavy babe in arms. Why had she asked to hold it? What on earth was she doing?*

She had agreed to see a colleague, a proper neurologist, after what she referred to as the "Hong Kong business". What he had said remained a blur. He used phrases such as "prolonged stress" and the "accumulative toll on the nervous system". She remembered his Scottish brogue and sailing metaphors: "you're a fine strong woman and a fine doctor, but this... er this ... event has plunged you into new waters. You must have a skilled navigator." He had been firm, and kind; the metaphors something of a relief.

She hated the idea of submitting herself to such a personal encounter with someone she knew nothing about, to something so unstructured as psychotherapy. She hated the thought of her childhood being raked about. There were so many things she had successfully buried. She comforted herself by hoping that Dr Max wouldn't be any good and she could just leave.

*But she couldn't leave. This time she couldn't leave.* This time it was truly serious. Her future career, her relationship, her freedom, were no longer secure.

*She saw the image of the child again: a small bundle, wrapped in blue, suspended in the air over the waters of Hong Kong Harbour.*

She banished it immediately.

*Sink, swim or be saved.*

She had refused to see a woman. Far too emotional, and competitive. Most of her colleagues were men and she preferred dealing with men. She hoped that Dr Maxwell, with his neat black-and-white appointment card, was properly qualified for what he had to do and would just get on with it. No messing about. Sort out what had happened, give her a prescription. Then she could carry on her life as she always had.

*Just stay in control,* she advised herself. Do what the doctor orders. It was what she said to her own patients. But there was the fear: *a shrink might make things worse.*

* * * *

The room was painted a pale green. It was the shade of green she had once been told that butcher's chose for their shops. It made their meat look rich – juicy pickings.

Dull, flat, pale, a butcher's green.

The furniture coverings and worn carpet cushioning the stone floor were also mainly shades of green. There were muslin curtains at the one small window that looked onto the heath. The two battered looking chairs had old-fashioned green print covers, and the couch was covered in dark olive-coloured velvet. *I will never, never submit myself to that!* There were books on the green shelves, mostly hardbacks with faded gold lettering, a filing cabinet and a few rather strange pictures.

But soon after entering, she felt the room begin to blur. Suddenly she was alone with another human being, where *she* was the patient. She started to feel very cold.

He invites her to sit in one of the green chairs, identical to his, placed at a slight angle. This means that she does not have to look at him. She feels wrong-footed in front with no doctor's desk or table in between, and then irritated by the modern fad for informality in the professional workplace. Her desk was her fortress and sanctuary. Behind it she had authority. It gave patients confidence. And here she was within toe-touching distance of a strange man who could see her whole body, and she his. He had smiled mildly after opening the door himself, and she was alarmed that he looked about her own age when she was expecting someone much older. His dark hair and brown eyes seemed oddly familiar. His crumpled corduroy trousers and old tweed jacket were too big for him. He needed a shave, and the collar ends of his blue checked shirt were frayed. In contrast, she wore a smartly tailored, plain grey suit with straight skirt and oyster pink silk shirt. The pale blue Murano beads reflected her blue eyes and complemented her pale complexion and fair hair. She was proud to cultivate the classic English looks she had inherited from her English grandmother. She crosses her long legs and waits for him to begin.

He sits very still, his hands resting lightly upon each other in his lap, and silence opens between them. He has one paragraph from the referral letter in his mind "she has been involved in a tragic accident with a baby". He notices the feel and energy of her and wonders who she really is and where she will take him. Still, he says nothing, and as she cannot think of anything to say, her irritation rises. She wags her crossed leg up and down. For heaven's sake! She is furious at the lack of format. It confirms her belief that psychotherapy is a contrivance for self-indulgence. Totally unscientific. How on earth could this sort of thing help?

But as she drums her fingers on the arms of the chair, waiting for him to do his job, her fire subsides, and the earlier coldness rises, leaving her with damp sweaty palms and uneasiness.

Aware of her discomfort, Max speaks. "Welcome, Dr Pierce." He is looking at her clearly and directly, relaxed and at home with himself. "Alan Mayers suggested you come."

"Yes," relief makes her speak quickly, "he's my colleague from King's days. I suppose he believes in all this." She sweeps the air with her arm.

Max looks mildly interested. "All this?" he asks.

"Yes, all this ... this talking cure." Perhaps if she quoted Freud he would know she knew a thing or two and get on with it. But he remains looking at her seriously and she begins to be concerned she's been so flippant. There is a new awkwardness, and then, rage. She's not going to let him think she's a fool and can easily be taken for a ride! Just get on with it, she thinks, then I can get out of here!

"Do you mean that you don't?" he asks, still serious. For some reason she cannot answer. Silence again.

She struggles on, her body cold, her mouth dry, wanting to leave. "Surely you've read the report from Alan Mayers," she says sharply, haughty now.

He is looking at her thoughtfully, sizing her up. Quiet. Slow.

"I wanted to meet you and hear about things from you first."

She is taken off guard. Her mouth opens, but words do not form.

Then something strange happens inside her body that she presumes is to do with digestion. The pale green room watches what appears to be a substance like jelly manifesting inside her stomach. Saxon feels the green walls swim; she feels sick. When the sensation does not go away she worries that something unknown is trying to force itself forward. She might even throw up. She must not let this happen. She blinks, holding onto the green arms of the chair.

"Would you like to say something about what's brought you here?" asks Max. His voice is quiet and slow, but solid.

"Do you mean to say you really don't know? Don't people get properly passed on in your profession?" Through speaking sharply she brings the room back in focus.

His brown eyes study her, and he says firmly, "I'd like to hear from you, what has brought you here."

"But you know about what happened in Hong Kong?" Her jaw is tight, her voice icy. The unpleasant sickness threatens to return. She feels a boiling heat. *Cool it down, cool it.*

"I know that you have been involved in a tragic incident in Hong Kong." Intuitively he does not say the word 'baby'. "Will you tell me about it yourself, how it all happened?"

*Incident. That's putting it mildly. Body ice cold now, overheat, green room definitely swimming. Green ice over the heated cauldron. Those tall glass buildings pressed close to the harbour waters.*

*Long silence. Only just breathing. Dr Maxwell invisible.*

*Once again three years old, surrendering to the inevitable, trying to be brave, trying to tell the truth. Knowing that no one would believe.*

"All right," she says through her clenched jaw. "If I really have to." Her breathing is chaotic; rapid pulse and pressured arteries making every breath an effort.

"There was a kid," voice almost a whisper, dull, flat. She gulps, then gets bolder. "Stupid parents. Gave it me to hold. Next thing I know, it's in the filthy water." *Defiant. Fierce. Ice green retreating. But, in the unnamed, unknown space inside, something else. She cannot place it.*

*Then an image: Three years old, woken in the night by shouting; stumbling along black night corridors and an open door, onto red and white ...*

The green room holds both images for a few seconds

then they quickly disappear. The energy has become sticky, like the wet leaves outside. Secrets are being touched and awakened. The room holds all in its pale green balm.

He is still looking at her, listening. Listening in a different way from doctors. She feels stupid. "I'm sorry," she rushes, smoothing the fabric of her skirt, wanting the room to grow arms to envelop her in simple acceptance, never to have to speak again.

Then another image, linked to the sensation of softness: *A floor of moss, bright green, furry with little hairs, and spores lifting from the emerald pile. So soft, touching her face. Her secret. Sitting under the arms of tree branches. A space to breathe, a place to be little.* She strokes the silk sleeve of her shirt under the jacket, still looking down.

Back in the room she feels stupid again, years of professional training out of reach. And what for? Where is this getting her?

"Stupid parents?" he says, the question hanging in the air.

She stares at him, and then at the green floor. In a flat automatic voice, she answers: "They were all agog ... you know ... the way new parents are. This ... brat ... was everything, apple of the eye ... all that stuff. Ogling it. Everyone had had to hold it, coo at it. They made themselves look so stupid, all fisheyes and open mouths, billing and cooing."

He stays with her as if he too is imagining the scene.

"How did all that ... billing and cooing ... make you feel?"

"I don't suppose I have any feelings about it at all," she says hotly, the unknown interior force under control. Jelly nowhere to be seen. The room feels more normal. "I can't abide that sort of thing; it's all so unnecessary." A nannyish tone has entered her voice. *Body hunched over, closed, like a dog grounded. Green walls have sharp edges. Room seems larger.* The room had a patience that was unending.

"And the brat?" He uses her word.

She pulls a face. "Just a brat I suppose." She looks down. *Body cold, fist, clenched, eyes hot.* A long way off she knows he is measuring her, but with what she cannot tell. A long way off she senses something nasty coming.

He takes a risk: "What was it like holding it?"

She gets up quickly, and walks towards the door, hands clasped together away from her body as if they do not belong to her, not looking at him. "No!" she yells, blue eyes tightly closed, fists banging against fists. "No!" She is close to the door. Her breathing is heavy and strained. Then, suddenly, as if some internal observer clicks into place, she breathes in deeply, lowers her voice and turns around. In a new tone, quite different from before she says, "Is all this necessary? You haven't asked me any proper details about myself. You don't know me, about me." She jabs her finger into her chest. She shakes her head as she speaks, as if shaking herself back into life. "I'm a professional doctor like yourself. Dr Saxon Pierce, forty-five years old. I work at Albion General Hospital, specialising in cardiology. I like the work very much. I'm good at it and I get good results. I'm not married. I have no children and have never wanted any. I have a... a... companion. I have a very nice house in Notting Hill Gate. My parents... I can tell you about them and then you can get a picture of me and make your diagnosis in the same way that I do..."

She tails off as if suddenly losing steam. Despite her impressive credentials and smart suit, she looks young and lost.

"Please, sit down." Again, that firm, kind, assured, knowing-what-he-was-doing voice.

She sits on the edge of the couch rather than back in the green chair, which means that she is opposite him, nearer physically, but she does not appear to notice this. She wraps both arms around her chest, and remains looking down with head bent and the toes of her elegant high-heeled shoes point inwards, each touching the other.

There is a time between them, not too uncomfortable, both evolving a way of being together similar to that of animals as they sniff around each other after an initial standoff.

"This is an exploratory session, to see whether and in what way psychotherapy can be of use to you," he says. "It can be an uncomfortable process when you are not familiar with it, and we work in very different ways from the medical model. My task is to help both of us make sense of what has happened to you, without judgement. I can see that just being here evokes really difficult feelings for you. I understand that there was a baby involved in this incident. This is an extremely traumatic experience, and I understand that just yet you would not be able to speak of it."

She cannot look at him even though some part of her knows that his brown eyes are kind. "I can see that my questions about the accident are premature, and I am sorry for this, but this has also indicated to me that if we are to work together we must go very slowly." He pauses and it was all she could do not to run out of the room.

"I understand that your Health Authority has asked you to take some time out from seeing patients and that the assessment with Alan Mayers suggested psychotherapy. Therapy only works if we both work together. I am not a surgeon who cuts bits out and replaces worn parts with new ones whilst my patient is unconscious. The work of psychotherapy is about healing wounds that are not usually visible." He speaks slowly, wanting to engage with her, part of him repelled by her cold dissociation but his heart already stirred by her suffering.

"I can see that my questions have made you anxious," she opens her mouth to deny this, but he carries on. "I can see that what happened in Hong Kong has had a big impact upon you, that it has triggered feelings that are most probably linked to past experiences."

The pale green of the room has taken on a soft, almost luminous quality.

"It feels as if there is a part of you which might be very fragile and which feels a bit out of control, and that this is a frightening prospect when so much of your life is spent having to be in control." His voice is steady, relaxed, it holds her there.

"The hope is that in the time we have, you and I can begin to understand the nature of the fragility that has been brought to light by what happened, and what kind of help or, healing, this might need."

She thinks she might cry, which she hates, and she fights hard to control herself. She must not let him win. She hates him in his corduroy smugness. He doesn't have this nightmare hanging over him! She hates him and his kind for what they do to people. The first appointment. So soon, so near to tears.

Any serenity in the room evaporates and the sharp green edges return. But that something inside her about which she knows nothing, something small and animal-like, begins to stir as she leaves the room.

\* \* \* \*

Earlier that day Max had seen another new patient who had come reluctantly, and about whom he felt unsure.

She sat so still it was hard to believe she could be breathing.

Her idea of what was supposed to happen in a 'shrink's office' came only from the movies. Barbra Streisand and Nick Nolte in *The Prince of Tides*. The therapist was always powerful. Nick Nolte had ended up in Barbra Streisand's arms. That would serve Alistair right! She took a sideways look at Max. He was powerful in a doctor sort of way, but badly dressed. Nothing matched. His jacket looked as if it hadn't always been his. He looked tired, badly shaven, with bags under his eyes.

Max could smell the fear in her, the immaculate hair and bright red suit an attempted defence against terror. Her black-stockinged legs were held tightly together, dainty feet in very high heels tucked under the base of the chair.

He says: "Welcome, Mrs Dodds. How are you?"

She does not know how to answer. She does not know what she is supposed to say.

Apart from *The Prince of Tides*, what she knew about the process of therapy came from the problem pages of magazines and her friend Coral. Counselling and therapy were always on offer immediately after any crisis; or it was for people who had been abused, had an eating disorder, had become depressed. And yes, her heart sinking, people went to a therapist when their relationships went wrong. It was everywhere now, radio, TV and magazines, the scores of rejected women screaming.

But Vera would not scream. She wanted to cope, and to wait. Wait until Alistair came to his senses. She was not weak; she had no need to talk to a stranger about her personal life.

Under the sharp edges of the tailored fashion suit she wore a black cashmere sweater, which tucked into a wide leather belt at her waist. A black lace-edged bodysuit moulded her firm-breasted body. Her black hair was thick and sleek, framing her olive complexion; her make-up was perfect. She had schooled herself in perfect presentation and proper behaviour. She would betray no outward sign of turmoil.

She had been waiting for a sign from Alistair, that he was feeling guilty and was regretting leaving. It was he who had made this contact with the Dr Max he had known of at Oxford. She was going along with it because it might be a bridge, a connection back to Alistair. She wondered how she should play it. Should she act broken and suicidal so that Max would tell Alistair and make him feel bad? No, that was what her mother might have done. Should she try to make Max want her, make Alistair jealous? Could she still do that? She had never looked at another man since marrying at eighteen.

Max decides to be practical: "I realise that it is probably strange for you to visit a therapist – not something you would normally choose.

"Your husband and I were at Oxford at the same time but have not met since. He sought me out on your behalf, and I know that it was his suggestion that you come here, and not your own. But this hour we meet in is your own. It's completely confidential and I will not be speaking to him about anything that happens here."

Well, that rules that out then! She was on her own here.

"I just want to say that I am sorry to hear that your husband has left the family home."

*Pompous or what!* she thinks inside her red shell. But she remains sitting very still. The smell of fear grows stronger.

"How are you managing at home?"

She has no idea what's allowed. She was no complainer: she just got on with it.

"I'll be alright I suppose," she says in a little voice.

Max smiles. "Does all of you feel that?"

His smile gives her courage, and permission.

"I miss my boys. It's dreadful. The whole thing is a terrible shock. They don't know yet. It's a mistake." She speaks in bursts, awkward, her heart racing.

Max watches her, wondering what is going on behind the doll-like mask.

"What made you come?" he asks.

She is very quiet. Then she turns her head and says, "Well it's something, isn't it? Something he's offered. He's not offered anything else. No thought of me or what is to become of me. I don't even have his telephone number!"

"That must be so very hard. I am sorry."

She is not used to sympathy. "He just doesn't care anymore I suppose." She says it as if she has only just realised it. She feels shocked, and then, ashamed. She is just a rejected woman, on the scrap heap like so many other women past their sell by date.

Max senses her feeling of shame.

"I can see that it has hit you very hard. I know that you have known Alistair a long time, and been married —"

"Twenty-one years," she breaks in. "Twenty-one years. I put my heart and soul into it!" She suddenly looks at him directly for the first time. Her dark brown eyes are full of intensity and passion. Something in her look stirs a memory. Max nods. They sit for a while in silence.

"And now …"

"He's gone off, hasn't he? Some smart upper-class woman. I'm an embarrassment and an inconvenience. I don't fit his Tory Party aspirations. I'm working class and born the wrong side of the blanket."

Max hasn't heard that phrase for a long time. He is struck by the refreshing robustness under her mask that shakes off the fear and shame.

Then she says, again shakily, with hurt in her voice, "I suppose he just doesn't care about me anymore."

Max pauses, "What's that like for you?"

"It's… it's … awful." The realisation, through words, intensifies her feeling. "And it's … it's not fair. I've done nothing wrong!"

She looks at him and he sees passionate eyes carrying the despair of a wounded animal caught in a cleverly set trap. Puzzlement, and hurt. For Max, another memory.

"I don't know what will become of me," she says quietly.

Max thinks: you discard your loyal wife of twenty years and send her to a therapist. How insulting. How cunning.

"Let's discuss how these sessions might be of use to you, for all that you are going through, if indeed they can be of use – because you don't have to continue to come if your heart is not in them. The most important person here is you." He pauses.

"Thank you," she whispers.

"Do you have a sense of what might be most useful for you? What do you feel you need most at present?"

"I should have thought that was bloody obvious," she says tartly, her flat Northern vowels coming through more strongly. Then, hand over mouth, "Sorry, I didn't mean to be rude."

He realises his question is foolish because she has no idea what she needs other than for life to go on as it always has, in Alistair's shadow. He wonders what she was like before Alistair and how much she has moulded herself onto his needs. And before that, as a child, how did she play, to whom did she relate? Now that she is sitting in his room he remembers seeing her once at an Oxford reunion, across the long dining hall. She was heavily pregnant, and her olive skin glowed with health. She looked radiant, happy and beautiful. At that time Max was about to take up his life with a monastic order in Switzerland and beautiful women were a curiosity. What he did remember were her hands; that a woman, so petite and doll-like, had such strong hands.

Vera doesn't like the silence of not knowing what to say. She doesn't know what the point of coming here might be. Her friend Lucy from school had said in her last Christmas letter that she was having therapy after a breakdown and had used the expression 'inner life'. Coral, a trained yoga teacher now, often used that phrase. What was it, and did she need it? Was an inner life now the requisite of women on their own?

"How did the separation happen?"

"He just said it. In the car of all places. Ninety miles an hour. After we had taken Luke ..." Her body bends forward as if she as been punched and she closes her eyes against tears. She's not ready yet to speak of the event.

"How had things been between you up until then?"

She sighs and shrugs, slowly sitting up again. "I thought they were OK. But that's it isn't it, that's what every woman says. Always the last to know what's really going on ... I just thought we were really, really different." She says this firmly, as if she held a secret. Alistair had hinted at something dark until Max had stopped him from revealing more if Vera were to become his patient.

"I knew he'd had other women. But I just thought that's what men did." She looks at him out of the corner of her eye wondering if it was what Max did. "Why does this one have to be different? To make him leave his wife and family? It's not what I want." Her tone is flat and dull.

"No, I see," says Max. He feels tired suddenly. This would be hard work. He wonders again why on earth he has agreed to see her.

\* \* \* \*

Later he stared at his lined notepad and tried to record details of the two new sessions. He felt unusually unsettled. As he rubbed the page with his thumb, he noticed the worn edge of his shirt cuff. The image of another man's tight-laundered creases and gold cufflinks appeared. Alistair. He remembered his smooth voice on the end of the phone late one night: "Looked you up on Google – pretty impressive. Quite the professional expert I see!"

Why had he picked up the phone that night? It was a month ago. His re-entry to work after a long, glorious Suffolk summer had been difficult. As well as his regular patients coming back from the summer break, a colleague at the health centre had hanged himself after being stalked by an ex-patient. His garage had been broken into and his bicycle stolen, and his bad leg was getting more difficult to manage. Sometimes he limped badly.

Too much, and not enough space to process it all. That night he'd felt as if he'd had no summer break at all. He'd opened a bottle of red wine.

Alistair was apparently "just round the corner". Max heard again the purring of the Jaguar outside... recalled the smell of the expensive after-shave when Alistair came in. Not only did he look Max up, he looked him over. Whatever credentials had impressed him on Google were soon eclipsed. Max saw himself now through Alistair's eyes – shabby by Armani standards, tired, living in modest accommodation –– on the wrong side of the river. The threadbare rugs and drab walls, the old armchairs covered in blankets. And, if he had known it, a sick wife in bed upstairs.

Although Max felt repelled by the world of commercial infighting and greed that Alistair inhabited so comfortably and successfully, he recognised that the man's energy and certainty stirred him.

Now he had met the vulnerable, innocent Vera, who was to be discarded so that Alistair could move on. And Max was to be part of it, to make sure that Alistair was seen to tick all the boxes, could not be accused of failing his wife. Worse was that Max suspected that Alistair might use Vera's unstable mental state as a reason for divorce.

Thinking about it now, he realised that Alistair's 'smash and grab' was like a hand grenade tossed in his direction and out to explode something in Max's own life. It felt like war. It felt personal.

What was he getting into? There was a tight feeling in his chest. He sat still in his chair and allowed the sensations to reveal themselves. He breathed into them and the out-breath began softening the hard edges. The feeling under the sensation was pride, and then, fear.

An image: a young lion alert and lonely in the night plain. He did feel alone, despite the people in his life.

When he stood up he felt again the extent of his fatigue. Through his consulting room window, he saw the outline of the maple trees on the street, at the beginning of their journey to full autumn glory and smiled. Here it was then, the herald of change, written into his body response, picking at old wounds, creating anxiety about the future. Life's relentless rhythm meant no resting on laurels or coasting. One had never arrived.

The sensations continued and he allowed them to move in and out of him like the tide on the beach. Sometimes urgent, like water released after being held behind a rock. Images soon followed, offering him connection to a deeper understanding.

He returned to his notes about Dr Saxon Pierce. What a strange name. She was defensive, in denial. What had so terrified her?

The image of the baby hovered, as it must have hovered

over those Hong Kong waters. Those desperate parents, the people on the boat helpless. Who would ever know what had really happened there?

His mind wandered. Shoes with a shiny stripe, the red suit and then red rock. Ayers Rock, the Australian aboriginal Uluru, where some years ago a baby disappeared, and became the focus of lawsuits, miles of newsprint and a film. Because it involved a mother, a baby and a dingo. 'Strewth, the dingos ate my baby!' said some teasing voice in his head. Which of them had killed? It was a subject that invited the storm of victim and villain and a primitive thirst for revenge. If this Saxon Pierce story got out in the press here, would it carry the same fervour? Would he be dragged into it? He and his childless wife?

He could not concentrate. Images of that new-born baby were interspersed with images of Vera, her dark beauty packaged into Alistair's desire. Plucked so young to be fashioned in Alistair's ways. Little sense of herself without the shape he formed for her. And yet the relationship had lasted over twenty years.

He had agreed to see Vera for all the wrong reasons, but he would not let smash and grab win. Right now he wanted that Goya beauty to have a champion, he wanted to help her become strong and stand up to the bastard.

Was he going to get too involved? Wasn't this exactly why therapists didn't work with the family or friends of friends? Too much contamination! He chided himself. And he smiled and thought of those who considered him to be too holy, too untouchable. He was right now just a vulnerable human being feeling his way, maybe getting into deep water. And was it fate that he did have an unexpected space for a new patient? One of his patients had left suddenly, believing the answer lay outside Max's green room – with a guru in southern India.

Max rubbed his large hands over the top of his head, and over the bristles on his jaw, left from shaving in the dark in order not to wake his sleeping wife. Both women had left him with something and the sense of much more to come. What could psychotherapy offer either of these women? And where might they take him?

*The Pale Green Room*

# 2

VERA walked out of Max's green room in her black leather shoes with their red striped backs, feeling churned up inside. She had allowed herself to think something good might come of her appointment, in the same way that when you went to the GP you got a prescription to make you well. She realised now that she had imagined this Dr Max might give some advice that would make Alistair return, and she and her sons could relax back into normal life. But that was what Coral called 'magical thinking'. It had not been like that in the shabby green room, so unlike the rooms of Harley Street specialists with their gold-framed certificates and chandeliers, waiting rooms with copies of *Tatler,* and composed receptionists who signed you in.

The idea that she might have to think and talk about herself in a personal way, what she thought or felt, was discomforting, shocking. "What's the point?" she thought as she opened her car door and wondered what to do next. She slumped in her seat, realising she was south of the river, a long way from anything familiar. No shops for miles. The east wind was tearing the leaves from the trees, casting them off from the security of their branches. She watched them fall to the wet ground, to be trampled by the feet of strangers. She was being cast off too. Her whole life was changing. It was change she hadn't invited and didn't want.

Perhaps nothing could soothe the agony of rejection. And what could she do with the rest of her life? Her eyes filled up and smarted and she was afraid. So far, she had not given in to tears. If she allowed herself to cry she would never stop. She had to cope.

She drove home more or less on automatic, taking wrong turns and losing her way several times. She eventually reached her Pimlico street, noticing her reluctance to go home. This feeling intensified as she registered the space left by Alistair's Jag in the shared car port. A space with the rebuke of something no longer shared.

She sat for a while in the growing darkness, alone in her car outside her now empty home; a home once full of life, colour and noise. She did not want to turn the key onto its current unlit emptiness.

She had taught her boys it was important to 'make welcome' for those returning to a house in darkness. She would turn on the lights, draw the curtains, light candles on the table in readiness for Alistair when he came in from work. She would change from her daywear into clothes for the evening, have a meal ready and ice in the silver bucket. She realised now, from her witness point outside, that as Alistair had returned home later and later these rituals had had to be modified. Too many suppers had congealed in the oven or been cast out in the bin. On too many nights she had gone to bed without him, her evening clothes carefully returned to the wardrobe.

Now she had not the heart to make welcome for herself. By the time she braved the house it was very dark. She made it into the hall without turning on the lights and sat on the bottom stair, resting her head on the expensive dark brown wallpaper with its embossed silver trees. She lifted her hand and traced her fingernail along the silver fur of a branch as she might have done as a child. It tickled her skin and made a slight rasping sound. She had never liked it.

How she had quelled her own opinions! If she dug her nail in deeper, she could peel this wallpaper, now exposed to her awareness as actually hideous, and get to the soft Laura Ashley floral patterns she had pasted on herself when they were newlyweds.

She heard the deep voice of Dr Max from that afternoon asking her about her life with Alistair.

This house had once fulfilled Vera's dreams. Three storeys and two bay windows, two bathrooms, mouldings round the ceilings and skylights lighting the large attic where her children would grow and play; enough of a garden for a cherry tree and a place for the boys' bicycles. And in a street not dissimilar to the one she had been born in, in her grandmother's house in Manchester. Similar, but poles apart.

Her eager, enthusiastic Northern self was excited by making a home. She collected catalogues from magazines and the Ideal Home Exhibition. Alistair was building up his father's business and not interested in décor. She remembered him being quite proud of her homemaking activities. How awkward he could be then around social things, a basically shy Northern boy thrust into the light of London life.

Vera was not fazed by hard work or domesticity.

She was a naturally easy mother. Dominic and Leo, born so soon in the marriage, when she was still so young, the sons Alistair wanted. Then Luke, her last child, had been born here just nine years ago, when Vera turned thirty. He came into life in the bedroom she had shared with Alistair, the room where she could no longer go. Luke. The child she had hoped would make all the difference.

After his father's death Alistair inherited full control of the family retail business and built it into a multi-million pound empire. As his prosperity grew so did his confidence. Pimlico was being gentrified and the Dodds with it. A roof garden and a house 'make-over' involved decorators from the Fulham Road. A drawing room in bronze and turquoise, with swoops and braids imported from France, and the hall of dark brown and silver with mirrors were the result. They mocked Vera's basic homely charm but she subdued any internal protest and silenced her tastes and views. This is what Alistair wanted. She must move with him and find a way of meeting their London status as well as his new chill. Alistair was becoming flash with money, but he cut corners. The ostentatious wallpaper at £50 a roll was put on at weekends by a shifty looking handyman, who had not removed the original paper first. Now, she felt curiously relieved that her gentle Laura Ashley print, fashionable from the 80s, was still intact on the walls, under the decadence.

One visit to a therapist and already I am thinking about things differently, she said to herself, puzzled. These people churn you up. "Do more harm than good if you ask me," she heard her mother's blunt northern tones. Her mother! What did she know based on the perfunctory hospital psychiatric assessments after her suicide attempts. Her mother! She would not contact her mother until she had Alistair back again.

"But," she thought, "how much has changed!" Along with the flounces and tassels came criticism of her, and most hurtful of all, emotional withdrawal. And now Alistair was to replace her as if she too were the old decorations up for renewal. Worse was that her last point of warm human contact, her son Luke, had been sent away to receive the same expensive English public school education as his brothers. She had fought hard against the system that scooped up young boys at a tender age as if their mothers might be poisonous to them. Luke was different from his brothers, who were robust and hearty, sportsmen like their father. Luke was small, asthmatic, sensitive. But she had lost.

Vera remained sitting at the bottom of the stairs thinking about how she had fought against boarding school and how Alistair had interpreted it as her wanting possession of their son. "At least I fought him on that!"

She remembered that when Dominic and Leo had been destined for public school, their names put down even before they were born, she had been proud, still thinking in the way her mother would. But it always felt hollow. It frightened her. She felt swept along by something inevitable that she did not understand and about which she felt helpless.

Somewhere inside her she knew that to send young boys away to boarding school was not right. She wished that Luke could have gone to the local school with Jason, Coral's son. Coral! Where are you now! But Coral was travelling with friends in Sri Lanka, taking Jason with her, not fazed by sending her son back to school late.

It was agony that no one was here. There was no comfort, no routines. The house was abandoned, the boys' rooms silent tombs full of memorabilia – posters, half-made gadgets, evidence of past life. Her aloneness was more cruel for its timing. She had lost her husband at the same time as she had lost her sons.

Just yet, she could not go up the stairs. She wandered into the kitchen and opened cupboards, asking herself if she was hungry. Opening the fridge, she saw a half-used jar of pesto. She had cooked favourite family food, pasta pesto followed by a treacle tart, not knowing this was to be the last meal her family would have together. Their last supper. Alistair had been in jocular and generous mood, shoving cash onto both his older sons. Leo was off to Tanzania on a gap year; Dominic to his first term at Bristol. Alistair had presented Luke with a new flute, but Luke had sat white-faced and silent. The two older boys, hardened to boarding, had made raffish jokes about the food, the masters, the lavatories, and the absence of women.

The next day Vera and Alistair had driven together to take Luke to his new prep school. She knew that something was very wrong between them, but she didn't know how to speak to him of it. She had tried over the past six months, but Alistair accused her of pestering him. She presumed he was preoccupied with his work and deals he did not want her to know about. A long way from those early days when she was his confidante and her basic common sense a real asset to him. She had helped him to form views over what to buy, whom to employ. She had listened hour after hour to his worries and fears as he built up the company.

She knew he had had other women, but she had learned from her mother this was what men needed to do, that it was not in men's nature to be faithful, so a woman just had to learn to be canny.

They had been together since she was 16. What she knew then of the ways of men and women was from the movies, or from the parade of men that came and went in her mother's unsatisfactory life. She had worked in the department store owned by Alistair's father. The boss's son – he could have had the pick of local girls, and he had chosen her. Vera knew that she had kept his interest at least for the first seven years of their marriage and she still did all the things he wanted. She had after all, made herself in his image; or, allowed him to create her in his. Even after three babies she still had a trim waist and small high breasts. She knew she was still attractive in her dark, rather exotic, Spanish-looking way, with olive skin and long dark hair, deep brown-black eyes with long lashes. She had never known her father and her mother's information was vague. As a child, she had secretly hoped her father was a prince.

She dressed well for Alistair, in the styles she had learned about which she knew he admired. She knew how to please him in public, when she went out with him or attended his official functions; and she knew how to dress for him in the intimacy they had once enjoyed. Whenever she felt uncertain, she reassured herself that she did all the right things.

She turned away from the kitchen, and returned to the bottom stair, unable to go further into the house.

That day! Max had asked her about it but she could not speak of it. That day in the car!

She had needed a handkerchief to dab her eyes. She could still see her baby, her little Luke, standing pale and obedient in his new uniform. Packaged into a crisp grey-and-blue striped unnaturalness and hard new shoes. The face of compliance but the eyes of reproach. How could you do this to me? It caused her heart to tighten. It felt harsh and cruel, and the thought of his silent weeping at night was unbearable.

Alistair handed her his own perfectly laundered white handkerchief, monogrammed with A. "You've got to be tough," he said. "You've got to for him, the boys all need to see you tough and strong, then they will know that it's right, that it's all for the best. It's how they get steeled to become proper men. You can't give in now to your sentimental tendencies."

She would have liked some comfort, the feel of his hand on hers, but she said nothing. She wondered if he was right; he had been through it all himself, and so had most of his friends, and, as he said: "It never did us any harm, it's made men of us."

They had driven on in silence for some time, Vera quietly sobbing but at the same time trying not to spoil her make-up and thinking about the lamb she was to cook for dinner.

Then he began speaking:

"There's another thing that you have to be strong about." She winced internally at the slight menace in his pause. "I've met someone else."

Vera saw 95 on the speedometer, but the expensive car gave no idea of speed. The edges of some leaves on trees and hedges were just turning, hints of red and yellow. The road was a blur. They were passing other cars. She looked into them at other travellers getting on with their private thoughts. Their forms were strangely vivid. She became quite still, almost not breathing, wondering where she was and how she got here, not sure exactly what she had just heard. She looked down into her lap; a tear fell onto her still, white hands.

"I think it's going to rain," she said, in an odd little voice.

"Didn't you hear what I said?" Alistair went on, sounding irritated.

Vera's breath came in gulps, in between holding on.

"You've met someone else." She sounded bland.

"I've met someone else and I'm going to live with her." Definite, non-negotiable. He paused, moving slightly in his leather seat but keeping his eyes firmly on the road as his speedometer slid to 100. He clenched his jaw and the knuckles of his hands were more obvious than usual on the grey steering wheel. He was the man in control of what he wanted and what he was going to get, as ever.

"Our marriage was finished before Luke was born, you know that, Vera. I always knew you had Luke to try to keep it alive. Totally unfair of you. I've told you that before." He paused, looking at her from the corner of his eye. "I've kept things going until Luke was ready for school."

The image of Luke swam before Vera's eyes, standing at the doorway of his school with his brave, shut-down face.

"My poor little Luke," she whimpered, slipping her shoes off and curling up her toes.

Alistair thumped the steering wheel. "Vera, you're deliberately not listening. I'm trying to speak to you seriously."

Vera caught sight of the expensive label inside her shoes. Something about the label soothed her, helped her feel some control.

"That's not true ... and it's not fair ..." She felt the first trembling of panic not far away, like the start of a motor both deep inside her and also somewhere outside of her. What would she do if she could not stave it off with her usual methods? What would happen if she could not steel herself to cope as she had done with so many other changes enforced upon her?

There was a long silence between them, with no sound except for the soft purring of the car's engine. Alistair stayed coiled and set, eyes fixed upon the road, heart hardened.

She thought now, sitting with her back pressed onto the silver trees of the wallpaper, that the whole thing had been surreal. To end a marriage at 100 miles per hour! She was captive. She remembered looking out at other drivers in other vehicles wondering if they could see the momentous destruction going on.

She was trying to keep control of herself but couldn't help her voice rising and trembling. "I've known you had affairs, but I've always taken it for granted that it's what you had to do. What's different about this one? Why does this one mean you have to end our marriage? And what about the boys?" Her voice moved higher in pitch. She was cold and terrified inside, helpless, on the edge of panic. Before her were images of her sons: one abandoned to the barrenness of school; the others setting off to start their adult lives away from home – one at the other end of the world. And none of them knowing what was going on with their parents as they travelled at 100 miles per hour on an English motorway. Not knowing that their father was in the process of destroying the fulcrum of their lives.

Alistair found her voice and inevitable weakness irritating.

Vera remembered trying to cling on, to what she was unsure. She had tried to make her voice more protesting: "You can't do this, you can't do it to your family."

She thought now that what he had said next was pompous. It was all about his ideas, his future, his development, his changing needs. She had heard much of the themes before, but then he wanted to impress her and to keep her in the place he had reserved for her: his admirer and his servant, grateful for his patronage. He had wanted her to be impressed and to wait upon him, and in return had kept her and sometimes been nice to her. What he was saying now was no different, but he had removed his need of her admiration. What had passed for love was gone. Without this he emitted a brutal chill. Now someone else was there who could give him fresh reflection.

He couched his rejection by telling her that he had had high blood pressure for some time. He hadn't wanted to worry her of course, so he hadn't mentioned it. His doctor had pressed him to tell about what problems and stresses he had in his life that might be the cause. And so of course it was his marriage that fell to be scapegoated. Vera was to blame. She wasn't an able enough wife and companion. She came from the wrong background, was unable to deal with the challenge and opportunity of rising with him. He had tried, of course, tried to instruct her in his needs, but she had failed. Alistair was just a harassed, hard-working, busy man with more of his fair share of troubles and not properly understood by his wife. He needed a new start, Vera held him back; she was in his way. He needed a better set-up for his political career, and he had to get it going before there was an election. His blood pressure had been better since he had made the decision, Vera would be pleased to hear.

Vera was protected from the full realisation of what Alistair was doing by her hard-learned survival strategy of shutting down over painful emotion and going numb. She had nothing that might fuel the language of protest. She only knew how to please and cajole. She knew dimly that what Alistair was saying was all to do with him, and what he needed and wanted for himself, and how he had grown out of her and did not need or love her anymore. She was to be discarded like a worn-out suit.

Of the children he was matter of fact and proprietorial. He would provide handsomely for them. Leo and Dominic were off his hands in terms of the everyday. He would visit Luke and share the holidays. Sons needed a father more than a mother, especially as they got older. He would probably take a more active role in the future, depending on how his new partner coped. He had already organised provision for this too. *Fait accompli.*

She could still see the marks made by digging her manicured nails hard into her palms. By then she was out of her own body but still so aware of his, there in the car next to her, his intensely physical presence, always so very sexual. She was used to being able to slide a finger over the hair of the back of his hand, igniting a shared passion. She knew that it was she who had awakened this in him. She had accepted the nervous, inexperienced mother's boy and helped him grow into a confident, sexually aware man. That was the place they had started at together, the place where they always met, where they never argued, where they were an equal match.

Her tears began slowly now, in her stairway reverie, as they had this afternoon. She realised that even her one private certainty about Alistair, that whoever he had been with, he would always come back to her, was gone. Although he was still so very sexual to her, he had shut down on her. There would be nothing for them now.

In the car it would have taken an extraordinary effort of will to touch him anywhere. If she looked at him it would have defeated her. How she had loved that abundant, soft hair that fell forward over his face when he moved his head as he spoke! But she did not dare to look at him now in the silence of his rejection.

But, surely, surely, his need of me and what I know of his need will call him back! A flicker of hope was created in her. Then, I wish I could hate him. But she had seen what hate does in her mother's relationships. The shouting followed by the hideous silences; the rows and physical violence fuelled by hatred that had punctuated her childhood. She had raised her life above that.

How good it would have been to explode! And in that damned car, to make a scene, to shout, to throw herself out or grab the steering wheel and crash! But she had retreated still further, into cold numbness, shrinking inside her red suit.

By the time they had reached the darkened buildings of outer London she had become set and tight. She imagined that she might sit immobile in the car seat forever, frozen, glued there by invisible forces, like a victim of an air crash.

As Alistair opened the door, she caught sight of his slackened mouth as he fumbled with his house keys and she came alive with the thought that this was all one of his sadistic pranks. He was just setting her up! Why hadn't she seen it before. For God's sake. She allowed an edge of hysteria to rise inside and followed him excitedly into the house.

She remembered now how she had closed her eyes in anticipation! Her excitement! Her hope then that as she followed him into the house he would turn round in the hall and grab hold of her collar before ripping off her clothes and screwing her against the expensive wallpaper, right where she was sitting now, as he had once done before. He would be saying that it had all been one of his jokes, his little teases, just to frighten her, anything to get her going and wind her up, and she was his wasn't she and she would take anything from him wouldn't she.

But once inside he had run swiftly up the stairs and started packing his bags.

She had shut down again in herself, the now familiar coldness closing in. No words. No feelings. She remembered how she had made her way automatically into the kitchen. She had opened the fridge, taken out the lamb. She had wondered if he would still be wanting it.

* * * *

Saxon drove over Hammersmith Bridge again the following week. "I must be really desperate." She had agreed to an initial six sessions. She had to keep the peace with Lewis and Daniel. They were determined she stay the course. "This is a real opportunity, Sax," Daniel had said. "I know it will be strange for you and it will probably irritate you at first, but just stick with it and you will learn something new, and really interesting." He had paused, looking at her gravely: "Then we will see all of you," he had added, mysteriously. Lewis had been very quiet since her return from Hong Kong and her suspension from work.

She clamped down the fury she felt inside. Just get through it. Then get on.

Her foot hit the brake as the rear of the car in front appeared in her windscreen and her car lurched and stalled. Her head swam. Damn, damn.

The claustrophobic press of 5 o'clock traffic closed in on her again. Her brain registered the iron grip from the back of her neck down through each individual vertebra. It had become a steel vice over which she clamped her mind, busying it with thoughts. Do something, anything, but do not feel the weakness of pain. Get out. Go.

But she was stalled on a bridge, suspended between two opposite sides.

"I've got no choice, if I can get this thing sorted then I'll be let off the hook. I can put Hong Kong behind me. Feel in charge again."

She moved her gaze through the car window with its murky autumnal moisture and then down to the grey-brown swirling depths of the Thames. *"Thank God it didn't happen here."* From out of the mist emerged the shape of black-headed gulls foraging for a last morsel before dark. They became the baskets known as weirs of the cleaning junks of Hong Kong, harvesting the harbour for litter. *What treasures might they uncover? A basket of peaches, a pearl of great ...*

She blinked and shook her head, turning up the volume on the radio.

When she realised she had missed the turning off the

Common she felt rage hit her again. Shit. All the one-way streets, No Entry, T-junction. She was going to be late. As she parked her car in Dr Maxwell's cul-de-sac, she scraped her front wheel on the kerb. The keys felt clumsy in her usually dextrous hands as she clicked the central locking. For God's sake.

*She would not run. On principle she would not run. And her body wouldn't let her anyway. All slow motion and walking through treacle. The click of her high heels on the pavement of the quiet tree-lined street sounded like bullets on a firing range, betraying the silence. Although Dr Max's premises were only a few houses away she felt as if she would never get there. And in that street. The eyes that might be watching. Judging.*

*At the green door she froze. It seemed that hours passed before she was able to push the circular bell. Had she got the time right? Was it the right day? Would he remember her or would she be an intruder, a nuisance. Her heart beat very fast. Perhaps he was asleep, and she would wake him, making him cross. What sound would the bell make deep inside this house that was growing bigger by the minute? Mole and Ratty pulling on Badger's bell having fallen over his foot scraper, hidden by snow. Snow – the longing for sleep.... Mole and Ratty.*

*She was indeed losing it. Calm she said, settle down, breathe. Be in charge, not like last time. Just stay in charge.*

In the room the all-over green is waiting. The fact of her lateness, almost unmanageable for her, is embedded in the tension in her jaw and the stiffness of her spine. Her mind is busy organising thoughts. It was others' fault anyway, making her give up time to be in this ridiculous place. And there sits Dr Max, still and calm. Also waiting.

She hates him for his smug poise. She will not apologise.

The opening silence unnerves her once again. She rolls her habitual linen handkerchief in her right hand, checks her skirt is straight and her feet neatly placed together. She wonders if she has caused her brow to sweat by rushing. Then, without looking at Max who has said something to her she has not been able to hear, she leans back in the chair.

As the iron stiffness in her back meets the green softness of the chair she becomes mute. All the feelings she had fought off when last here slip in, as if they have been waiting within

the soft fabric folds of the green chair for her return. She has not felt them since, but now, here they are again, inside her like some monstrous jelly fish rising from the depth of the ocean. *The mass of murky water, swirling under the Chinese junk, the water that would not stay still. The murky water of my under life.*
"He's going to die. He's going to die in that filthy water."
Minutes tick by. Her body feels formless.

Dr Max says something again: "How are you?" But she does not hear him.

"What's happening?" He is leaning toward her, listening and watching intently. Her mouth opens, but no sound comes. He is following her closely.

Her body and brain have been taken over by the jelly. No thoughts, no voice, no shape to go on. Dr Max is surrounded by a silver fog. Her muteness is merciful.

He must have been telling her to try to concentrate on her breathing.

Gradually she becomes aware of the rise and fall of her chest and of shiny points in the brown of his eyes, beaming in her direction through the silver fog. Then that brown becomes the brown of the Indian floor rug, which starts to swim into focus and her eyes engage in following the circular movements of its patterns. A rug illustrating the tree of life, with birds and butterflies on branches. This activity brings some order to her brain and the power of the jelly fish recedes.

"No. What?" she says eventually, in a small, hoarse voice.

He repeats his words again softly, watching her intently, aware of how severely she has been traumatised.

"Coming here makes you feel things," she says in the odd, young voice.

She is struggling with the impact of the jelly with its strange formlessness, and the breathlessness inside her tight chest. She cannot form the right words, it is as if her brain has been reduced to pulp. It is surreal, so vague. Her limbs are cold, her heart racing, but the hot blood was not reaching where she needed it to go. She shakes her head as if trying to shake sense and order into it. Why was being here so difficult?

She tries to organise her thoughts, to speak of what was

happening.

Time passes in silence. The room waits.

Then inside, a sudden surge of fury. *I don't want this. I just don't want it.* She turns to Max angrily, her voice steely and clear:

"It's all a trick, isn't it? Trick cyclists –that's what we called you in med school. You set it all up to make fools of people, to make us look stupid and then you can pounce." Her blue eyes blaze into him. The jelly is getting firmer, she starts to feel some control.

Max meets her gaze steadily.

"I am certainly not going to pounce," he says, "and I do not wish to trick you."

"I just want you to get on with it," she flashes at him.

He says nothing.

She looks cornered, stuck. Then, appearing afraid in the movement of her eyes, she blushes slightly and smoothes her skirt in a way that is becoming familiar to Max.

The room falls into a difficult silence again.

"I can see that something comes forward when you step into this room that as yet has no name and is not your usual experience." He is treading carefully, wanting to engage her, not wanting to increase her fear and thus her fight, her flight, or her freeze. "We do not know what that is yet and we do not have to know for now. The first important thing is to acknowledge that something – probably fear, arises here and shuts you off from your usual operating methods. The second important thing is to help you feel safe here."

She remains with her fixed stare, saying nothing. Then something moves inside her, something a bit like a small fist inside her chest. She gasps a little and looks at him from out of the corner of her eye. He looks bigger Safe – of course she was safe, she kept in control didn't she. Except here. But what does he mean, safe? What was it, to feel safe?

"Can you identify a place or a feeling where you have felt steady, strong and safe?"

The small fist disappears. She flares up.

"I just can't stand all these questions! Trying to get under my skin."

He puts his hands on his worn brown corduroys. He is so tired. He has been awake with Emily's ramblings most of the night. He has asked Saxon a direct question too soon. He would have to go very, very slowly and also risk igniting her contempt. He chooses to appeal to her strongly defended survival self.

"I'd like to explain something to you about responses to trauma," he says and picks up a chart he has on the small table by his chair. "May I show you this?"

She cannot see properly what he is doing, but shrugs. In her resentful compliance Max sees a very young child, four or five, wanting to please.

Saxon feels the gasp again; something is happening in her chest. But she focuses on the paper with the chart as something scientific, subject to research and scrutiny. That's safe, she thinks. At last he is showing proper professional colours.

"What happened in Hong Kong is a traumatic event."

She opens her mouth to protest and he holds her firm with his brown gaze. Smiling at her he says: "As you know well, when we experience trauma our autonomic nervous system goes into action and produces our fight, flight or freeze response. It's possible that you've not thought to apply this understanding to your own recent experience. And this is because when your fight/flight/freeze response is dominant, and your body flooded with cortisol your thinking brain shuts down."

"I do perfectly well at my own work thank you," she says smartly.

Max carries on. "I think that under your strong coping self which is dominant in your own professional work, and therefore your preferred residence, you are experiencing some very frightening feelings you are unable to comprehend and this has made you try to clamp down further and try to stay on automatic. It seems as if these feelings become more present in this room with me."

It is still too much, he can see that. He directs his attention toward the cut-off frightened self within her that is trying to communicate.

She has tuned out and is staring at the chart with its straight horizontal lines and squiggly markings, not unlike an electrocardiograph.

She reads: "Hypervigilant", then, "Panic", "Shut down", "Mute". Images of her mother appear, followed by Aunt Frances throwing herself on the floor. Horrible.

Dr Max is explaining the effect of the cortisol, something about fear responses taking over and shutting out thinking and reflection. Then, something again about safety.

The word strikes her in a new way. Safety. Safe. She heard the deep notes of a song in Spanish. *'Las flores, las flores.'*

"Wanting to find a shared language for what's going on isn't a trick, it's something we need to do together so —"

"I'm not frozen," she protests. *Badger's bell under snow...*

He gazes at her thoughtfully. She is picking up words he had used several minutes ago. She has leaned away from him. He realises that now he is too near. He moves back into his seat.

"You are very wary."

"Of course," she says, with a hint of sadness.

The chart lies on the floor between them.

"Is it OK to continue?" he asks.

She shrugs, indifferent, the cold blue eyes not engaging.

"In the upper section we have a description of hyperarousal – when we keep busy and are on alert – a way of managing not feeling something we do not know what to do with. In the bottom section we go mute in order not to feel. These are all natural defences and very useful. We usually have both responses, so that sometimes we notice that we are speeded up and then we may sink into the more depressed response. When this process becomes habituated, we remain at the mercy of our chemicals, unable to think about what has happened to us or find other ways of coping with fear."

"I'd rather stay habituated."

Her arrogant avoidance is breathtaking. Where was her professional curiosity? He could get angry now.

"You're here because a serious event took place for which you have no clear memory, and a child's life —"

"Yes! Yes, I know. You don't need to go on!" she says tightly, putting out her right hand, the palm up, to shut him out and turning her head away.

He smiles. "You have just illustrated how it works. The slight mention of the child is a trigger to your cutting off, becoming brittle and angry, your body rigid and defensive. It's a defence against what feels unbearable. Whatever it is that happened is unbearable for you."

She closes her eyes.

*His wrinkled face was still imprinted with the tight womb sack from which he had been delivered. His naked head vulnerable, open fontanelle throbbing under his mottled skin. The tiny, perfectly formed hands lay still, the fingernails —.*

No! She opens her eyes, her heart beating fast.

"No!" she says aloud.

"It's really, really hard, isn't it?" says Dr Max simply.

"Don't! Don't be kind. Don't be kind. It's too awful," she cries in dry voice. *Whatever you do don't let anyone see you cry. Any weakness and they will move in. They will destroy you. Don't let anyone be kind, it's just a trick to move in on you. You can't trust anyone...*

There is another movement now, once again deep inside her. Max sees this movement and senses it to be a sob and leans further toward her. The room holds its soft green arms around her. The moment exists between them and is registered, but not by Saxon's consciousness. She sits up, sniffing and says stiffly, blue eyes in focus: "There must be a format surely. Can't you ask questions like I do so you can get a picture ... can't you tell me what to say ..."

Suddenly she feels really trapped, and so, so tired. She wants it over with. What it is that needed to be over she does not know.

Max is quiet, thinking how to engage her or indeed if he could.

Sometimes he used a questionnaire with new patients who were not psychologically aware because it helped them to formulate their survival behaviour patterns. It was her cut-off traumatised state that had brought her here so he must address this first, long before she would be able to talk about her life, or accept she had any emotional difficulties. She had survived her life by trying to make herself into a machine, with any feeling or difficulty sorted by logic. Whatever he gave her she would either ridicule and dismiss or use in an over-logical way. How to find a place of reflection?

He sits in contemplation, aware of his body's growing fatigue, and the level of exhaustion in the room. He directs his attention towards her most wounded self, to the lost child in her and the lost child in Hong Kong.

She wonders why he takes so long and perhaps he doesn't know what to say. Perhaps she is difficult or not playing by the rules. But she doesn't know what the rules are. Then she wonders whether perhaps he is stupid because he is so slow. She is comforted by this idea and begins to feel the warmth of her familiar energy returning. He did wear such peculiar clothes, the sort her father would refer to as worn by "weedy intellectuals" with no "male backbone". Soft fabric jackets in cotton or corduroy, waistcoats from some ethnic tribe in India, wide shapeless trousers, never a proper tie. She bet he wore socks and sandals in the summer. These thoughts make her feel better.

She sits up more firmly in her seat.

"I like my life very much," she declares in an authoritative voice. "I'm good at my job and I work hard. What happened in Hong Kong was really nothing to do with me. A pure accident. I'm sorry about it of course." She shrugs. "But it was, an aberration. I can't explain it. It's over now and I think I should put it all behind me and get on with my life."

Max feels the cold of shock, and then a very deep sadness. He also feels uneasy. He has the flash of an image. A knife cutting into soft flesh.

Her intelligent blue eyes are watching him, waiting for an answer, as if it were he who is on trial and she the one waiting to pounce. Her mouth looks tighter and there is something predatory in the way she is holding herself. Minutes ago he had seen a tiny unformed creature. *She can cower like a frightened animal, shiver like a formless jelly fish, he had felt that well of tears from her stomach, and she can also cut, dismiss and persecute.* He feels relief at getting this far with his understanding of her pattern of relating.

"Is that what you want to do, move on as if nothing important has happened?"

A stubborn look comes over her face. Her adult voice has a metallic ring. "I don't believe what happened was important. As I said, it was an unfortunate accident, an aberration. And I was very tired. I had just presented an important paper," she emphasises the word again, "an important paper at a conference and flown out to Florida to see my father before his bypass operation. I had been on the go for over forty-eight hours and before that for three and a half weeks without a break." She is getting fired up, bringing out concrete facts that could not be refuted from out of her fire.

Max hears it otherwise.

He allows a pause so that she can hear the echo of her own words ringing harshly within the soft baize quality of the green room. A room that allows words to grow, develop and extend themselves into understanding and at times invite compassion and transformation.

He decides it is time for him to get his own knife out. "Are you saying that you feel it was your level of fatigue that led to a newborn baby ending up in the harbour water?"

She appears shocked for a moment and her body rises, slightly arched like a startled impala he had once seen caught in the jaws of a lion at the foot of Mount Kenya.

Then she lets fly, nostrils flaring. "You see, there you are doing it. It's a trick. You ask me to speak and then you throw something like that at me." She is blazing.

He follows her quickly: "The something 'like that' – what is it, what is the 'like that'? Tell me more so that I can understand it."

"It's horrendous. How dare you." Body tight as a drum.

"Let us stay with this together," he says firmly. "When I said, 'so your level of fatigue led to a newborn baby ending up in the harbour water' – that was horrendous?" he asks again slowly and firmly.

She hears him differently now and blinks, swallowing hard. She looks terrified, then moves from side to side in her chair to try to keep herself from being taken over by the jelly fish. *Once again the image of a hunted animal caught in a trap.*

"You don't believe me, do you? You don't believe it was an accident. It was an accident!" she shouts. "I'm not a murderer,

I'm not. I'm not the mad one!"

She catches sight of the scuffed rug under her right foot. Max has moved quite close to her. She is aware of the silver again and the points of light coming from his eyes. Looking down she becomes sullen and her voice slurs. "You blame me don't you. It's all my fault. I'm a thoroughly bad person, a bad, bad girl who nobody wants or loves."

He looks at her intently, and then she says: "That's disgusting – look what you've made me say. I sound like a spineless winger."

"I am on your side, Saxon," he says quietly, intent upon her.

The use of her first name jolts. She does not look up.

He continues: "I am here to help you, and I want to help you unravel all of this. I do not sit in judgement of you. First, we need to clear a space here in which the painful story of that day can unravel in its own time, and safely. The fact that you are fighting me here is a sign that your own natural defences are coming into play to protect you. I am OK with your fight. It alerts me to something fragile inside you that you need to protect. And as you say, you have become habituated to cutting off from difficult feelings."

He knows that he must continue and let her have the benefit of all his thoughts, thoughts that he might, with a less tricky patient, have kept for later.

"I can already give you my professional opinion that what happened in Hong Kong was an accident waiting to happen. By this I mean that the event most probably represents the accumulation of many responses to emotional hurt that have been repressed and that day all these things came together. The result was the accident. What it tells me is not that you are bad or mad but that you have been trying to keep yourself together by automatic means and that the life inside you can wait no longer."

His tiredness is eclipsed, and he feels only the full strength of his heart feeling its way around something wild and unknown.

The movement that had begun on the first day in this room begins again. If she were able to recognise feeling in her body she would have noticed some tingling at the base of her spine, not unlike a steady heartbeat. It is strangely familiar, and oddly comforting.

"*Perhaps I am mad.*" She does not know what to feel or how to. Her fight continues: "I can't imagine what you are talking about."

Max sits back in his old, worn chair, letting its familiar shape support him. He thinks for a minute. "What do you want yourself out of these sessions?"

"I don't want to be here at all. It's not my wish."

Max nods. "I'm glad you said that, at least this is now spoken between us. You feel as if you are here against your will and it makes you feel angry and trapped."

She is silent. Sulky. Then unexpected humour arises: "So I guess we are stuck with each other." The way he keeps his gaze on her! She turns away from it.

"Could you allow us to experiment together?"

She frowns. "I don't do experiments, except on rats."

Another document.

"I wonder if you would read this during the week and let me know what you think?"

He hands her a small booklet. "It's something I've written to help patients to think about themselves and their behaviour; to have some sort of map of how the mind works. It explains how all of us have to adapt to the life we are born into and that sometimes this adaptation restricts our thinking. Usually, we don't question this until problems occur. Psychotherapy aims to help recognise these unhelpful patterns of thinking that lead to painful outcomes and find ways of revising and changing them."

"It's the thought of you trying to get under my skin."

"Your fear of being tricked?" he asks.

She does not like him naming it but he isn't fazed by her and she can admire this.

"It was an accident. Really!" ' Eyes are pleading now.

She cannot bear his sad look.

A deeper silence envelops them. The green walls of the room have contained many other silences, allowing secrets to become heard and embryonic life to find its moment of birth.

Max notes and breathes into the fatigue and deadness passed on to him from Saxon. Separating what is hers and what belongs to him restores him. He looks at her clearly and kindly.

"I was wondering whether you have any curiosity about what happened to you in Hong Kong?"

"I am a responsible person." Still tart, and tight.

"It is such an extremely unusual thing to happen for you, out of character wouldn't you say? This is only our second meeting, but you strike me as someone who strives to remain in complete control with an exceptional care."

So he has noticed her.

"Is this the first time you have been involved in anything that felt so out of control and character?"

She remains silent, and still, not looking at him.

Then she struggles slowly with words: "Yes," she says in a small hesitant voice. "I suppose it's the first time I've been involved in something…" she squirms at having to say it, "where there are …" she searches for the words, "consequences …"

"So, are you curious?"

She laughs.

Max continues, "I'm thinking scientifically. As a cardiologist you're curious about what goes on inside people's hearts…" As he takes a breath, she interrupts him with: "And as a therapist you look at people's minds. Not quite so exact wouldn't you think? Not a level playing field."

He just has to play along.

"So – why do you think you are here, having to engage in this way with all that has brought you to my consulting room?"

She wants to say "Because Lewis and Dan made me…" but catches herself in time. Silent again, a slight shudder inside. "I suppose you would say that it all goes back to childhood. I don't think I was abused, abandoned or undernourished," she says acidly.

Max feels angry. She is so contemptuous, so bloody angry, so damned up. He controls himself.

"If you think that you can withstand the fight you have to make here then perhaps we can work together," he says, the challenge understated. She looks at him sharply, suddenly interested. He continues. "For example, it may be that you believe that only if you are fiercely in control all of the time will you be respected and loved and that not being in control will have you floundering in a mess and being tricked. So you have tended to live at the control end. Very sensible and it has so far worked for you. But it can be very restricting. It means that you are unable to tolerate mess of any kind, which often includes feelings. And feelings are the messy stuff of living and relationship. You have just had an experience where difficult feelings were aroused and resulted in you feeling in a mess and out of control. We need to ask: is this a signal that there needs to be some rebalancing? This would allow us to understand and revise what has led you to be so dependent upon control and made you fearful of anything else."

She is watching him. Whatever this B movie of the body is, going on inside her, it is getting busy and she is starting to be more aware of it. An elbow prods her insistently and the tingling at the base of her spine continues. If she had been a dog this would have been wagging of the tail. Despite all this activity, which she fears is a sign of her going mad, she senses that what he is saying is right. She wants him to be wrong. The inside elbow wants him to go on.

"Knowing something of our inner landscape, how we think and feel, gives us a wider range of choices of how to be. Ultimately this helps us to feel more in control."

She has become thoughtful. "I've said I will come here six times," she says.

In the silent B movie, something is definitely pricking up its ears. Minutes tick by. She finds herself having a hysterical thought about a film she has never seen but whose title she remembers now: *Bodysnatchers*.

Max continues thoughtfully. "Earlier you said, "I'm not the mad one." Are you afraid that I will tell you you're going mad?" He wants to get this out.

"Yes," she says simply. Then she smiles. It opens up her face and he can see that she is quite lovely. For an instant she looks radiant.

She breathes a long out-breath. "Good to get that over with," she says, "but then you might decide that mightn't you? And you've got your report to write."

"Yes, I will have to write a report. But collaboration is the key."

She looks down. He can see the outline of her small ear as her fair hair falls over her face. So much a little girl, so much a forceful professional woman. He bet she fought hard for her patients.

"It would be the end of everything wouldn't it? All gone, finish." She shrugs and looks small and vulnerable. "A real mess ... terrifying ... and yet, at the same time ..." She does not finish, but he senses that she might have said that it would be a relief.

"I would not like to be mad." That's what the woman in the boat said. "You must be mad." Then, quietly, "I do fear losing my mind."

At last! She had shared something with him genuinely. He breathes out.

"Have you ever known anyone who has lost their mind?"

She smiles, a wintry, bitter little smile, wringing her hands, "I think my mother was not in her right mind most of her life, since she lost her son. She says, 'her son', as if this had been a stranger's child, not her own brother."

"You may as well know, but I don't like talking about it. My mother became an alcoholic. In and out of rehab." He is listening quietly. She continues, more reflective now: "That left just Dad and me. He was away a lot. I tried to keep things in order. We try to keep the sane end. We've had to. Not much of a pedigree, is it? You can't be surprised I try to keep the lid on irrational behaviour."

"Perhaps some of this is why you're really here."

She pauses, forcing herself to try to think reasonably about what he is saying. But part of her still wants to squirm away and bury the guilty secret. And talking about her mother has brought the B movie back, the jelly, and other things. Sickness that would surely lead to tears. But at the same time something else was happening in this green room that she could not name. An atmosphere that conveyed a feeling of inevitability, like watching the course of a river running on from source to sea.

She looks again at the chart that still lay between them. "What is this gap here?"

"It's called the window of tolerance," he says simply.

She repeats: "The window of tolerance."

She looks at the space and then at Max. She has the

feeling of a hand coming out toward her, from someone unafraid of what went on inside people. She sits completely still, hands limp upon her lap. Then there is the sensation of all the other people who must have sat in this chair and been this way and survived, even got mended. The word struck her with force. Was there something in her that was broken?

Max lets the feeling remain between them for some time.

*The Pale Green Room*

# 3

MAX closed his front door, noticing how the smooth brass handle warmed quickly in his hand. He carefully rearranged the heavy brocade curtain that concealed the door and protected the inner hall from draughts. This was always a good moment, when he could celebrate the end of the working week. He breathed out a long breath. As he walked back into his room he rubbed the nape of his neck and rolled his head a little, pulling back his shoulder blades. His large frame, with its muscular legs and shoulders, was not happy sitting in a chair all day. It growled, wanting the relief of exercise. His leg ached. Today he had had to forgo his early run across the Common, replaced by a conference call about a patient who was at risk.

After a day's work with patients, he would set aside time to think about them and make notes, then have a few moments of peace and stillness. Only then would he begin his evening with his wife.

He could recall most of what had happened during a session and would record a patient's feelings, images and dreams and ponder on what remained with him, and on his own feelings about the person. Some of these feelings would be described in psychotherapy as counter-transference, or the invitation to feelings that were connected with the patient rather than the person of the therapist, although this was always the challenge, assessing which belonged to whom. He pondered now, in the stillness of his room, on the mysterious technical term "transference", so often misunderstood. He understood it as the process where patients re-experienced the pull of strong feelings connected to old relationship patterns. The emotion embedded in these earlier patterns would be brought fully charged into the consulting room and be projected onto him, Max. He would be then invited into the relational dance, and the counter-transference, the feelings he experienced in relation to the emotion of the other person. With Saxon Pierce he was already sensing a brittle, demanding, critical self in relation to feeling crushed and denigrated. With Vera Dodds he could see that he could be invited to play the role of saviour to her victim. These experiences would offer the opportunity to revisit emotions hidden in repeated patterns of behaviour, and revise those that had become problematic. He loved his pale green room and the way it offered containment for the understanding and change needed within the therapeutic relationship.

He looked at the page of notes and smiled, enjoying the intimate ritual of bringing a blank page to life via the flow of ink. It was a rich accompanist to his solitude. Years of journal-keeping maintained within his monastic discipline had forged this intimacy. The practice of transforming the contents of his mind into written word had honed his writing skill. He used a burgundy-coloured Waterman fountain pen, and blue-black ink. These confidential patient notes were locked away in the old wooden filing cabinet he had inherited from his grandfather. The key he hid in the false bottom of one of the flowerpots he tended himself on the windowsill.

He knew that Emily looked for it often. The nature of his work both held her to him and drove her further into her paranoia. The demands of her condition had increased his rituals of control.

Sometimes he opened the door of the room at midnight and stood in the half-light, looking in. He knew, because of his own analysis, that he had recreated something of his beloved grandfather's study. The same changing sea greens, the books, the abstract oils without frames, the scuffed old kilim grandfather had brought back from Afghanistan upon which was woven the tree of life. He could become once again the young boy who had stood barefoot on the Eastern rug tracing the green leaves and plumage of the exotic birds with his toe, watching his grandfather writing with his gold-nibbed Parker pen. That mix of dark oily ink on the gleaming new gold; the faceted glass jar of Parker ink; the wooden row of pencils, nibs and pens; the tin of tobacco. Max's assignment, to keep the words clear on the virgin page, no blots or smudges, but a playing field on the pale green blotting pad of shapes like miniature tree roots. Grandfather would give a long sigh and say "thank you son, you did a fine job", and begin again to unite form and virgin page in thoughtful word by the twist of his ungainly longhand. Few words. Max's heart filled up in this place.

This is how it all might have been.

Now, each time he looked for a clinical text he was reminded of the younger Max. He had learned to hold a book open with two hands, and to use the satin ribbon to mark the place last read. His way of digesting the books he could not read was to press his face into the book's heart and inhale. This habit still remained, intact, with all its association.

Now, when his own room was unoccupied and still, Max marvelled at just how much it could take and still keep its own shape and its still presence. Some of what went on here had a visceral charge. The unearthing of past horrors sometimes meant shouting and weeping and dramatic acting out, beloved of Hollywood movies. Patients did sometimes throw themselves on the floor or at the walls. There was wailing and weeping. There were terrible silences. When the pain of past emotional suffering had been silenced it found expression through body symptom, through dream and image and through what happened between the person and Max, often in the quality of the returning silences.

He had learned that patients could re-connect with earlier losses, and within the safety of the pale green room take the knots and stones of pain into their hearts to be softened with compassion. Therapy offered the opportunity to experience joy in discovering what was eclipsed rather than lost. There was relief in the possibility of change. And there was the wonder of transformation.

He would often look to see if the room had changed, if it showed signs of pain or regret, of suffering. But the room held a constant presence; it was almost a holy place where the intimacy of lives was respected and allowed to unfold.

As he wrote his notes before closing his room, he wondered about his two new female patients. He realised there was unease under his detachment. He bent down to smooth the rug scuffed by the stiletto heel. He disliked the aesthetic of those sort of shoes, but he realised they came with a kind of thrill. 'Fuck me' shoes. "Are you married?" she had asked. Dangerous? And all that red? Alistair had said of Vera: "Manipulative bitch. Before I can raise my hand, she's got her clothes off and I'm ruined."

There was something else, an unnerving familiarity in her smile, the slightness and dexterity of her body and the way she moved it, her turn of phrase, the way she looked at him suddenly, imploring with her deep brown eyes. Max did not want to open this further. He had to let it just sting him, and to bear the tug at his past. He hoped it would settle as he got to know her as herself rather than the person, she reminded him of. Finding her attractive should be the last thing on his mind.

He thought about this now, but there were no sensations in his body. He knew that his colleagues were concerned for him, in view of his demanding marriage and celibate existence within it. To many female colleagues he was a challenge, a juicy oyster to try to prise out of its shell. "What the hell do you do when someone really fancies you, Max? What if you feel like having a bit on the side?"

He completed his notes and bent down again to smooth the scuffed carpet. Then, closing the door reluctantly, he went across the hall and entered the kitchen.

\* \* \* \*

"There was that time when creatures on the earth cut down all the trees in order to blow their noses, make cartoons, and the shells for cupcakes. They destroyed the earth, were made mad forever from the heat and snows and permanent sunsets and smog-filled skies. They lived in holes when they had once had fine buildings upon whom artists lavished their skills, polished woods, carved great beauties..." Emily's voice swung into a lilting chant... "then it was said that no one could cut down trees anymore, the rivers were full of animals' blood and the septic mud from the pale squares which haunted the sky with their chimneys of smoke... the seas were swelling, the earth's surface returning to rock. No green shoots, nothing flowering, not even the everlasting cactus could survive against the wrath of God... he has pointed his beard and smite us down ..."

Emily was seated at the empty table, wearing a white kaftan. He knew she had been waiting for him to finish for too long. There was no sign of food preparation, but unusually the newspaper was spread open on the counter next to the fridge. Max looked at his wife. She had white hair now, probably a mixture of premature ageing and electric shock treatment, which seemed to have turned her natural Scandinavian white blonde even lighter. The white kaftan reminded him of the white dress she had been wearing the summer he met her and become enchanted with what he saw as her purity and perfection. He was eighteen, about to leave school and take his place at Oxford. All the people he had loved deeply were dead. He wanted to move as far from the inside violence left by loss as he could. He wanted to change the world. Emily was his house master's goddaughter. She was fragile then, and special. To Max she seemed a sprite not quite human, someone so far removed from the bloodied reality of his life that he believed he could be saved. He knew now it was his youth, his idealism, and his avoidance of impossible and unbearable feeling that had directed his actions then, and that now he was having to live with the consequences. But he was starting to recognise that he felt trapped. Something needed to change.

For Emily there was no difference between inside and outside worlds, no boundary to keep things in or out. When he met her this had been compelling. Loving her was one of the ways to lose his pain.

"Green and lilac... green and lilac... the green and lilac will cover all... the white will be covered... lost..."

She watched him from her watery eyes as he quietly went to the freezer and took out a pizza. He had forgotten to do it earlier. As he sliced cucumber to go with the pizza that would make their meal, he realised he felt angry. He thought about the green and lilac. Yesterday it had been red and black, the day before pink and yellow. Those colours would accompany the evening and were the colours worn by one of his female patients that day. Somewhere in Emily's limp being was a robust self who hated the intimacy he shared with other women.

He saw that the newspaper was open onto an article about the murder of a young doctor whose dismembered body had been found under the floorboards of her rented flat. The man who killed her had answered her advertisement in a lonely-hearts column. She had been lonely, working long hours on call, and she had wanted to find a partner. He had killed her because after seeing him twice she no longer wanted to go out with him. He had killed her with a knife and cut her body into pieces. Max remembered a discussion on this case where the idea was mooted that she had become sexually involved with him before she knew him properly and might have seen that he was unstable. Perhaps this was why she had terminated the contact, but too late to defend herself from his emotional instability over rejection. Max shuddered. Who knew what lengths people would go to, to not feel emotional pain?

He sat down at the table, from which Emily had not moved, and noticed that she was gazing at him more thoughtfully than usual. Often, he could guess what she was thinking, could follow the pattern however bizarre.

"The woman with the pearl necklace and blonde hair."

Max was intent on getting some supper into his hungry belly now that the pizza had started cooking. He was also reflecting on the effect of the article headline. He couldn't anticipate what Emily wanted to say. He raised his eyebrows, sensing trouble.

Next to the article about the murdered woman was another piece about knife crime in southeast London among teenagers who would keep their knives sharpened and use them on reflex if they felt 'dissed.' He turned the paper over to close its horrors only to be hit by more headlines spelling violence. The war in Iraq was escalating and the US had ordered a surge of troops. Women and children were being slaughtered in the name of democracy.

He took out the pizza and cut into it hungrily. It was a mean pizza, undercooked, and under his knife it jerked and tore. He sighed. Too much difficulty and violence, too much horror and not enough comfort and pleasure. He was shocked that he thought in this way. But he really did want just to curl up and have some kind person tuck him in.

"The one who comes to see you. She came this afternoon. Blonde hair, grey suit and black polished high-heeled shoes." Max nodded, still not properly engaging. "She's trouble."

Max looked up at his wife in surprise. "How do you mean?"

He knew she watched the patients come and go from her lace-making seat at the upstairs window. He didn't like it, but he couldn't stop her. Some years ago she had taken up bird watching, going out into the parks on her own with binoculars. She would often sit on the half- landing looking our across the common and watch the finches. Now she made lace, flicking the bobbins in and out in the afternoon light, and the binoculars remained in the country, largely unused. She could watch the street from there without being noticed. She would curl into the deep armchair with the blue box perched on her knee and look out through the leaves of the maple. When the light changed and the tree pressed itself more deeply at the window, she withdrew downstairs.

"I saw her first in her car. A metallic Audi TT." Max was always surprised at his frail wife's attention to the make of cars. Something in which he was not ever interested. "She has come twice in her car, after the woman with all the black hair who comes in a small red BMW."

"What is it you see?"

"Black aura."

Max nodded but said nothing.

Emily smiled a queer little half smile. "You don't believe me."

Max sighed. Then looked at his wife clearly. "I do. I know you understand about these things. I know that you do."

"But you don't believe me".

Max shrugged. "What about this black aura," he said, trying to humour her, which sometimes was helpful at leavening her focus. "What should I do, my psychic friend?" he said gently, stretching his hand to touch her fine white hair.

Emily shrugged him off. "She will do you no good".

"I won't let the black aura get me."

Emily stared at him, not smiling, determined.

"And you won't let it, will you, my darling." He took another mouthful of the ungenerous pizza.

"You can't always let the light into a black aura," she said darkly.

Max leaned back into his chair. "Emily, we have had black auras before, haven't we? A couple of years ago there was that man who —"

"I know. But he wanted to be healed," she said.

Max began to feel irritated, and disconcerted. "You sense that this woman doesn't".

Emily nodded. "She doesn't, she can't, she is dead." She

spoke as if there was no question whatsoever.

Max sighed, suddenly more tired than ever. "But my love, Emily, she's my patient."

"But you don't have to see anyone. You can pick and choose."

"But I have started working with her. She has been involved in an accident with —." He broke off, remembering the baby, not wanting to say any more. Suddenly he was alarmed. He needed to take control. A twisted sly look had entered Emily's child-like face.

"She will take you away from me."

Max stopped eating. The look had gone and been replaced by something resembling challenge.

She got up then and put her arms around him, as graceful, purposeful and sinewy as a snake.

Some thought that Max was too good looking to be a therapist and that this would get in the way of the work. He was handsome in the way of traditional sportsmen, with the sort of clear complexion of an Englishman who looked most natural on boats or in cricket flannels. He was a man upon whom clothes hung as an irrelevance, the sort who could shrug them off in a hurry. The brown monastic robes had camouflaged this potential eroticism successfully, except for the unmistakable wide muscular shoulders, kept tight by exercise.

His open face had a ready grin, showing crooked teeth, and his thick straight hair often stood on end at the crown, making him appear young and boyish. He could also appear serious and intent and communicate this with expressive brown eyes that could flash with feeling or temper. He looked like someone it would be easy to both fear and trust.

His early spiritual discipline had trained him to recognise the power of sexual energy and to use it as a force that could be channelled into another passion of choice.

He was taken by surprise at Emily's sudden expression of physical affection, she seemed to rise up and move around the table without his noticing. As he felt her body against him, he was more aware of her child-likeness than ever. He had hoped she would grow, and mature, as he believed everyone could if offered the opportunity, but her wounds seemed too deep, too intransigent. What was he to do if he had to face the fact that she could never be a full-grown woman? He felt sad and he felt, for the first time, that it was wrong to touch her as a husband might hope to touch a wife.

Emily remained clinging to him after he had taken his arms away. She looked at him knowingly and his heart sank. He would have to find a way to speak to her about what was happening between them. He felt ashamed then that whilst he was fearless with strangers in the pale green room, he became silenced by fear at speaking to his own wife about his own feelings. Emily became sullen. "Don't you want me to warn you about bad things when I see them. And I do, Max. I do see things coming. I do have the gift, even if you don't appreciate it…" There was a terrible silence between them. "Don't you care for me anymore?"

His mouth was dry, his tiredness acute. "I do, of course." But they had just had a month in the country, and she had been impossible to approach. Max longed for his green room, for the sound of the cello and Bach, for …

Emily went upstairs to take a bath.

The remaining pizza had congealed. The feel of his wife's child-like body rebuked him. The image of the black aura hovered.

He turned on the radio, hoping for the balm of the evening concert, only to hear news read in sharp-edged tones telling of US troops gunning down an entire family at a lunch party in Baghdad. The horror of ordinary citizens dying in violence and being left with horrific injuries as they went to schools, to markets, to visit their relatives, in the name of a war so many in Britain had not wanted, was utterly unbearable. Even doctors were fleeing Baghdad and those who remained had to struggle on without supplies. Max felt enraged and helplessness.

Eventually it was the charged simplicity of Bach's cello suites that restored his mind. He went upstairs in the hope of speaking to his wife, but on putting his head around the door, the sound of her breathing told him that the effect of nightly sleeping pills was taking place.

He walked back into the stillness of the green room, always waiting, and sat in the chair he had had for over twenty years. It had been his grandmother's sewing chair. He wondered what was going to happen. A restless spirit had been ignited.

He thought of Emily, asleep upstairs, of her fragility, of her mental state. Who was she now, for him? Who had she been? There was a photograph taken during the summer they had met at the small leaving party given in honour of the boys about to go to Oxford and Cambridge. How curious to think of it now. He had placed it inside the *Tibetan Book of Living and Dying*, a book he had at one time read a great deal. He stood up to find the book and opened it. The first page opened straight onto the photograph. It showed a smiling Max and Emily, both wearing white, standing thigh deep in a field of poppies and meadowsweet. His heart softened, remembering the heat of that summer twenty-five years ago, when they lost themselves within and in each other. *The warm balm after the unbearable cold winter of death and dying.* He could smell the heady, sensual scents of hedgerow grasses. The sun's rays warmed and softened, opening every pore of the skin, confounding the dark touch and smell of death. He saw now what he had seen then, Emily as a gift from the earth's abundance, brought to him to make up for his loss.

Without discussion she had bound herself to him, and he had gone along with it, although the way forward was often blurred. He knew that he had avoided true intimacy because he feared he would not be able to tolerate its inevitable cost. To love was to be truly brave. It was to be open and defenceless in the face of hurt. But he could see that he and Emily had tried to remain together in an idealistic way that did not involve the mess and confusion of mature love. They were more brother and sister, trying to fuse their bodies and souls to barricade themselves from the pain of adulthood and its inevitable losses than they were active lovers. Their sexual relationship was always limited and costly in terms of Emily's stability. He shuddered. Could they now have become the Paolo and Francesca of Dante's Hell?

Her worried parents had sent her to a clinic in Switzerland during his university days and she had benefited from this place in the mountains. They exchanged letters but despite the opportunities afforded by Oxford life Max was already on his way to committing to the spiritual life. He continued with his doctoral studies whilst in the monastic order he joined after leaving Oxford. During those seven years living the simple life of a monk, Emily returned to Switzerland to be near him and to wait, believing that their union was pre-ordained. Monastic life taught him about the power of meditation to train his mind. But it did not offer him any balm for his soul or help soften the sharp edges wedged in his heart. After leaving, he had plunged himself into the rigours of an intense analytical training in the same way that he had given himself to the disciplined structure of the Order, hoping that he might find another way to be with suffering, his own and that of others. And he had married Emily.

In all these fourteen years together, Emily had developed no filtering lens that might protect, reflect, contain or reject whatever influence came her way. Her communication with him remained intense but became more labyrinthine, and focused only on him, so that now he was the only one who could fully understand or communicate with her. His analytical training confirmed to him the nature of her condition, and he had tried to be her analyst too, after appointments with experienced colleagues sent her into a flight of displaced words and actions for several weeks. Choosing his way of being with her as a path of compassion, he had taken on her suffering as a practice, thus bringing the precepts of the Order into ordinary daily life. After a disturbing emotional beginning to their married life, this practice had held now for ten years. And now everything seemed to be changing.

So far in his therapeutic practice he been able to contain easily and lovingly the experience of a patient falling in love with him. He knew that the feeling was not for him personally, but that he was a conduit through which a patient could experience their own capacity to love safely, and as something precious. He felt comfortable with the many different expressions of love and professional boundaries were a relief. The red-hot moments could feel frightening when so out of context from normal life. The room could feel sticky and frustrating.

There was a new, sharp interior voice forcing itself to be heard. "For heaven's sake, Max!" That's what young masters had said at school when he appeared so grown up before his time. It's what several friends had stopped saying now as if somehow it was all too late. And anyway, what did it mean, "Loosen up?" How did he do it?

He sat in his green chair and thought clinically in order to restore clarity of judgement. What was he to be up against? Something to do with women? Clearly something he did not know about, something beyond his control. If there were a falling in love, what would it be with? When patients seemed to fall in love with him it was not him because they knew nothing about him. But what if he was about to fall in love himself? Would that be loosening up? He could not imagine such a thing and laughed inside.

As he left the green room he paused for a moment in the open doorway and looked back at the place where he had tried to smooth the scuffed carpet. It had refused to be smoothed.

# 4

SAXON looked toward the radiographer to indicate she was ready for her to take the images. The nurse released a syringe of radio-opaque dye into the catheter inserted into the femoral artery. Saxon held the tube in place, gently against the patient's right leg.

The team of gowned theatre staff looked up to watch the televised movement of the outline of the heart appear on the grey monochrome of the screen. The great muscled fist of the heart pulsed blood through the coronet of arteries and veins in a dance that signalled life but might also be indicating death; an intimate dance upon which modern technology placed its gaze and made decisions. Trained human eyes would convert opinion into action. Cut, mend, stent, bypass and replace, insert, change, add, insert a pacemaker. Nothing can be done. Take pills for the rest of your life. Wait for a transplant.

This work was daily routine for theatre staff, and clear pictures meant that their contribution through radiography and technology had done its work well. The dance they had been privileged to witness would go on, hidden inside, until the next intervention. A wonder taken for granted.

Secretly Saxon marvelled at the mysteries of the heartbeat, but to speak of such a thing would not be professional. She bent towards the gowned patient, an elderly man with thin white hair and frightened watery eyes. "Are you alright, Mr Fletcher?" Her voice was a welcome balm to his fear. She looked him directly in the eyes. "It won't be long now."

The man seemed to warm at her voice, and whispered hoarsely "Yes, thank you, Doctor". His anxious eyes had rarely left Saxon's face. They now relaxed. His large, rough hands with thick blunt fingers rested in Saxon's finer ones.

"We've got some good pictures, and I can see that your operation will be going ahead as planned." She smiled and rubbed his arm. "We'll be taking the tube out in a moment, and then I will just put some pressure onto the place where I inserted the tube, to make sure that it heals up properly. You'll feel the pressure of my hands and then it's all over for today."

She pressed both hands firmly onto the cut she had made

directly into the artery. Then she stood very still. The body of Albert Fletcher, retired farm worker and market gardener lay in her charge. It was one of the rare moments in technological medicine when the laying on of hands was both an imperative medically, and also allowed a space for healing communication.

Relief at getting through a successful procedure released the room into action. There was noise and bustle: instruments into dishes, trolley wheels on the rubber floor, water running, wires pulling and flapping, metal on metal. Theatre staff wore white clogs on their bare feet, which clopped and shuffled against the tiled floor: wood percussion backing to the varied syncopation of voices and noises, the leavening of jokes and laughter raising pitch.

The uniform green cotton shifts and slacks were designed for the air-conditioned theatres, often ill fitting, and obscured by heavy lead aprons under which the body sweated and was pressed from shoulder to knee. The weight was familiar, it gave Saxon a sort of importance. But today the weight of the lead apron felt oppressive. It pulled on the back of her neck. On the knot of fear which was never far away. It throbbed significantly as she stood with her hands on her patient.

Her staff cleared up and chatted. Her dominant position gave her the chance to think alone in the relief of aftermath. She could unwind from the tension of the work, feel good about her ability to be in control. She did not chat.

The throbbing increased. She was moving, swaying.

*She was on the boat again; it was swaying, throwing her against the thumping riot inside her chest.*

Her heart leapt into her mouth. Her hands were slipping. Slipping about in hot stickiness. They were slipping about in the cut she had made in Mr Fletcher's artery. The cut was widening instead of closing. His blood was leaking out, over her hands, over the green sterile gowns, onto the white tiles. She couldn't hold it anymore.

*He was getting heavier, she could hardly hold him, and he was weighting down her whole body, taking it over. She could not breathe. She moved forward, to try to get relief, to get better air, to be nearer some imagined freshness from the water. She was sinking. The junk began to sway, then to roll. She tried to plant her feet more solidly on the swaying deck, to hold onto the leaden silk-wrapped bundle that was now hers alone, that had become fused within her... a child. A newborn. A baby boy.*

She spread her hands. They were bloodied. All that red. She had to get rid of it.

*"Just get rid of it for God's sake."*

Her hands were empty ...

Then blood begun to spurt, in small spurts at first, then in jets of fine spray, spilling wide. She heard screaming.

In horror and fascination, she watched the spray of deep red rare B-negative blood being pumped out by an inner force. Of course. The force of the heart. The heart she was supposed to be mending. She was after all a doctor. *"She's supposed to be a doctor for God's sake."*

The room swam. Faces, elongated, horrified, with open mouths, pressed against the sterile tiles of the white basement room.

Faces of the boat passengers, mouths open, paralysed by the image of the blue quilted bundle suspended over the dark waters of Hong Kong harbour. Screams of many merged into one. Saxon's jaw was being torn apart. Her heart was about to burst.

She sat up, awake, sweating. Palpitating. Horror. Horror.

It was three thirty in the morning. In the fragment of time between sleep and waking consciousness the impact of the nightmare remained vivid and held her. Relief that she was in reality in her own bed in Notting Hill. But what had she done? *The cut, the blood on her hands, the baby hovering over the water, the unstoppable haemorrhage.* Her body was back on that boat in Hong Kong, but her mind had no access to understanding its response. It became an adrenaline- and cortisol-filled space, all trembling in the limbs and bile in the mouth. As she sat on her bed, shaking and alone, she had a micro-second flash that something very bad, something involuntary and irrevocable, had happened.

*They were calling for a doctor.*

"She's supposed to be a doctor for God's sake ... you can't trust anyone these days... Someone she did not know had said quietly, "It's an accident, a terrible accident ..."

"It's my baby," said the father of the child. "My little baby boy. He's going to die in that filthy water."

Was it her fault? She could not, would not, go on with the unbearable thoughts. What else might reveal itself in her half-awake, half-sleep state, and unravel her completely.

But the images would not go away. They would not leave her alone.

She sat up and turned on the light. She knew she should touch something solid and drink a glass of water. She'd been shocked awake in the early hours before. By many things. But not for a long time.

She noticed her raised heartbeat settling and found herself thinking scientifically about her fitness level and that her heart could restore its rhythm within a few minutes. But what had happened in the nightmare was far from scientific. It was insane.

She leaned back onto her pillows and looked at the painting of Venice that hung on the wall opposite. The particular Venetian blue of the sky and the soft stone-coloured streets of Murano where they had made glass for hundreds of years in their fine tradition. She felt the movement of tears, but so fleeting and deep they never made it to the surface. Venice. She had been happy that holiday; one of her earlier times with Lewis, where he had bought the shoes, and the blue necklace.

Then, anger! Bloody hell. The damn therapy. That's what was causing this. Poking itself inside what should be left alone. He had even suggested she might bring her dreams to the sessions, and perhaps it was this suggestion that had triggered ... Dreams of all things, how very mad. She knew it would make things worse.

Why couldn't she just put the lid on it?

*"You will have to pay for what you have done,"* said a stern voice inside her.

Then another voice, *"Why couldn't it have been me? I wish it was me who was thrown into the filthy water to drown."*

But she was alive, only to be now tortured by the unbidden. Was that a life worth having? She was no good to anyone now. She couldn't work, no hands on. Suspended. Looking out she saw there was yet no sign of dawn over the park.

\* \* \* \*

She raised her head into the full spray of the shower. It was Thursday, a day for the green room.

Immaculately dressed and in control again, she closed the door of her apartment and walked down the stairs. As she opened the outer door her peripheral vision noted a movement to the left side. She froze, not turning in that direction but trying to make as much of the sighting as possible. Even this, this person following, spying on her. It was all like being in a horror movie. She was the target, suspended, on the hook, like meat in butcher's window. Who was he? She knew it was a he. What did he want?

\* \* \* \*

Max seemed solid, a corduroy presence in polished brogues. He rested his strong-looking hands, one over the other.

She did not know how to start. Where to start.

The familiar sick feeling that arose when her body met the green chair forced her into the peculiar 'otherness' that seemed to be the business of therapy. He had said to tell him of any dreams and so he could have it.

She spoke then, because it was right there in front of her still, and also to play the therapy game and for something to say. The possibility that she might be helped did not arise.

"I had a dream in which a patient exsanguinated."

He is surprised, and gratified, that she seems about to offer him a dream and that her unconscious is starting to speak, and so soon into the work. He concentrates on the word exsanguinated – then asks her to tell him about this word.

She shrugs again.

"Is exsanguinated the same as bleeding to death?" he asks.

"Oh, that's a much more dramatic expression," she says briskly.

"But is it accurate?" he asks.

She shrugs again. "Actually, it means to drain of blood." As she spoke, she looked at him. She realises that speaking the meaning is in fact much more sinister.

Again, the silence, in which Saxon fights to stay in

her chair, fights to remain rational when there seems to be a cacophony of elements inside of her. The jellyfish, the sickness, the fog and also an uncanny feeling at the base of her spine like the wag of a tail; but she has no tail.

Max feels concerned. "Could you tell me the dream's content?"

She stumbles through it, holding her breath, avoiding his face, missing out the reminders of the boat in Hong Kong.

Max is thoughtful, being presented with such a dream when he knew so little of her. He says quietly, "Thank you for telling me such a powerful dream. I am aware that looking at dreams seriously is probably a completely new territory for you, but dreams often give us a real sense of what is not yet able to be in the conscious mind. They always present dramatically, especially when there is something important needed for homeostasis – for balance."

She is about to leave the disturbing quality of the dream and scoff at the idea of taking dreams seriously when he says: "What was the feeling of the dream?"

"Isn't it obvious ..." she starts. Then she realises her habitual defence.

"Try to stay with how you felt when you woke from the dream," he says firmly.

"It was half-past three. Dark. Wind rattling the window frames. Cold. Nothing steady, nothing to hold on to ... Hanging from the butcher's hook," she says slowly.

"Suspended?" asks Max.

"Yes," she replies, surprised at his awareness.

"So there is some aspect of the dream that refers to your current suspension from clinical work?"

She shrugs again. "Maybe, but ..."

"In the dream", Max continues, wanting to engage her in the substance "your hands get bloodied, and you are left with this. What was that like?"

"Oh, I'm not afraid of a bit of blood," she says quickly. She is about to continue with some quick and witty line when Max comes in again.

"Yes, I understand that, but here the dream is presenting you, in your doctor's position, and in a situation that is familiar to you, with a bleeding you are unable to control. I was wondering what this was like for you? And I am not trying to trick you with my question, I am trying to reach into what the dream might be telling us about how you feel deep inside."

"Do you really mean you use dream material as actual information in your profession?" she says haughtily "Look – I had this dream, its obvious isn't it?"

Max smiles. "Tell me," he says.

"Well – of course I don't like being out of control, no one does surely. That's why I'm here, isn't it? To get back some control."

"Yes, I think you are onto something there. Control is very important to you, isn't it? We need to know a bit more about what is at stake, about just why it's so important."

There is a pause between them.

"When you were telling me the dream you sounded very matter of fact, when the content is shocking and upsetting," he says. "But I noticed that you held your breath a lot and avoided eye contact. You gripped the chair a little more strongly. I wondered if this is a way in which you have got used to trying to keep control of your feeling through tensing your body."

*The things he noticed!* "Of course, it's a doctor's nightmare," she says, "making a cut into the artery is a serious business and of course it's a terrifying thought …." She falters and her voice becomes smaller "I might not be able to stop the bleeding. I might bleed to death."

They share the moment together, and the "I". But Max did not think that she had heard herself: that it was she who might bleed to death. She also had not registered with any curiosity his suggestion that instead of feeling emotion she had body experiences. She had no words for feelings.

He decides to wait before returning to the matter of bleeding to death and marvelled at the creative expression of her mind, to which she was currently oblivious. He proceeds along another tack: "The suspension, what's this like for you?"

"Hong Kong all over again," she says unexpectedly and then immediately regrets it. She looks at him in horror. He looks at her with compassion.

Here I go then, she thinks. Giving him the stuff he

wants.

"That boat. Planting my feet on the deck, it started swaying, I thought it would go on forever, the dark, the water, the waves."

Max can feel her fear, and something disembodied. "I want us to go very, very slowly and be careful. It feels as if you are beginning to relive some of what happened on that boat in Hong Kong. Remember to use the steady breathing we did last time if you notice your heart rate rising too far or when you feel overwhelmed. Just notice," he says firmly.

She looks serious. "It was like that when I woke up this morning."

"I can believe it was!"

"It's all meat and potatoes to you, isn't it?"

"A bit like cutting into an artery for you, I guess," he says.

They smile at each other in appreciation.

Max can see that her eyes shifted into a faraway look. He waits, watching her.

"That Chinese junk, a tamed species," she is ruminating, "like me. Neither one thing nor the other, neutered, suspended, from everyday flesh and blood life. These junks were once the glory of the China Sea. Red canvas sails. Now they are used to serve expensive buffets to visiting businessmen or drug companies." She shudders.

*Gold leaf had been brushed by hand onto the red carved supports of doors; it decorated the frames of the many mirrors; it lay in bathrooms and lavatories. Walls were covered in silk traced with bamboo calligraphy. Deep pile gold and red carpets silenced the plimsolled feet of the Chinese staff offering the mix of food tastes, stir fry, curry, salad, roast beef and ham, imported salmon and champagne. All to impress the foreign and Chinese business community living in or visiting Hong Kong.*

*She had preferred the open space and air of the deck, even though in June it was so very hot. She had moved out several times to find relief from the suffocating social press of people and food below. Too much, too many, too tightly packed. The unnatural freeze of air conditioning dried any moisture. Again, there was the familiar grip across the back of her neck* and heaviness in her chest. Body tension created by having to be polite and make small talk with dull strangers never to be seen again.

She rubbed the back of her neck.

She was stretching her neck from side to side, rubbing it with her right hand as she watched the busy water crater of Hong Kong harbour, with the splash and zip of taxies, ferries, sampans, boats of all shapes and sizes. A frenzied womb of water enclosed by glass skyscrapers, reflecting green, blue and gold. No interface between water and glass-walled slopes. A mighty city built upon a bubbling cauldron. Despite the heat she had shivered in her formal English clothes.

Max did not know how far her recollection had gone. He asked an ordinary question: "Why were you on this boat?"

Her hosts were an American drug company marketing a new treatment for cardiomyopathy. Her social obligation took her from the air of the deck back down into the belly of the junk to talk in empty phrases. She had no appetite for food. As soon as she could she returned to the deck to find that the junk was moving amongst the slightly wider spaces of Aberdeen. Still stretching her neck and trying to breathe out the tightness from her chest she watched the far-off fishermen and women.

"I watched the fisher people," she says. "They reminded me of the matchstick people I made as a child, automated into activity."

They were bent double, their bamboo cone hats covering their heads. One group was pulling urgently at their nets in staccato rhythm, stick bodies rigidly upright, then they would bend like hairpins before rising up and folding down, again and again.

"Did you know that *coo-li* means fierce labour?" she asks.

"No, I didn't. Does that also describe you?" asks Max, taking a risk. He had seen her child-like self, but had she ever been given the freedom of childhood?

"I think that I felt like them that day, sort of doomed into action, imprisoned. I know that I felt extremely tense." She sounds very sad.

*That day she felt as if the slightest whisper could break*

her in two.

"Do you feel OK about saying more about what happened after you returned on to the deck away from the guests?" Max is watching her breathing. Her hands are gripping the arms of the chair. The dream has opened something, and he needs to help her go with the natural flow in a way that could contain the feeling and arousal and protect her from her fear of bleeding to death.

*From time to time the junk lurched under the swell of a passing hydrofoil wake, which made her stiffen more. Standing on the deck of the Chinese junk she was more tense than after a day working with her cardiac patients. And the noise. She couldn't get away from noise. Everywhere she went alien sounds stabbed into her as if she had no protecting passage between inner and outer ear.*

"The noise was terrible," she says now, lifting her hands to hold against her ears.

*On the return part of their voyage, back to Queen's Pier, the harbour had become deafeningly noisy. The alien sounds of Chinese language pierced her ears and rose above the gruff roar of diesel engines as orders were exchanged.*

"Can you describe it?" asks Max. He wonders whether she had suffered a small seizure on that boat in Hong Kong.

*All around her were water sounds made by speeding engines, waves, water pipes, and the splash and dip of oar. As they became more amplified, she began to feel as if she were held inside a watery cave. Smells were strong, a mixture of engine fumes, dead fish, dubious waste products. Litter bobbed incongruously in and out of waves, in abundance, before being harvested by the cleaning junks in their baskets called weirs. The open mouths of the netted booms hungrily scooped up all. More bulk, more dollars. Saxon wondered what treasures they might find when their catch was unloaded. A box of peaches, discarded pages of* Gray's Anatomy; *maybe even a pearl of great price. A wry smile creased the taught page of her tired face. "Dream on," said a voice inside her.*

Max is collecting her repeated phrases and images. The jigsaw puzzle fragments of her inner world. Trapped and imprisoned. Suspended. Fierce labour; exsanguinated; drained of blood. Something inside her had given way on that boat, as if the different pieces, too long forced together in a bad fit, were being blown apart, far away from home. A migraine, a seizure, a breakdown.

It would be a while before they could get to it. He wants to keep the pace slow so that her understanding could come alongside the events. He notices that she is sweating.

*Behind them now, and beyond the floating restaurants of Aberdeen, every hillside was covered with matchstick cities made by the matchstick people; They were like the nests of sea eagles, bundles of sticks carried from far to form a precarious perch. 'Home' to thousands of families trying to hold together. The continuum of some eternal life effort meant that when they were swept away by winds, or crushed by those wanting the place cleaned up, they were immediately replaced.*

"They do all this, and will repeat it all tomorrow, and the next day. And for so little," she thought, "and there are so many of them." Her breathing felt leaden. "What is it all for?"

He feels that he is losing her in the reminiscence. He thinks she has had enough for one session and there are only ten minutes left. He says:

"I have been noticing the effect talking about Hong Kong has on your nervous system and it feels as if we have done enough for today. I'd like you please to keep a notebook of any feelings, images, sounds or other things you might normally think as odd occurring in your every day, or indeed through dreams. Then we can look at it together next time and return to what you came with today."

To himself he wonders: she is afraid, she feels bad, but she has no language other than repression and the effort of will. He wonders about guilt, whether she feels as if she had blood on her hands. He thought it more likely that she carried an old, entrenched guilt, guilt for things from childhood which could not be her fault. This would get in the way of her being able to connect to any guilt about the baby which could provide her with the relief of remorse.

But it is too soon and too dark and challenging. Her feelings are too drenched in feelings of badness.

He has to stay with what she can manage. "Before we

## The Pale Green Room

finish, I wanted to ask you what are the terms of your current suspension?"

She shudders. "If you must," she says tartly. Max understands now that this tart defence is her way of normalising herself and keeping control and that it would be important to be able to return to this kind of normality after the destabilising power of re-visiting Hong Kong memories. "I'm not allowed to work with patients," she says in a furious tone. "But I still go into the hospital every day and get on with research. I draft clinical papers." She stops. "The hands-on ..." she looks at her hands. They were clean. They could have blood on them. "The hands-on duties and the taking of examinations are forbidden."

Even though she was so skilled, so thorough. She would never hurt anyone; she would never put a foot wrong. The injustice, just because of one incident a long way from here that was nothing to do with patients, nothing to do with her integrity as a doctor.

And now she was seen as someone who might put others at risk. And, oh the emptiness! The dreadful sickening emptiness!

\* \* \* \*

Vera had agreed to the six initial sessions. Max asks her how she is spending her days. She cannot tell him. It was the weekly appointment that forced Vera out of house. It made her get out of her exercise gear and think about what to wear: dress properly, wash her hair, put on make-up. She had to think about what she would do after her appointment. She would be outside, in a strange part of London, with no one else to meet, no plans, no one to go home for.

She can only tell him of activities. Her default position was to go shopping. She would drive under Hammersmith Flyover into Shepherds Bush Road and along to Holland Park and the Bayswater Road. Once away from the mysteries of South London she felt more ease. She would park in the underground car park in Cavendish Square at the back of Oxford Street and enter her paradise.

Surprised at Max's interest in what she did, she tells him how Oxford Street offered her comfort.

"I like to wander in and out of the big stores. I can look

at everything without anyone bothering me."

She didn't say: *I like to touch the silk and satin, press their soft colours to my face. I used to like to try on evening gowns as if I were Princess Diana (God rest her soul). I can go to the ladies, eat a snack, even buy something, all without having to speak to anyone.*

She loved to look at the displays and models, at the colours and decorations, at the fantasies created where everything mixed and matched and looked wonderful.

"What is it like?" asks Max.

She pauses, looking down at her hands.

"It's nice," she says slowly.

"What is it that attracts you?"

It's this interested "tell me about it" style about ordinary things that encourages her. She becomes thoughtful.

"I began my working life in the shop in Manchester. Dodds," she says. "My name now, and of course it's all much bigger" and she makes a faint smile.

She thought how Alistair did not like her to reveal that she had once been a shop girl. At Harrow he had begun the process of camouflaging his own Northern accent, then later, at Oxford, he tried to complete the obliteration of his background.

"Did you know, did I tell you before, that I'd worked in a shop?" she asks Max nervously, even now wondering if she was betraying her husband.

But in this green room she was being actively invited to step back once again into Dodds, and gain access to the energy of the girl she had been then.

For Vera, a girl in the 1980s, Dodds was a paradise all on its own. It was the place where, through her imagination, she could become a smartly dressed young woman who had an independent life. A girl who did not have to live in constantly changing rented accommodation with a mother whose moods were unpredictable, and extreme, by whom she felt both resented as a tie, and depended on to sort her out when needed. She could imagine having a shop or salon of her own where she did not have to wait upon demanding strangers. The store was the nearest she got to family life. And ultimately it turned out to be the gateway to a completely different life.

"When I started, I was just sixteen, straight from school. I had two "O" Levels – in domestic science and English." This proud reporting, as if to a headmaster, accentuated the rounded vowels she had learned and practised by listening to tapes, the rounded vowels that separated her from her mother's dialect.

The green room opened its arms for Vera to glimpse her earlier self, walking down the central staircase at Dodds. She knew she was pretty and that her dark bouncing hair lit up as she moved. Her deep brown Latin eyes were full of wonder and fun, and her large perfectly formed mouth did not need words to speak. Her natural dimples, freckles and humour, had not yet been compromised by plasticised charm and effete manners.

"What was it your mother wanted?" asks Max.

Vera gives a surprisingly deep-throated laugh – then puts put on a traditional northern accent: "A woman can't make it on her own, not in this world. You need to find a man to operate through. Always please a man, but never trust one. Always go for big blokes, the ones with the cash, and especially the ones with a good family. Once you're in, make sure you stay in." She had answered quickly, on automatic. Her mouth set itself a little.

The room is startled by the shift in accent. Max feels his ears tickle.

"So you met Alistair in the store?"

The Alistair she first knew now joined her in the pale green room. The awkward son, expected to make up for being an only child. Always eclipsed by a larger-than-life father who owned the store and "half of Manchester". Alistair's grandfather had begun importing fabrics from India after being out there in the army. His small stall in Manchester market had grown to a business, which included made-up clothes, leather goods, bags, belts, and jackets. They were all rather exotic for the early twenties; trimmings, beads, fringes, anything sparkling was novel and in demand. The eventual store to which Vera went for her first job was a successful development from this enthusiastic love of luxury and Grandfather Dodds' natural business intuition. It had survived take-over attempts, buyouts, fires, and strikes. It was an indulgence of over-the-top northern grandeur for an entire cross-section of the vast Lancashire area it served.

Inside the green room her mind was opening up to vivid images of her past, as if she had stepped through CS Lewis's wardrobe. The image of herself as an eight-year-old, with her mother, standing at the bus stop. White ankle socks and a Fair Isle beret. A second-hand wool coat that scratched the back of her neck. Her mother stiffening at the sight of a sleek black car, whispering: "Get a good look at money, Vera. Without staring." That first glimpse, through lowered eyes, of Alistair in the back of his father's Jaguar, wearing a maroon school uniform blazer with gold badge, a large cap that looked odd on top of his floppy hair. He must have been thirteen.

The Dodds were a family her mother whispered about, in envy and in awe. She whispered gossip: "That boy, that Alistair – silly fancy name – most likely spoilt rotten. He'll be a mother's boy." Alistair was the precious only child. His mother had suffered miscarriages and infant deaths. For all their wealth and opportunity, fate was not kind in giving the Dodds what they most wanted: a large family of children.

"I've heard tell", whispered Vera's mother, "that he's an odd one too. Been seen beating his dog and horses. Mind you," she straightened Vera's beret, "he's a good catch for a girl."

"My mother always thought Alistair a good catch," Vera says to Max.

"And you?"

She shrugs and smiles her soft wistful smile. "I realise, sitting here, that I am very tired," she says. "This chair, this room, it makes you stop doesn't it? It makes you think and feel things. It's like going into the magic wardrobe – you know, in *The Lion, the Witch and the Wardrobe?*

Max smiles. Oxford. CS Lewis. The legacies.

"Got children, have you?"

"No," he says.

She looks at him, alert, but does not comment. She wonders if his childlessness is a sadness.

Then she thought about the day Alistair first noticed her. His face. It was a summer afternoon, and she walked her practised walk down the wrought iron central staircase which ran through the department store. "I was very young then," she remarks to Max.

"What were you like?" he asks, curious, interested.

She smiled happily and entered that happy afternoon once more. "I walked slowly, I was sure of myself. I held my head high. I had a shirt-waister dress, pale blue. I loved that dress. My Mum's friend had made it for me. She said that it complimented me. It showed off my ..." she falters, shy, "my waist, you know ..."

She remembered the feel of the soft cotton and the wide petersham-backed belt. She remembered the swing of her hips and how the movement of the full skirt showed off her small waist and slim legs.

She brings her hand up to her throat. "I had these pearls even then. They were from some distant bloke who took a shine to me and sent them in the post. Friend of my Mum's. But he was the one person who did something nice. Who didn't want to..." she stops and looked sharply at Max.

They are silent together, sharing the feeling of the many 'uncles' and mother's male friends who were 'not nice'.

Max imagined how very fresh she must have looked. He pondered on her talismanic wearing of the pearls. "Do you often wear them?" he asks.

She smiles. "I go back to them, over and over. Alistair, well he used to buy me all sorts. Bought stuff in Bond Street that was a bit too ... well formal and brassy sort of, for me. I really like these pearls." She fingered them as she spoke.

"They suit you," says Max simply. "And I can see they are one of the few good things to have lasted from difficult times."

She looks down, unnerved by his understanding, and scared. If he knew, knew what those bastards had made her do ... Could he see through her, to then, back into the past? Could he see what all those awful uncles did, her mother in the next room, knowing. Would Max not see her if he knew they had tried to make her into a little whore?

If he could he was not showing it, and maybe even if he knew he would not judge. Now that was a powerful thought!

The room is now offering her something else, another perspective on understanding her relationship with Alistair, that there was possibly something hidden about her that had charmed him. She, like him, was not all that she seemed. There was also the shared sense, never spoken, of being only children and wanting something different from the demands of their roots. She was not eager to impress him as other local girls had been, nor was she bothered about his family's standing and material wealth. She wanted to train as a beautician and have her own salon and had secretly decided to save enough money for the evening classes. She might even one day have her own products. She wanted to become independent in a way her mother never had, and to be able to hold onto this whatever happened with any man.

"When he first asked me out I was sixteen and he just twenty-one. I laughed and said, "You don't have to do that you know." Max could imagine it, a sweet tinkling laugh, her black hair bouncing. Now, in this green room, Vera felt pleased that at first she had refused Alistair, despite repeated requests, stirring his need. The room was allowing her space to remember the sixteen-year-old self, who had her mind set on independence, who was amused by his advances, finding them earnest and immature after seeing the behaviour of older men in her mother's life. She did not take Alistair seriously.

Then, a harsher image appeared, of returning home one evening to the storm of her mother's rage. She had found out that Alistair was in pursuit and that Vera was playing, in her mother's words 'a hard-to-get little bitch'. "After all I've done for you and now you're throwing away your one good chance, you little idiot," she yelled.

As Vera looked around their shabby room with its smell of stale cigarettes and beer, its cheap leather sofa and stained rug, she was unable to tell her mother about how she hated their life, how she hated what the uncles did. She was unable to tell her mother about her own dreams, of independence, of having nothing to do with men.

The campaign started that day. The pressure became too much to bear. The only way to escape her mother's world was to become as far removed as possible, and Alistair offered her a way.

"My mother seemed to want better things, but not if it meant her being what she would call 'shown up' and feeling small. I think the Dodd's family made her feel small," says Vera candidly. Max listens deeply, offering a faint smile, encouraging her to go on. "She became, well, spiteful," Vera says with difficulty. Her voice had changed now, it was softer and sad. "I was getting in with people Mother had nothing in common with. When I started seeing Alistair and it became serious, I think she got scared."

There is a long silence.

"Anyway, she disappeared for a time."

Another silence. Vera was remembering, but it was hard.

"She disappeared. I didn't know what to do. No one seemed to know where she might have gone. 'Good riddance to her, love,' many people said. I didn't tell Alistair because his family were the sort who'd get the police involved or something official, and I knew that would be hopeless." *Of course, it also suited Alistair that her rather common mother had gone missing. He would not have to suffer the inevitable confrontation between the parents. His parents were always completely against it all.*

Vera was not sure yet just how much she could tell Max about Alistair. She found herself thinking all kinds of new things in this green room but she did not want to be disloyal and, after all, what if he came back and she had aired all these new thoughts. Once spoken about who knows where the seeds could fall? So already there were two new voices – one, not so new, said "Be canny, box clever, don't let them know what you think or feel"; and the other new voice that said "Alistair used me to get at his parents, to be different. He was not going to be dominated by his parents' choices and he used me to rebel against them as well as have good sex." She kept quiet about these new inner voices.

She said: "I think she went because she was embarrassed and scared."

Max is impressed by her understanding and insight, and her lack of criticism at the obvious envy of a mother for whom he could feel distaste rising. He wondered if Vera had even been shown her own true value, whether she had ever been given space to think about how things affected her. It seemed as if, in order to survive, she just had to manage others.

"And then I got a note saying "You've got lucky. You'll

be alright, not like me. You've got something for yourself now and you won't want to be bothering with the likes of me." Vera looked sad, "It was as if she blamed me for having something she claimed she always wanted for me."

"Were you worried?"

Vera smiles, turning the corners of her mouth downward. "I was for a while, and, guilty. I felt guilty, I worried about her harming herself. She had made suicide attempts before. Then there was all the rent and bills and debts that kept coming to the flat." *As well as the hideous drunken ex-punters looking for a shag.*

"But I couldn't find her. I didn't know what to do."

"You were also very young," says Max thoughtfully.

She looked at him as if she had never thought of that aspect, or as if it didn't count and she shouldn't have minded being young. She had always been rather grown up.

Max asks: "What happened then?"

Vera is thoughtful. By the time her mother had disappeared she and Alistair had become an important part of each other's lives. It was more than just attraction. Each offered the other an escape from the grip of demanding parents.

The room allowed her now to see the nature of this escape. It was also beginning to allow her to see in Alistair the son of the father for whom Vera was a challenge, an available rebellion. Through Vera, Alistair had outwitted his father and begun to be his own man. And of course, Vera's mother had sent word, to wish her daughter good luck and had turned up again, as if nothing had happened, just after their wedding.

\* \* \* \*

After her session, and more tired than she was aware, she wandered around the John Lewis department store. Today it lacked comfort. There was nothing she needed to buy. She felt disorientated, without purpose or shape. She looked around hoping something might suggest itself. She might buy a new tapestry, or cushion cover to complete, but her house was full of them. She hadn't made her own dresses in years, but now she found herself looking at materials and then standing in line for the pattern books over which she had pored as a girl. She remembered saving up to buy from the *Vogue* catalogue she then shared with three other girls. Memory was welcome, and warm. She wanted to talk to the other women in the line, to ask them what they were making, or planning. Was it for a special occasion? Was it for themselves or their mothers, their friend, their little girl? A little girl to make dresses for. The miscarriage she had had after one of the more violent rows with Alistair. That might have been her little girl.

Those memories of her past fuelled her nostalgia and longing. She felt the sting of withdrawal from that life, and the regret that she had allowed Alistair to train her to reject, even despise it. Apart from Coral I've got no real friend here in London, she thought. My life here has been a front, to keep in with Alistair. I don't belong here, I never have.

At one of the mirrored pillars, she caught her reflection. Her cheeks were hollowed, her eyes lacked sparkle and lustre, her jacket wasn't straight. She hardly recognised the image staring back at her. She felt stuck there, her mouth dry from lack of food. Despite her thinness she felt heavy and bloated; walking away from the mirrored pillar seemed too difficult, her feet felt as if they were sticking to the carpet. Greetings cards were all around, with rows of wrapping paper and matching ribbons, candles and flowered boxes. Their messages of celebration seemed to mock her.

"If only I could cry." Had she said that out loud?

She looked down at her hands. What had Max said? "I sense that you are a practical person, you have strong hands." She was alarmed at the time and worried that her nail polish might be chipped, and she had pushed them under her thighs out of sight. She remembers Max's curious smile. Quite quickly her hands had started throbbing, they would not be sat on and she had pulled them out and looked at them as if for the first time. Perhaps he was right. She could put her trust in her own hands as strong. After what seemed an eternity, she forced herself to move on and out into the now darkening square, where she collected her car and drove home.

# 5

SHE was talking again about the black hole of suspension.

"Does it link with what we were discussing last time, when you told me the dream, of being drained of life blood?"

"As if the black hole was moving in and taking over?" Saxon shudders. How horrible. "It's a sort of death."

"Yes," says Max and looks at her keenly.

"I don't think I'm ready to talk about death," she says.

"We could talk first about symbolic death," says Max. "Being suspended from work, does it feel as if it's the doctor part of you that is being drained of life blood and that this part is in danger of death?"

She looks up and smiles surprisingly. "Sort of, yes. I think I can see where you are going with this now."

She leans back into the chair. The green room becomes blurred again.

"We are in this together," says Max in a firm, steady voice.

The feeling of the words registers, and his calm is as slight as a feather's quiver.

The black hole. Exsanguination. She wasn't afraid of a bit of blood for God's sake. She allows herself to ramble in a way she has not done before, her voice soft and almost whimsical: "Who am I without my work? That's it isn't it? Without meaningful work as a woman, you lose identity. You become invisible."

She thinks to herself: "Women who do nothing. Trussed up chickens, waiting to be sold and eaten." Then she says with cynicism: "A woman who does not want children has no place in the home."

Max is unsure what he is being told. "Whose voice is that?"

A smile. "Mine, of course." But inside she hears another voice. "A home is for children. What's the point of making a home if there are no children. What point am I if I have no …" She stops the memory there because the voice is her mother's and she did have children, just not the one she really wanted …

"Have you ever wanted children?"

"There might have been a time …" she trails off. Then,

looking sad and in a quiet voice she says, "I have a dog, she's called Alma."

Max is surprised. He had not imaged she would relate to an animal. He worries about staying with the events of Hong Kong in order to assess its severity. But he follows what she brings, and children have been mentioned without her cutting off.

"Do you want to say more?"

She looks up and hugs her chest with her arms. "No. Not yet."

"So, identity without work."

She shrugs. Surely it was obvious. Emptiness. A worm. Despised by all. The lowest of the low. Kicked around by anyone, spat upon, laughed and jeered at. No form, like a jelly. No place.

Her hands and face are moving slightly. Something was becoming active in the mysterious energy around the green chair. It was revealing, under its dark green cloak, some words she did not know she had, and attached to aspects of her body she could not diagnose.

"I can see that you are feeling something. Where do you feel it, this emptiness?"

She looks blank. Feel it. Being empty? Everywhere.

"In your body, where do you feel it?"

Was it in her body? Then, a hand, her hand, on her solar plexus. Under it, something.

Max follows the hand. She has not said a word to him.

"What is it like?"

Awful. Sinking, falling, falling forever, lost. No one, nothing there, nothing to hang on to, no form, no substance, only the blinding of anxiety. She grips the green chair and odd thoughts come in, in between the swirling feelings.

If she stays here, she will be lost and falling. She must get out. Soon she would not be able to breathe.

Max knows now that her identity has been based upon achievement. She has no idea how to just 'be', indeed she may not feel that she has the right or place to just 'be'. He senses that she associates ordinary emptiness with annihilation, such as death, where her life blood is drained away and she ceases to exist. Helping her to feel safe enough inside to just 'be' will be a complex and timely task, and require her to allow it.

Her hand on the solar plexus generates warmth of a sort, a life raft over the rapids. Then she remembers.

She looks down, shaken. Max sits with her in the silence. She looks up and smiles.

"How do you feel?"

She cannot speak.

She smoothes the fabric of her dress, along the sleeve. "Sometimes I can feel my heart."

"What's it like?"

"Sore now, and heavy."

He repeats her words warmly without question and his voice is soothing. He is just there, with her in the rawness, no questions asked.

"Do you feel it might be trying to say something?"

"That's a novel idea." She takes a deep breath.

"You know a lot about the heart."

"Yes I do, but not this kind of sore heart."

Max senses that it will take time for her to bring something vulnerable into the room voluntarily. For the first time he is feeling the level of her fear and the depth of her defence against it. Whilst he now knew some of the events of Hong Kong, they had not shared the holding and losing of the child. He was concerned. This was the fifth session and he had only a hunch about the build-up to the accident and what had been going on inside her. Was he missing something? Was he trying hard enough? Or was something happening secretly, without her being able to say, and that one day, as it had happened a myriad of times in his practice as a therapist, she would just bring her connections and surprise him.

Emily had said: "She will take you away from me." It unnerves him that her words enter this space at this moment. He had to trust that he, and the room, would hold the space for whatever she could manage.

"How did you get interested in hearts?"

She sits very still and engaged, and Max is encouraged that, for now, he is walking the right path with her. There is something reverent about the way she holds her hands together. "It was when I first saw the heart coming off bypass. There it was, a grey and white bloodied mass that had been worked over, fingered, sewn, bits cut out and bits added. It looked dead, just a mess, you couldn't imagine that life could come into it. But it did, it started pulsating. Medicine had given it a start, a bit of a shock, and then it continued beating all by itself. It went from grey to pink, then red with the blood." She pauses, "I thought it was so brave."

Something seemed to be speaking through her, giving her different words. She had stopped her fight for now. Somehow, they had got to the other side of it and found this sensitivity. He warms to her.

"The soreness in your own heart, what do you feel it needs?"

"It needs courage," she says unexpectedly. "And it needs to be less heavy."

"Do you know what has made it so heavy?"

There is a pause.

"I'm thinking that you might be going to help me find out," she says.

\* \* \* \*

As Max pulls back the curtain and opens the door to the street for her she remembers the figure of a young man in a crumpled suit at the top of the seven steps down into the junk. He was there again when she was doubled up against the side of the boat after the baby had gone. He had watched her with such kindness, as if he knew her. She had hung her head, unable to meet his gaze, and when she did look up, he was gone.

Max hears her say what queer things she remembers here.

\* \* \* \*

Once Saxon had made it back over Hammersmith Bridge, the conversations in the green room had disappeared from thought or exploration, as if neatly excised by a scalpel. Despite her rational command when away from the pale green room, she could not control what happened inside it. The very act of having to cross into the relative unknown of London south of the river threw her sense of order. The knot of pain at the bottom of her spine would grow and she would begin to feel disorientated and lost. The appointments did not lend themselves to becoming part of her organised structure, on a par with going to the gym as she had initially thought. They made her feel things she did not want to feel or own and behave in ways she considered childish. She had spent her life organising things to work like clockwork, to get away from being one of those women who had feelings that required understanding or needed others to confirm their worth. She could see that her chosen way of being reflected her father rather than her mother. If she had repressed some aspect of her 'feminine side' in order not be to be like her mother it was not surprising. The suggestion there was something hidden or split off in her that was trying to signal and break through seemed extraordinary, and hard to grasp.

As she turned into the hospital car park, she realised that she didn't really want to understand what had happened to her in Hong Kong, or find out why, she just wanted to put it behind her and carry on. She parked neatly, in her reserved named space. Her mouth was set, her thoughts practising her distaste for the current collective vogue for understanding, for counselling, for alternative medicine, gazing into crystals, astrology, meditation. She had been shocked to discover that one of her oncology colleagues had set an exam question for students on: "How does unhappiness get into a cell?".' It was followed by: "How does happiness get out of it?"

What was it Max had asked her about her own heart? That its soreness and heaviness might be trying to 'say' something. She knew that some part of her had said 'courage' and she felt embarrassed now at the romanticism. She thought about her studies and training. She thought about William Harvey and how he had challenged and disappointed the eighteenth-century Church for whom the heart was sacred to God when he discovered that the heart was nothing but a pump. Harvey relieved us of sloppy romanticism, she thought, clicking her central locking. God and mysticism had nothing to do with it, they were just excuses for lack of knowledge, although until Christian Barnard performed that first transplant in 1984 the heart was still seen as a no-go area for doctors because of its religious connections.

She tightened her grip on her briefcase and turned towards the entrance. Before she could get into her stride she saw the movement again, behind the big sycamore. That familiar dark figure, bearded. Waiting for her. She froze.

Nearby a young mother was lifting a baby dressed in blue out of a car seat. Saxon's heart took a swing. "Have you ever wanted children?" Max had asked, and she had been deliberately vague.

She looked again toward the tree, ready to move forward and challenge him. But he was gone.

Some stuff from that room was leaking out here, in her hospital world. She must not let that happen. Yes, they had established she was stressed, or had been, and for a few minutes she had been touched by Max's show of concern and intrigued by the idea that her heart needed courage. But now, back in reality where she belonged the whole idea of symbolism was fanciful and ridiculous. She just needed to get on and do what was necessary for her review in February when her period of suspension would be reconsidered.

As she entered the hospital corridors, alive with a buzz of people from all over the world, she comforted herself by thinking that by then she would have the whole thing under control.

But the process that began in the green room would not leave her alone. In the lift a young Ghanaian nurse wheeled in an emaciated old woman with a once-lovely face and no hair, her stick-like arm linked to a drip pole, her feet swollen and bandaged. Another dream triggered. She had started having the most awful dreams.

Max had indicated that dreams could be important for homeostasis. He spoke as if the unconscious were some part of anatomy, like the liver or pancreas. "I would assess that you are having these dreams because your psyche – meaning the whole of you, has been given a space here. And those things you have had to bury can be allowed. Dreams often shock so we take notice. Bit like a wakeup call." He had smiled, showing the gaps in his teeth. "It's actually healthy." She had had to smile at his attempt at humour.

The lift had become very full, and Saxon was pressed against the West African nurse bent over her charge. Her heart accelerated as images from the dream and the patient in the wheelchair connected. An old German rhyme came into her head, as her German nanny had translated it: "You're a crone, all skin and bone, ever to be alone, or moan, moan, moan. Nobody wants you, old crone, all skin and bone."

*The Pale Green Room*

# 6

FOR the first couple of hours after her session in the green room Vera would feel churned up inside. She would go over and over what had been said and how she had behaved. Driving home after her fourth visit she turned on the radio, hoping for distraction. She chose Classic *fm* – less talking. Berlioz: the Symphonie Fantastique. *How much of her life had been fantasy?* Yet with the bright, hopeful quality of that first movement and its waltz rhythm came the realisation that something quite new was happening to her. She was not on edge in that room, wondering what he thought of her and waiting for signs of judgement. Dr Max seemed not to think of her as a bad person or a failure because Alistair had left her for someone else. It was novel, as was the feeling of being taken seriously as a person in her own right. She even dared to think that Max might be someone on her side. He took all she said seriously and treated her with respect. In the green room she heard herself saying things she didn't know she could say, or even knew about.

But it was hard for her to maintain a connection with these new feelings or new thinking. The effects of the sessions, and the hope they inspired, faded, like music. When she was alone in her own home, without her usual purpose, her days were long and empty, the family house large and silent. She washed curtains and covers, wiped down walls. She returned to her exercise routine, but with a heavy heart. What was the point of keeping her figure unless she were to get Alistair back? A voice inside told her she needed to be strong whatever happened, but this would give way to an obsessional urge to try to use her body to outwit what had happened, and on really bad days she punished her body for letting her down. It had failed to keep her man.

On gentler days, she would find the energy and focus to read or listen to tapes that focussed on self-help techniques. Over the years she had used all kinds of self-improvement techniques, for fitness and appearance, then, later, for her nerves, for her nightmares, and sometimes panic attacks, and for boosting her confidence. She had not returned to them since Alistair's leaving for they seemed to mock her efforts as failures. Learning and being inspired was one thing; putting these pearls of wisdom into practice was another. And she saw no one to speak to properly; she kept the secret of Alistair's leaving.

Sometimes she would catch sight of the yoga mat she had bought this recent summer, kept in the corner among the books. She would flick it out in the way her teacher did, taking the three breaths before stretching gently as she had learned, then trying to remember the poses. When they came back to her, she felt cheered, and she even considered returning to the class. But how would she explain her absence?

It was very hard to leave the house. She wanted to be there, ready and waiting for when Alistair might return. If he came and found her out he might go away again and she would miss her opportunity.

She sent texts and emailed her sons, giving them news from their Pimlico square and the local markets, events she made up to amuse them. She made out she was well and happy, not mentioning their father's defection. It would soon be Luke's half-term and first permitted visit. She waited to see what Alistair would to do. She made a plan to make her own way there in her own time if he did nothing to include her.

Alistair was clever and devious about his means and had the use of experienced lawyers and accountants to make financial arrangements. Within two weeks of his leaving he was demanding that the house be sold.

Vera stopped answering the telephone unless she recognised the number, and the mail collected on the small table by the front door, unopened except for those with Luke's handwriting. She cleaned out the fridge, eating up whatever was left, and at peculiar times, when she remembered. At night she lay on the sofa, her brief episodes of sleep interrupted by dark images, half human, half insect, in a ferocious chase, and there was often a feeling of falling from which she would be shaken awake, suddenly.

She was unable to return to the shared bedroom, where the sheets remained unchanged, still holding the memory of Alistair's physical presence, in the marital bed where he belonged. When she pressed her face into the familiar smell to gain some comfort, she breathed in all that she had lost.

All she intended to hold on to.

They had made love – or was it just having sex? – early in the morning they took Luke to school. That he could do that and be planning to leave her the same day was beyond her. She picked at the memory. Had it been different? She didn't think so. The ferocity was the same. Should she have known? She went over and over what had been said between them before the scene in the car. Over and over how it might have been different, how she might have known, and forestalled his leaving.

Sometimes, the physical actuality of their being together only a few weeks ago meant that she could be a little bright. She could comb her hair and do her nails and have some hope of a future life. But it was short-lived. It would be replaced by the snarl on his lip and cold in his eye, the way he pushed passed her in his hurry to be off without any sadness or feeling. This cut to the quick. It stripped away hope, and the memory of her physical connection with him would no longer hold. She kept falling into the dark.

Her nights began to take over her days. Nights when it was not quite dark because of the glow of London streetlights and thus impossible to sense the correct time. She would doze for an hour and wake believing it to be morning, relieved she had managed to get through. But it might be only three or four o'clock. What came with her waking was the sickening ache, and her heart crushed and pressed down by some leaden weight.

\* \* \* \*

It was session five and Max was looking at her with those steady brown eyes in which she was finding some comfort.

"How are you?" he had asked. He felt she needed encouragement and ordinariness until she was ready, if ever, to look more deeply at psychological patterns.

She didn't know how she was, but she found herself saying: "My whole body feels as if it has been mauled by a lion."

Max nods. He sits still and Vera feels again that he takes her seriously, that her strange statement is not at all strange to him. She feels his concern as he considers the image that speaks of being played with like a prey, continually bruised and teased. Together they sit with these sensations.

Vera hesitates. Then she says: "I have this strange image,

an image of the lion's paw like a bandaged hand."

Max looks at her intently. He sees her look of concentration and senses that another language of communication is emerging through visual image and body sensation.

Vera closes her eyes and it's as if she is now very little, lying still, hoping to stay asleep, hoping her mother would settle down.

There is a mewing sound. She covers her ears.

Dr Max leans forward, kind.

She senses him near her and moves into current time. Without looking up she says: "I'm getting some awful images. Is it my memory playing tricks?"

Max has seen and sensed her body tension.

"It's horrible. It makes me feel sick."

Max pauses, each of them allowing the presence of the physical reality.

"The sickness you are feeling, can you tell me where you feel it in your body?"

She holds her stomach with her right hand. Max follows her closely.

Vera becomes aware of touching the feeling with her hand. So tight in there.

"It looks as if you are holding your breath."

Vera nods, her eyes are closed.

"Can you allow your breathing to move into the tightness as best you can?" he says.

"How?" she asks

"Concentrate on the feeling under your hand as it lies on your stomach. When you breathe in, imagine that you are directing the useful oxygen into the tight feeling. When you breathe out, breathe out the tight feeling, let it go as best you can. You can breathe out right into the earth, the earth can take it."

Vera follows him exactly.

"It's easing." She feels a strange happiness that someone is telling her what to do.

"How is the sickness now?" asks Max.

"I still feel a bit sick." The acceptance in her voice tells Max that she is trying to work something out.

"I think I'm having what the books call a 'flashback'," she says.

Max smiles. He did not know that she read those kinds of books. She continues, immersed in her own curiosity. Max finds his heart lifting, to see her beginning to listen to the knowledge inside her. That most precious experience of curiosity was the road that led to freedom, and occasionally to wisdom. It was what gave him hope.

Vera continues with her voyage of discovery inside the hidden memory carried by her body, now hearing sounds. An ambulance siren; a deep gruff voice; being held against a rough navy sweater; the feel of something like concern, and more difficult, kindness. Then words: "How old are you, lass?" A flash of mixed emotion inside her chest, coupled with thoughts. Something she would later link with the kindness of strangers toward a little girl; and something dark and difficult Max might call shame; then anger toward those that would pity.

There is more. Others have gathered.

"Poor little mite," she hears them say. "What a life."

Now Dr Max is there too, listening, hearing it all, even though Vera was not speaking. He knows that she is experiencing an early memory, embedded in the body, come to light through the image of the being mauled by a lion and the feeling of nausea. Max wonders why the image of a lion, and which bullying lion has mauled her so badly and so early, leaving her with so many bruises and difficult unprocessed feelings.

Her six-year-old self is now more clearly in the room with them. Max witnesses her little legs in their white ankle socks, the dark pigtails in tartan ribbons. Every now and then, out of the child's body, rises a startled, grown up beautiful face.

He imagines her childhood: the many moves, school in fits and starts; getting in the shopping; all the 'uncles', the clink of bottles and smell of drink; slagging off men and people in authority.

Then the green room clears a space for the memory of Vera coming home from school at six years old to find her mother lying in a bloodied bath.

Max and the green room wait, supporting her with their presence.

Vera turns her head from side to side. "She didn't sign the paper. She was asleep. I wanted her to sign the paper. An outing to the moors. I had it in my hand, ready. But it got … it fell. It got red. Daffodils." Her mouth is dry.

Max says "This feels a painful memory for you. It feels very near to us right now."

"Damn daffodils. I hate them. I always have."

Max is not sure how much she is remembering. "What are you experiencing right now?"

"I'm holding onto my safe place like you said. It's a circle of stones. I made them as a girl when I did get to the moors, and I brought them home in my pockets."

Time passes whilst Vera wrestles to make a boundary between the memories and her safe place.

Max says: "It feels good that you have the stone circle for now. Can you just spend some time feeling the safety of being in the circle for a while, and give the memories a rest. We can come back to them later?"

Vera smiles with relief. She can see the stones, solid, beautiful colours, ancient, once part of something and still connected to something.

"Thanks," she says.

Then she sits up in the green chair and allows it to support her, as Max suggests at the beginning of each session, letting the chair support her body and feeling her feet being supported by the ground beneath. The earth can take it, he had said. She liked this.

She tries to start speaking, but the words will not form themselves. She tries again.

Max feels for her "You sound weary, and as if there's been quite a struggle".

"Yes."

"Do you want to say something about what you just experienced, so that we anchor it in words, try to make sense of it so that it does not have to live quite so much in your unconscious?"

Unconscious thought Vera. I'll have to read up on that. "The 'unconscious' – what is it?" she asks.

Max smiles, but they are getting away from the subject.

"Anything that's not in the conscious mind is unconscious. Many things happen before we become consciously aware, but our bodies and our unconscious store them. They tend to be carried in symbolic language, through metaphor and image, and come to light in this way too, or through dreams. It's often a crisis that activates them." He pauses. "Unconsciousness also protects us from what might have been unbearable."

She looks at him keenly.

"You mean in our earlier lives?"

He nods.

"Yes," she says, knowingly. "I see." Then: "Will I have to go into all that?"

Their eyes meet and the image of the many uncles and what they might have done with Vera is unspoken between them.

Max says, "We allow space for whatever is appropriate to be honoured and respected, for the purpose of healing, that is all."

Vera sighs. "I don't know how much I said. Just now. But it was like ... remembering something horrible. It was that first time, I was about six or seven. I'd just started to make friends. She never helped me. I came home and found her there. All that red. I couldn't bear it. Then the yellow, it got so bright in there. I probably cut off, didn't I? I went next door, and they got the ambulance. They took her away and my Nan came."

"You're talking about your mother?"

Vera sighs. "Yes." She looks up at him, absorbed in these emerging memories. "She was often trying something – to kill herself. People felt sorry for me. I hated it. But I couldn't stop her. Nan said Mum could never settle and she was always in trouble over a man, and that's what did it." She pauses, adding "Like me, now," in a limp, defeated voice.

"But your situation is very different, isn't it? You have had a stable twenty years of marriage and have brought up three children." Max is firm and definite.

"It's still rejection, isn't it?" she says quickly. But she felt his solidity. "You make it sound ... decent ..." She is quiet before looking at him. "I've not seen it like that," she says.

Max smiles: "Do you feel now as if you are like your mother?"

Vera shudders and laughs unexpectedly. "No – no," she says. Then, "All that was my mother's world. Not mine."

Max is impressed. She had become victim to Alistair's bully in their marriage. But without a bully to spend energy on placating and getting a sense of self that way, the raw feelings of the repressed, rejected child self would be revealed. She had become a mother by being one, but would she be able to mother or look after herself as she needed to now?

She had separated herself externally with steel dividers from the chaos of her previous life by developing a persona that tried to emulate admired others she assumed were superior, like Alistair.

Max is also alerted to the power in this childhood memory of her mother's suicide attempt, revealed so early on in their therapeutic work. This was her mother's response to rejection from a man, and it could therefore be, in Vera's unconscious, a possible model of behaviour.

"Have you ever thought of trying to end things in this way?"

Vera looks surprised. "Killing myself?" she says. "No. Why? Do you think I should?"

Ah yes, thought Max, that early symbiotic tie with her mother could indicate how, in relationships, she might not be able to distinguish between her own voice and need, and that of others. She could easily take his questions as paradigms for action. He must be careful.

"I do not think you should at all," he says firmly. "I ask because these images of suicide have come into this room, and I feel they have had a powerful effect on you. Right now, you are vulnerable and the question of how to be with and bear the painful feelings of loss and rejection is important."

He feels her watching him, hanging onto every word. He wonders why he sounds more pompous and formal than usual. But he has to press on. "Talking allows us to bring things out of the dark into the light and it can also give you choices. Your mother has shown you one way of coping with crisis created by the loss of a man. Now you have a crisis of your own. Sometimes we feel pulled, unconsciously," they smile at each other, "into following what we have been shown, especially when we cannot see any other solution. I would also like you to know that if you have any suicidal feelings, you may bring them here for us to share."

She shakes her head. "You don't need to worry." Was this 'no' her real feeling, or an automatic response to please and take care of him? "I know right from wrong. I would never do such a thing because of my boys. I know what it's like to have that hanging over you when you are little. I lived in dread of coming home from school and finding her like that again. It put me off school for a while and I didn't dare go. Social Services got involved. I reckon I missed a lot because of it; never got a proper education."

"You got the two O Levels though – you did well." Vera warms. This clever man who went to Oxford valuing what little academic success she had been able to achieve. "You're not taking the piss, are you?" She peers at him again.

Max laughs. "I wouldn't dare. No really, I am serious. I think you have braved a very difficult emotional start in life with great courage and nerve. And I can see that you are a great mother to your sons."

Another piece of information about Vera's past, that she had become phobic about school, fearing that her mother might harm herself when she, Vera, was not there. Max wondered how much education she had missed.

"Think of how awful it would be for them".

Max warms at the generosity in her. But he is concerned over her self-imposed isolation.

\* \* \* \*

*Why on earth had she answered the door?* It was her neighbour Michaela, collecting for charity. Michaela straight away registered Vera's loss of weight and uncharacteristically dishevelled appearance. Usually competitive, Michaela decided now upon a friendly stance. She had herself been rejected by Alistair in the past and saw an opportunity to harvest revenge. She sat down at Vera's kitchen table. Ah, the juiciness of another's tragedy.

"What brought all this on? How did it happen?" Trying to be thoughtful but dying for gossip in the drama of the aftermath.

Vera couldn't speak about it.

"He's just a shit, Vera. You know that... I've always presumed you knew that."

Vera stared at Michaela's made-up face, the tight Hermès shirt, the Gucci gold jewellery. "Why? Why is he a shit? Why do you say that?"

Michaela retreated. She shrugged in an exaggerated way, saying "Sorry, Vera. I didn't mean to be rude. I mean we are neighbours. But you see, I know his type. I could see how he eyed people. Women. My girls." She made it up.

Vera looked startled. "You don't mean..." Things were worse than she thought.

"Oh no, no, nothing happened, I made sure of that." Michaela would have to be a lot more careful. Vera was such an innocent.

"Look, I'm sorry. I can be a hard bitch at times but then life's made me like that and you could do with a few more skins yourself."

Vera felt exhausted. She shrugged and began to breathe in the steam from the hot coffee Michaela had insisted upon making. How can she talk to this woman now she has lost so much.

"He's my husband." She croaked. "He's the only man I've ever been with. Ever ... loved." Her voice tailed off. Her eyes were too dry to weep, their edges burned.

Then her voice got higher. "We have ... had, so much and been through so much. And the boys, Dominic, Leo, are away, I don't know what he's told them. And Luke," she broke off, the tears welling. "That's when he told me, just after we had left him at that awful place."

Have you no shame, girl, said a voice inside her, but she no longer cared to keep up an appearance for this nosy neighbour.

"They're my whole life. My family. I've given my all to Alistair. I helped to make him what he is today." She stopped abruptly, exhausted by these few sentences and the newness of talking about her problems and herself, her shame at being seen as a rejected woman, her fear of moaning. She never moaned.

"What am I going to do?" she whispered into the air.

Michaela pursed her lips. She had taught her girls never,

ever to make themselves completely available to any man.

"You gave too much, Vera. Men like Alistair move through life like an experienced consumer. Discarding as they go. Who's this other bitch?"

Vera gave a small animal growl at the back of her throat. "I never thought he would go off. No. Never. Had affairs, yes." Michaela took an in-breath. Did Vera know about her? "But we were together. We were the same." Vera's face had taken on a dreamy look. "We're the lion cubs in the lion club."

Michaela frowned. "What on earth are you talking about, Vera? Lions?" Was she losing it?

Vera started talking. To whom she did not know. Anyone would do, right then. The few sessions, the self-help tapes and books, a flesh and blood neighbour whose daughters grew up with her sons, the warmth of the coffee – her defences were down.

"We had the same background. The same past. When I met him he was a shy boy who'd had a hard time at public school. He was teased about his dad being 'in trade'. It made him hard, I know. But we were together. We were the same. We both had to overcome our past."

Michaela noticed something break into Vera's voice that was unfamiliar. A hint of Northern speech. The poor girl never had a chance, she thought. She encouraged Vera to eat, to talk, to contact others. "Who's here for you Vera? Shall I telephone your Mum?"

No, no one could know, especially her mother of all people. Her mother would see it as Vera's failure – and how she would crow, because now they would be even. They would both have failed.

Vera refused to make an absolute fact of Alistair's departure. His clothes were still here. His shoes. His sports gear. They were still married. She knew him. Better than anyone. He was having some sort of fling. An early mid-life crisis. He would get over it. He would come back. If she held on and kept herself together, he would get over it and come back, and he would be so sorry, as he had in the past. There would be daily flowers and he would beg her on his knees to forgive him, his little lion cub. The thought of their lion play revived her. She grinned then at

Michaela, a stiff, non-convincing grin.

"I need just to hang on. He'll be back, you'll see. It's the shock that's affected me. It's all so ... so ... unexpected, and the timing. On the day when Luke started school." Tears again. "It's so hard for me because of that. I'll work it though; I'll get myself back into better order. I'll get him back. You'll see."

Then she remembered Dr Max.

"He must care still because he's sent me to this doctor friend of his." Suddenly Vera was proud. He had done something hadn't he? He must care.

"Who?" asked Michaela, not really interested.

"Dr Max Maxwell. I think he's quite famous". Vera didn't really know but thought it sounded good.

"You mean a shrink? Huh. I tried that once. Psycho-bloody-therapy. Went on and on about my father and what he did or didn't do to me. Awful. Didn't believe a word of it. Dangerous if you ask me." Michaela stared at Vera in a hostile way. "God, Vera, you aren't going to fall for that one are you. Don't let Alistair try to make you mad. That's what men do to stop themselves having to feel guilty – make out their long-suffering wife was actually mad and that they, the men, were the poor, sad victims!"

Vera didn't want to hear any more. She stood up. "I'm glad you came, Michaela. You've helped me to think more clearly. Thank you." She was unsteady on her feet.

In spite of herself, Michaela was concerned. "You must eat," she said.

"Yes," said Vera, "I will." But she had to keep her figure didn't she, and you could never be too thin.

Michaela started looking through cupboards to find something for Vera to eat. The woman always looked half-starved while it was all Michaela could do to keep her figure from its natural desire to spread. There had always been something a bit odd about Vera. Would she be all right? Should Michaela call a doctor or something? No, she was already seeing a doctor. Thank God for that. What was Alistair up to? What sort of doctor was a friend of Alistair's? She would go and see Alistair at his office. Get the truth out of him. Make him pay. She might even have a word with one of his colleagues. Make it look bad that he had left a fragile wife and three sons. And what if Vera started thinking about suicide? Alistair wouldn't like that added to his pedigree.

Vera was trying to smile. She smoothed her shirt and pulled the thin cardigan around herself. She'd better begin attending to her appearance. Yes. Alistair was sure to come back. He would make it up to her and she would be gracious.

Vera sat down again and watched Michaela move about her kitchen. There was something incongruous about the bronzed arms with their gold bracelets reaching for old crisp bread at the back of the cupboard, trimming the first signs of mould off cheese she hadn't touched for days.

She began to realise that she needed to form a plan. She did not want Alistair's going to become concrete. Other people's knowing meant making it manifest. People would have opinion, would take sides. And then there were the boys. Nothing had been said about how or when the boys would be told. Vera did not want the boys to know what their father was doing, destroying the lives she had carefully woven for them. No, she would hold on. To what she did not know. Because in fact she was losing everything. And she was losing her grip on every day. On her hair, her body, her sense of reality. How many days had she sat here at the kitchen window watching the finches?

Now Michaela had startled her awake. She hung on then to the fact of this woman, here right now, making food and wanting to do something. With the warmth of the coffee reviving her, she breathed in more comfortably. Just then she felt sure that in time Alistair would come back. He wouldn't be able to do without her, particularly the way she knew how to administer to his particular needs. He would realise the enormity of what he had done. He would come to his senses.

These ruminations began to stir her. But there was more. Things she did not want to hear. Michaela seemed to know about betrayals and rejections, she had had three husbands and knew about arrangements and money and the future. She knew what procedures had to be completed to get the best out of the guilty party. She spoke the dreaded word 'divorce'. Vera put her hands over her ears. But the woman took them away and spoke to her directly, the Gucci gold dangling about her face and arms.

The very next day she insisted on taking Vera to a good female lawyer and sat with her whilst she was forced to speak of what had happened to her marriage. She spoke like a robot, on automatic. Most of what was said to her about her rights bounced right off. She did not want to speak to a stranger about Alistair's current desertion, of his unusual habits and desires that others would call cruelty, of the details of their married life about which she had never ever opened her mouth. They didn't know! They didn't! Vera had to have control, she had to make it all right. Her dark brown eyes glittered as some vestige of life and fight began to be returned into her.

She had not considered how she would cope for money. How she would pay her bills, how she would get about. She was totally dependent upon Alistair financially, and drew as she wished on their joint account and used the credit cards he had given her. The horror that this might now be removed from her! She had not ever had to manage money beyond the time when she gave her mother rent out of shop wages and saved enough each month for her beauty treatments. But now, this was more than just money. This was identity. Alistair, by his actions, was threatening to snuff out the reality of Vera, Mrs Alistair Dodds, and she did not deserve it. She had done nothing wrong. She could not, would not, think about an end. She would hang on, but to what she could not say.

Michaela had found the unopened pile of letters by the front door and sorted through, taking those from Alistair asking for the house to be sold to the solicitor's appointment. Encouraged by the lawyer, who could clearly see she needed help, and her newfound friend, she agreed to hand over any communication with Alistair on these matters to the lawyers. It bought her time. It meant that she did not have to speak to him herself and be wrong-footed because she was so needy of him.

Vera told the lawyer she did not want a divorce.

She would be patient and wait until Alistair realised what he had done. It might take months, but she felt sure he would miss what bound him to her. She felt better when she realised consciously that her silence was her only power.

Michaela said, "You won't do anything stupid, Vera, will

you?" And Vera had given a strange little laugh. She supposed she worried about her slashing her wrists or taking an overdose. "You forget I've got my Dr Max," she said.

She had told him that she would never harm herself because of her sons and this was true. Slashing her wrists could be what Alistair might expect. He knew it was what her mother had done. A gloomy thought arrived: perhaps that was why he had sent her to Max, to get her off his conscience. Did he not realise that she had not spent all these years grooming herself for a better fate than her mother to destroy it all by acting out the obvious? She knew it never worked. People only thought the worse of you afterwards; you were seen as weak and manipulative. Unless you succeeded of course. Who knew what happened to the dead?

But she was also aware that she had recently had quite desperate moments when she could not imagine how she could go on and that suicide might become all too seductive, the only way to obliterate the pain. But she didn't want to die. Funny that, to realise it. However much pain there was, she told herself as she closed the door of her house after visiting the solicitor, she would not die. There was life in her yet.

And then she thought: I wonder what Alistair *will* expect from me now? And more chilling was the thought that he might not even think of her at all, nor be concerned for her welfare. No. She realised with a sinking heart that he had stopped being concerned for what she was feeling a long time ago.

*The Pale Green Room*

# 7

*IN the dream the crone had been slumped in a lopsided wicker chair. Her oval face had once been beautiful, but the dead eyes stared vacantly ahead. The stick-like limbs with their sharp points gave the impression of a giant spider. She was naked, and Saxon saw that her crab-like hands were holding the plump body of a young infant. In the dream the crone was trying to push the nipple, still surprisingly taught and dark in the slack elongated breast, into the child's mouth.*

Lewis was away and Daniel had rung and was coming round that evening. Saxon wondered why. He was mainly a friend of Lewis. They did men's things together. What could he want with just her? Had Lewis put him up to it?

She shook her head as if trying to unleash the permanent knot in her neck and found her hand checking for the roundness of her stomach. That morning after the dream she had seen her reflection in the bathroom mirror and thought she was getting fat. She had pounded what she felt to be extra flesh, pulling it away from her bones and screwing its softness into her hand in desperate fury. She must fight off unruly glutinous flesh. She resolved to set her alarm earlier and step up her exercise programme more vigorously. She resolved to be more watchful, and to be alert for any hated fleshiness in her breasts and thighs. Her diet would become as rigorously pruned as her wardrobe. No milk in tea, no bread, no butter, nothing cooked in oil. Vegetables only in the evenings and fasting at weekends when Lewis was away.

She wondered whether to tell Daniel about her stalker.

Daniel brought a bottle of Chablis and was about to open it when she declined. He looked surprised. "It's your favourite." She felt bad, "I know, but …" She did not know how to answer. "Not Lent yet," he said playfully, knowing she was not religious. He looked her over keenly. "You fasting, Sax?"

She sighed and rested her head on one of the white cushions of her sofa, closing her eyes. All this concern and care of her, what was she to do with it? She would be completely undone. Her little dog, Alma, watching, put her head on one side in concern.

"It's the therapy, isn't it?"

She opened her eyes and stared at him with hostility.

"Jesus! I didn't know you could look so *very* cross!" he said, still playful.

She frowned. "It's awful," she said plainly.

"Oh dear. You poor thing. What is it that's awful?"

"That pale green room. That man. The things it makes you feel. The things it unearths that you want nothing to do with."

Daniel was thoughtful. "I remember when I first started in therapy," he said. "I remember wondering what the other bloke thought, wondering if he'd like me, if I would be good enough, if I'd make a good client." The silence between them was intense.

"Then I realised – and he probably indicated as much, but that's the real skill – to let the patient feel as if they've done all the work, letting their own realisations arise naturally so that they always have ownership. Well, I realised that was how it always was with my dad. I could never get it right. I was always waiting for rebuff and rejection. When I saw the connection and realised that this bloke wasn't going to do that, he was actually just there, listening, no judgement, quite empathic actually. I felt such a relief, and I felt that I could be, well, just OK as I am, without having to try so hard."

"I just don't care what this Max thinks of me."

"Really? Perhaps you haven't bonded yet."

"I don't intend to bond," she said coldly.

"Why not? He's been carefully chosen for you. He's very experienced, well known, deep and thoughtful. And he knows a lot about trauma …"

"I don't care, Daniel. It's not a process I respect."

"Oh dear," said Daniel. "And it was my idea too." He was watching her, concerned. "How many sessions do you have left?"

"I've had five, and despite my horror I've agreed to continue into the New Year. I felt duty-bound until the internal assessment by the Health Authority in February. But God knows what I'm going to say or do in that room until then."

They were silent. Daniel sipping his wine, Saxon leaning

back on the white covers. Alma still watching. Daniel felt she was keeping something from him.

"Anything interesting turned up so far."

She sighed. "Just awful dreams and nightmares, lots of feelings I don't understand and don't have when I'm not there. Stuff about my mother of course! Always that, blame the mothers!"

Daniel nodded. "It is a mysterious process I know. Especially for you being trained in the medical model which is so focussed on being rational and precise."

"Yes. Not a very precise profession, is it?"

Daniel was thoughtful. "Actually, from what I've read, it is. It's got a base and structure and is quite rigorously regulated now. But what I think is confusing and difficult for people is the therapeutic relationship. That's why Lewis, Alan and I, we were all so keen on your going to the right person, for the chemistry, you remember?"

"Ah yes. Chemistry."

"You're falling into sarcasm, Sax. It cuts you off from your softer side. We'd all like to see more of that." Daniel started walking round the room straightening already straightened pictures and waving his wineglass. He was working something out. Alma started watching his movements, every now and then returning her focus onto Saxon.

"What do you mean 'all of you'?"

"No, I don't mean there's some conspiracy. But Lewis and I, we love you. We've seen how you've got increasingly under stress. And now you and Lewis don't ...."

"So that's what this is about! Has Lewis put you up to this, to try to get me back into our living together?"

"Saxon," he called. Then "Saskia ..." he came toward her, putting his hand on her shoulder. "Please, you sound so angry, so defensive. And it makes me wonder whether you are really, really depressed."

She breathed out heavily and stared ahead. Alma looked startled and laid her paw on Saxon's thigh. Saxon began to stroke her.

"Perhaps I can tell you something of my own experience?" He took her silence for acceptance.

"Back to the chemistry and why it's important. This mysterious therapeutic relationship is the space in which the patient rediscovers old, learned patterns of relationship and then has the opportunity to experiment in letting go of the more problematic patterns. I'll give you an example if you like. As I was saying earlier, I was this brown-noser, this pleaser, always wanting to make everything OK and this of course got on people's nerves because I wasn't being real. And another thing, I couldn't say no. I couldn't even make a decision when I first went to therapy because I might offend someone. I was in a real trap, and very lonely and depressed.

I started to notice this pattern in myself, and I had homework to notice and stop, and then to try something different. It was all about awareness and practising awareness and then having the sessions to report back. But the most effective part was being with someone who didn't judge me but allowed me the freedom to find out that I could let go of old patterns that didn't work anyway, and that I was a decent, even loveable human being."

"And it's lasted," she said softly and wistfully. "I can see that. It did you good."

"Thanks," he said raising his glass.

"It is very hard for me to trust anyone," she said slowly. Her little dog's eyes were closed as Saxon rubbed her ears and neck.

"It might take some time. Is Max someone you feel you could in time trust?"

She was thoughtful. "Do you know I have never considered it. I suppose you're indicating an act of faith. I haven't much of that."

"You have had to be so self-reliant all your life haven't you? It brings such a loneliness with it. This business with the child in Hong Kong. Is there any chance that it's connected to some vulnerable part of yourself that is really hard to hold?"

"I can't do this, Daniel, I can't have you and Max digging away."

"I am sorry, really sorry. It's not my place. I am just wanting to help."

The silence between them felt crisp and Daniel cursed

his question after he had seen her soften in recognition of what he had revealed of his own.

"Is there anything you are aware of that you'd like to change?"

"For Hong Kong to have never happened!" Her hands were back in her lap.

"Yes, of course you do. But that's it isn't it. It happened, against your conscious will. And it was shocking. To everyone."

She tensed. Everyone again. There was a conspiracy.

"So, were you shocked, Daniel?"

"Yes." He looked at her directly. "Yes, I was shocked to hear about Hong Kong, Sax, although I don't know the whole story. I know Lewis is really worried about you."

"Well neither of you shouldn't be. I am doing all the right things, even against my will and I will be fine. It will all be fine."

Daniel was quiet, and unnerved.

"I remember when we first met," he said. "You were so fascinated by the drawings. I was making a study of artichokes and grasses. When you spoke, your whole face opened up and there was that evening we all shared, when Lewis had baked the soufflé."

"Ah yes," she said. She had felt more open then, and relaxed, even maybe, hopeful, that her lonely, ordered life as a doctor might change, and some of the ordinary everyday things she watched other people take for granted and enjoy might be available to her. But that was before she realised, she couldn't cope with intimacy.

He came and sat near to her, not touching, as if he knew this would not be appropriate.

"I just hope, Sax, that you will continue with Max. There's obviously something pretty big going on and I beg you to stay the course."

"That's what he said: 'something important going on'."

Daniel, prevented at every opportunity for opening, decided to change the subject.

"You're losing weight."

"No. I'm putting it on."

Daniel felt the extent of her isolation and delusion, even

paranoia. He felt the agony of her closing off as if some part of her had begun descending into a bottomless pit where no one could follow or help. He feared for her and what might happen.

To break the awkward silence, she asked: "What made you go into therapy?"

"Well, on the surface it was because I was too depressed to work. After my father died, I got very depressed. Had to stop work," he looked at her ruefully thinking of her suspension, remembering what it was like to not have the identity of work. "I hadn't a clue what it was all about. I'd been fine up until then and it wasn't as if I'd really known him properly. He left us when I was sixteen and I had just presumed he was fed up and that Mum and me were too much of a bore."

"And you found out that you weren't boring but loveable?" she said, longing to change the subject completely. To speak about Philip Glass, Francis Bacon, the war in Iraq.

Daniel sighed. What did Lewis see in this woman? He knew that he loved her, or had. But recently she had become very hard to love. "I found out that I was multifaceted," he said after a long thoughtful pause. "And that this was OK. That I was worth something and that I could be me and feel free just as I am myself."

"Was this Max your therapist then?" she asked, surprising him.

"Actually, yes. I wasn't going to say as I didn't want to prejudice your freedom. But maybe it will help? It was a long time ago. I send him a card at Christmas, and he always replies. He's been like a wonderful wise father, even though we are probably similar ages."

She is quiet.

"It helps to have an open mind."

She sighed, "I know. And I know that you and Lewis really want me to make a go of it."

He smiled a big smile "That's right, but not in an ambitious way, but to us you are an intelligent, very clever and witty woman who we love and we think you could use the insights into yourself, when they come."

Daniel was alarmed by her shut down responses, the obvious anger, even rage embedded in her fixed stare and stiff neck. He suspected she was not sleeping and eating, perhaps in an attempt to stay in control. He sensed that somewhere she was quite desperate and afraid.

He did not mention that Max also had an understanding of spiritual matters that had been invaluable to Daniel. Having a difficult and often absent father meant that he was easy prey to charismatic figures, self-styled spiritual gurus. He had followed several, as far as India, even beyond, only eventually to be rejected and disillusioned when natural questions arose. So often he had returned home empty and angry. Max had helped him to connect with his own capacity for spiritual experience, in the present moment. This had become his guiding principle, his authority. He so wanted Saxon to have some of it.

"What shall we listen to? How about the Glass second violin?" he said.

"Oh yes, lovely," she replied, relieved. His words "you must be so lonely" echoed into the music and the rest of the evening.

\* \* \* \*

*The child, about six weeks old, was already chubby, pink against the woman's grey. It flailed its little arms and legs against the stick limbs of the spider crone. Living and breathing against her deathly stillness. There was no sound. The crone opened legs to release a flow of dirty red. In a micro-second of long-dismissed genital pleasure, not quite orgasm, angular spider crone became fertile woman, then the image closed. The child had stopped moving, and dust, like snow, began to fall from an overhead beam.*

Saxon remembered the disturbing feeling of the dream that very morning, lying in the murky half-light, the bed covers warm around her but her body cold, aware that her arms were stretched out to take the child. Once more fully awake, she had chilled at the image of the monstrous spider woman. There was revulsion, she felt sick, and afraid. Her heart was beating unusually fast, sweat gathered in the creases of her body. She felt disgusting.

Lewis had stayed over, the night before he began his long lecture tour in Finland. He was sleeping soundly and silently in the next bed and appeared normal and safe. She wanted to touch his sleeping pyjama shoulder, to confirm he was warm and mortal, here and now. Dawn gave the room an eerie half-light, both thrilling and threatening. The dream's images shattered her rationality, and she was at the mercy of her unsettled heartbeat and feeling of panic somewhere between her throat and solar plexus. Her thinking was woolly, and vague. Was she menopausal? At forty five, was this all the early onset of that change? Was it possible microscopic hormones were to blame for the Hong Kong incident? And everything else. Perhaps this was what it was like to go mad. She looked again at Lewis, at his solid back, his firm neck holding that sensible head on its shoulders. She wanted to cry. But she never cried. "You're my good little Anglo-Saxon aren't you, Saskia?" her father had said. "Saxon, that's what I'll call you."

Now, with Daniel gone and his words reverberating in her head she wondered again what was really happening to her. Daniel felt real, and alive. But Saxon did not feel like this. She felt frozen, half dead; she felt as if she lived behind glass and that flesh and blood life were never touchable. Was this all biological? What did she really know of women's hormonal structures other than her praise for HRT and the avoidance of menopause? Her mother hid herself in her room each time the monthly blood arrived. She had been unable to conceive again after her son, and every time this was confirmed the atmosphere in the house became very dark, and sometimes violent. They had lived in different countries as her father set up new and pioneering commercial ventures. She could almost chart her mother's descent into alcoholism by country. In Spain, where they lived until Saxon was six and where her mother had lost her son, the despair, rage and alcohol dependence were hidden, but there were peppermints and muffled sounds behind closed doors. Saxon overheard family friends saying that this loss had fractured her mother's creative but fragile personality, and the relief she found from the bottle was all she had. She had even indicated it was her link with a romantic Russian ancestry, for her parents had come to America from Russia, bringing with them nothing but ragged clothes, weak chests and a ukulele. Grandma Vischa had never learned to speak English, but Saxon's grandfather had gone out and tuned pianos for a living and learned to communicate in their chosen foreign land.

In Germany, where they lived five years, Saxon had entered school. She owed her scholastic drive to her German foundations. She relished order, the demand for excellence, the heady sense of success when her efforts were praised, which increased her drive. This was in acute contrast to the marshmallow life at home, her mother's increasing sentimentality, maids always leaving, doctors being called, doors slammed on tears and wails by a permanently angry father who turned increasingly to Saxon for reason and escape. Her mother hated Germany, fuelled by their destruction of twenty million Russians in World War II, but mainly because she couldn't get on with the language or the people. *And because even the clever German physicians could not help her conceive a child.* When she thought of this now her heart gave another jerk. Each month when there had been no pregnancy there was such drama in the house and Saxon felt shut out and, yes, she had probably thought it was her fault somehow. Her mother also became bawdy and reckless. The alcohol, its acceptance within the elegant drinking society, with the freedom and money to continue unchecked, accentuated her recklessness. Saxon remembered now how uninhibited she had become. Her streaked blonde head thrown back, a long pillar of cigarette smoke escaping from her lips, the uncontrolled exhortation of the intimate physical life of being a woman. Saxon's mother embarrassed and enraged her. Was it this that had confirmed in her the need for control at all costs? The more her mother deteriorated into the despair and chaos Saxon would learn later was associated with alcoholism, the more Saxon developed her own protected world.

When Saxon realised she had been ruminating for over half an hour she became alarmed, and left the bed quietly. In the bathroom mirror she saw a tired face which for a minute felt as if it did not belong to her. She saw that she was trembling. Beyond this bathroom window stretched the garden, now lit by early morning light. Dew caressed the shrubs, flower beds and lawn. It looked like the down on a newborn baby's head ...

She made tea and thought again about the awful dream. The crone and the child. Perhaps she was that old crone, all skin and bone. Perhaps the child was some innocent other, she could not hold. Her mother's dead child came into her thoughts. She had never seen him, and she wondered what he had been like. Perhaps there was a simpler explanation to the unpleasant dream, perhaps she had started an early menopause and her psyche, or whatever Max had called it, was playing tricks on her. A darker thought was that if what he had said was correct, then the things we deny or bury return to haunt us. "So, I have to pay a price for what I have done in the past," she thought, "and for the life I have denied."

She sat in front of her laptop feeling numb, out of herself, displaced, somewhere touched by a sadness she thought would never be eased. Her automatic pilot would speak words for her, organise her day, stay on track, smiling at others, getting things done, being there for others, even knowing others' pain. An automatic pilot to see her through life but never to actually live. Not to feel, or if feeling, remote, far far away, behind glass, protected and cut off at the same time. To be with others in pain and in others' hearts, but never to know her own.

* * * *

On her return from her session with Dr Max, Vera placed a card on the hall table. She had found it in the newsagents near his rooms, where she had stopped for milk. On the front was a photograph of a stone arch reflected in a pool of water, the whole forming a circle. This was to remind her, every time she passed, of that safe circle she was trying to create inside herself. She touched the picture and resolved to go out and look for stones so that she could build her own circle, in her own shape, with her own hands. She did not know where she might find such stones, but hoped the place would come to her.

The house seemed cold, frozen, inhibiting of spontaneity. The card was something – something new, something of herself. She crossed the upstairs landing into Luke's room, full of souvenirs of his adventures and creations. She sat among his Spiderman and Superman trophies, then picked up one of his small amethyst crystals and lay down on the single bed staring up at the planetary constellation on his ceiling. She thought about the way he had been conceived, in violence, the result of Alistair's selfish sexual need, forcing himself into her without protection when he knew she was struggling to find a contraceptive pill that suited her and was vulnerable. He had refused to wear what he called 'wellington boots.' She had begged him to wait until it was safe; she did not want to go through another abortion. Keeping her eye focussed on the belt of Orion she thought that she had probably given in to Alistair ten years ago because she wanted to keep the peace. He had probably tired of her then, all that time ago. So when she found herself pregnant again after the assault she knew that she wanted this third child, especially the chance of a daughter, and she had refused to terminate. His white rage followed her throughout her complicated and difficult, painful pregnancy. He accused her of having another child for her own ends. He was impatient with this third son from his birth onwards and never bonded with him. Everything Luke did was seen as evidence of Vera's trickery – even his artistic temperament was an insult to Alistair's need to make men in his own image. Luke was so different from her other sons. He was quiet, sensitive, shy. He had learned to read early. He liked to draw and had bought second-hand art books with his pocket money. Sometimes he looked directly into his father, which unnerved and angered him – "Just what do you think you are looking at?"– especially when he had said something sharp to his mother.

Luke in that starched boarding school! He would certainly need the energy of his superheroes right now, and the crystals, fossils, robots and dinosaurs that lined his shelves. He had taken so few of his own things to this new school, as if he had stripped himself in preparation for confinement.

She thought now, what if Luke had been a daughter? Would it have been different? Or would it be this new woman who would now bear him a daughter?

It was during her lonely pregnancy with Luke that she had met Coral, a single mother-to-be who had been abandoned by the father of her child when she was six months' pregnant. They shared their loneliness. Coral introduced Vera to yoga and to self-help books, which she had merely flipped through without much enthusiasm, never imagining that one day she might need them. Coral assumed that Vera was in thrall to Alistair, a bastard like all men, who just used women for their own gratification. But Coral enjoyed her visits to Vera's large house and the activities inside it; she enjoyed taking Jason to play with Luke. In Coral's eyes at least Vera had a paid-for roof over her head and a man standing by her. She would be sympathetic at least, but the thought of explaining and listening to responses made her feel exhausted.

Vera moved into Dominic's room and sat on the red chest, looking around at his posters: Cold Play and Manchester United. Another series of interplanetary posters, stars, suns and their constellations. He had taken his expensive telescope with him to Bristol. Squeezed in between his copies of *Wisden*, the remains of a battered *Winnie the Pooh*.

She and Alistair had been such proud parents! A healthy boy, named Dominic after a distant cousin who had made good in the City, born at exactly nine months after their lavish wedding, organised by Alistair's parents. And then, within ten months, another son, Leo. Alistair had been determined to break the only-child stigma he believed he had suffered. "No child of mine is going to be an only." At first, despite their horror at their son marrying 'beneath himself' even Alistair's parents were grateful for Vera's youth and fecundity. And even they could see that, surprising given the sort of mothering she had received, Vera was a natural and truly loving mother. She would prove to his parents that she was up to her job. The two boys were like twins; both pale skinned and freckled like Alistair, and with his straight fair floppy hair, but each with the burning deep brown Spanish eyes of their mother.

Vera remembered the chaos and exhaustion of new motherhood, and her determination to keep her babies and herself looking healthy and clean. She would never have it said anything was too much for her. And Alistair was so very proud of her, then.

Her in-laws had been silent these past weeks. Vera had had little to do directly with them over the years, all contact was through Alistair. She imagined that they would be siding with their son and might even be glad to be free of their common daughter-in-law. But they could not cut her off as if she had never existed. Their grandchildren also carried Vera's common blood in their arteries and half their genes came from her background no matter how much they might wish to eradicate.

She knew they had wished their son and heir had not felt so compelled to marry her. They had tried to make him keep her as a useful plaything, someone to satisfy the peculiar physical need that had come upon him during adolescence. His mother sensed that Alistair's father, Douglas, was the same but she'd had no truck with it and he'd fortunately kept it in control or at least out of their marriage. Douglas thought it was all a reaction to boarding school, but secretly he was proud to know this about his son, and relieved that Alistair's mother hadn't made a wimp out of her only child.

Vera wandered from the boys' rooms and into the small alcove at the end of the landing. This upstairs corner was one part of the house that looked as if there might be life going on. A low table was scattered with papers to do with school, catalogues, magazines, cottons, a ball of knitting wool, a small array of paperback books and, more recently, a computer for learning email and a tape player for talking books. Since Alistair's going, this is where she had lived. She could put her feet up on the window seat and look out at the square. She read magazines. The radio had hummed a background blur until her recent discovery of Classic *fm*. She was surprised, for she and Alistair had never had music in the house.

Vera was born in 1967, before the publication of *The Female Eunuch*. Her mother despised and dismissed Feminist literature as anti-man and causing trouble. And Vera had taken this line as her own. She had amused guests at an elegant dinner one evening by proclaiming that it was women like Germaine Greer who broke up marriages, and she had a lot to answer for. She thought then that it was true. In Vera's adolescence during the early 1980s when the women's movement had gained momentum and status, she was busy, with her peers, concentrating on improving her looks and gaining a man. She thought that her dedication to pleasing and keeping a man and holding onto her role as centre of the family structure was right. But now she was not so sure.

In her lonely moments she had started to read the books passed onto her by Coral with more interest. She would open the page at random and just pick out something. The book that started her thinking was *Women Who Run With the Wolves*, written about ten years earlier and a favourite of Coral's. The first story about Bluebeard startled her. She read it over and over as if trying to shake herself awake.

She went downstairs to make herself a cup of tea. She felt hotter than she had for a while, a kind of burning. She wondered what was happening. There had been letters from Alistair, pushed through the door at odd hours, intended to bypass her solicitor and wear her down over the sale of the house.

"They're just threats, don't give in to them," said Coral, who had turned up on her doorstep one morning, just like Michaela, wondering why Vera had not returned her calls. When she heard what had happened, she put her arms round Vera in a bear hug and held her there until the sobs subsided. "I've been away, but why didn't you call me on my mobile? I'd have come straight round, you know that." She looked upset and at the same time felt that now they were equal. They were both women left by men, and single parents.

Vera's solicitor had advised her not to give in to threats but to sign the measured, firm and clear letters written for her. She had rights. She had the right to her contribution in effort to the home, even though the money had been all from Alistair's family. She had a right to a home with her remaining under-age child. What was he thinking of, imagining that she could live in a small, terraced house by herself with her three sons left to roam between their two parents. She knew it wasn't Alistair's idea. She knew it was the bitch he had got in with, who had expensive tastes and high and mighty designs and a fancy name. Vera fumed and seethed and then retracted her feelings. She mustn't give in to these emotions. She had read that it gave you lines and wrinkles, and made your hair drop out. She would just sit tight, keeping herself intact, until the spell this upper-class thief had woven around her husband had worn off. Until Vera's own magic began to work its way again into Alistair's being.

She returned to the landing alcove with her tea, noticing the photograph of the stones and gaining some strength from it as she passed. Just this summer she had returned to Coral's yoga class. How she wished Luke was there at the local school with Coral's son, Jason, his friend from birth. She realised now that she had not used her yoga mat properly since Alistair had left.

She pulled it out from the rack underneath the small table, lay down on her back and stretched, feeling a flood of relief. She really needed to get her thoughts in order, and she needed to keep in control.

She stood and made the sun salutation, breathing in and out steadily with each following pose, allowing her breathing to soften any tightness in her joints and muscles. She was learning in that pale green room and her conversations with Dr Max that perhaps she had played down her own intelligence in order to keep Alistair. Well, damn fool her. She bent forward, allowing her arms to reach toward the mat and her fingers to splay out onto it. She leant into her hands, those strong hands that took her body weight as she felt the burning sensation enter her wrists and arms. Now she needed every ounce of strength to make the platform pose, the best pose for strengthening the whole body. She would be seeing Luke at the weekend, and she needed him to see her strong. She did not want to worry him. Sometimes in yoga she had a feeling of strength, of things feeling OK even when they weren't OK outside. Coral called it being centred through creating mastery. She made several more poses until, in the child pose, she found her face wet with tears.

\* \* \* \*

That evening Alistair watched the house from the warmth of the car. The landing light she used when sitting alone was lit, and when he saw the hall light come on, he knew that she was inside.

Alistair had anticipated hysterics and screaming, as he had seen her mother behave in this way. By sending her to Max he had prepared in advance for this eventuality. He was more unnerved than he would admit by her withdrawal. He did not want to think that Vera might have really loved him, and that his leaving had opened up a real wound in her very core. He turned off his car radio and swung himself out of the driver's seat, pressing the locking device as he walked across the road and with his other hand pulling his house keys from the tightness of his trouser pocket.

He needed to sort things out. He needed answers. He needed to get on.

He was used to doing everything at an oiled run, so when his house key did not slide immediately into the familiar lock on the front door he fumed and swore. It took a few moments to realise that Vera had changed the locks. His key, his *own* key wouldn't work. Damn it! His own house! He felt enraged at whoever was advising her. She would never have thought of such a thing herself. She would have him back like a shot.

He stood on the front steps, his hand on the heavy brass lion knocker, one of the first things they had bought together early after their marriage, for their first house. He remembered now how he had picked it up and held it fondly near to her face, saying "We should have this because we're the lion cubs together." They had pawed each other, four arms and hands making arcs in the air, feet scraping alongside. He shuddered now at the memory of his banality. He shuddered too at the games he and Vera had played. The descent from play cubs into something more serious and depraved: the once delightful but then dreadful scratching, biting, baiting, taunting.

He shivered, and his hand sweated. He held back, alert, his whole body tense. He was being watched through the spyhole. Vera. The familiar animal scent of her body. Lion cubs. The way they had been. The creature he had to shake off. He had to shake her off.

Sweating still, and not unafraid, his rage swelled. He made a harsh, whispered sound, as near a shout as he could, not wanting to attract neighbours. "Vera, let me in for God's sake. I need to talk to you."

Nothing happened.

"Vera, I know you are in there, I saw the light come on upstairs. We need to talk." He was thinking on his feet. "I'm not going to be difficult, and I hope you won't either. It's much better in the long run if you co-operate. It's in the best interests of the boys after all."

Silence. He became nervous of neighbours eyeing him; houses were so close in this Pimlico Street. Then, with a physical lurch, he wondered if some witness might intervene, wanting to take action on Vera's behalf, should he be seen as the deserting husband upon whom revenge was due. He hadn't thought of that. That there might be people who took Vera's side. People who were stronger and more together than Vera, who might take up her cause and stand against him. Stand against him and what he wanted. Worse, he might even be seen as an intruder by a passing stranger who thought he was after something that was not his.

But Vera was his.

Alistair wasn't imaginative, but visions of being body tackled as on a rugby field filled his mind's eye. He straightened his tie, smoothed back his hair. He should have bought flowers. His own doorstep for God's sake.

Vera had been watching him through the spyhole. At last. At last, he had come back. He was here. She let the strength of the sight of him on their doorstep surge into her. At last. She breathed deeply and held her hands against her silk blouse. Thank God. Now, how should she behave? What would be the best way? She had not organised a plan, although she had rehearsed conversations in her mind about what she would say and particularly what she would wear when she saw Alistair again. But those ideas had worn thin over time and as her emptiness had grown. She found it hard to remember what she needed to say and how she needed to behave to make sure she really held him. She was breathing deeply, her eyes scanning the mirror for how she looked. She mustn't hurry. She must capitalise on the situation where, for the first time since his going, she had the upper hand. Here he was after all, standing on the doorstep waiting for her to let him in. Changing the locks had been a good idea. She had been against it at first, because she wanted to leave the door open for him to return at any time. To let him know she still wanted him and loved him and it was his home.

But his waiting made her clap her hands and smooth her skirt. It fired her up. To see him having to shout and ask, to plead even, just to see her. The thrill of seeing his distorted image through the fishbowl lens. She could peep out at him, see him, but he couldn't see her. She was peeping out at a peeping tom. How they had done this together! How they would do it all again! She felt like a wild animal. Excited. She must calm down. She must give nothing away.

Through the spy hole his slim body appeared truncated and squat, his legs tiny, his head like a potato. She feasted on her position of command: she would make him plead more, beg even, say he was sorry, that he had made a dreadful mistake, that he loved her really and was coming back. Her eyes widened, she breathed fiercely. Perhaps he had a suitcase in the boot of the car; perhaps somewhere at the other end of the city was a weeping woman whom he had just discarded, as she herself had been discarded six weeks ago. Now that bitch had her come-uppance. Vera feasted and feasted her starving self and relished these thoughts. She watched herself in the hall mirror as she smelled his sweat through the door. Thank God she had been to the hairdresser, and the manicurist at last. It was Michaela's idea. "Keep your chin up, Vera. Keep your hair and nails done properly. Don't let him get you down!" It will do you good," said Coral, "But do it for yourself, love, not for him. Self-esteem is always important."

Also, she was going to visit Luke at school. She did not want her Luke to see her as other than completely reliable in the way he had always known. She did not want pity from strangers. She also did not want that Dr Max thinking she was a poor thing. He was trying his best for her and she wanted him to see her at her best. She looked steadily at the card of the stone arch and its mirrored reflection in the still water then smoothed her hands across the swelling of her breasts under the silk blouse.

"Vera, I know you're on the other side of this door. Do you want a scene where the neighbours come out? Do you want Jack's parents to see what's going on?"

Jack was another of Luke's close friend. Vera cared about that. Just a few more minutes relishing Alistair's impotence and refreshing her lipstick.

She had had to stand on tiptoe to see through the spyhole and her feet and ankles had begun to throb. She sank down onto the deep orange carpet and rubbed the circulation back before slipping on her shoes. Then she looked at herself again in the mirror, straightened her belt, patted her lips, and opened the door, keeping the chain in place.

Alistair went to try to slide the chain back, but couldn't get his hand through the gap, and Vera was holding the door against him. It was the first time she had seen him since the day he left. Six weeks ago. Six weeks in which she had been driven to question her very existence.

The shock of seeing him in the flesh was electrifying – the man who had been her husband and lover for over twenty years. The physical look of him filled her up. That soft hair. Those hands. She could weaken and simply fall on her knees in gratitude that he had come back. She might beg him to stay and be with her always because they belonged together didn't they. She might make even more of a fool of herself than she feared had been made already, without her knowing why or how. The card with the stones fluttered in the draught from the open door.

Resolve not dissolve, she said to herself. She must remain strong, and firm. The stone circle, her safe circle gleamed. Yes, good things were in place. She must not let him take her straight away.

He was still sweating, despite the chill of the night. "For God's sake, Vera, what's the matter with you?"

Vera laughed a harsh laugh.

He put his hand on his hips, a gesture which made her focus on his belt – no longer the one with the lion motif she had given to him but one with a designer symbol. She was getting more filled up with the sight of him. She found herself thinking of his legs wrapped around her. Her heart was beating rapidly, fluttering like a moth at paper.

She opened the door. The card with the stone circle was blown back by the movement of air and fell down the back of the hall cabinet. She turned her back and began to walk slowly through the hall.

"You should know what's the matter with me, Alistair. You started it all."

He sighed, shutting the door carefully, looking round his own hall in shock at the sight of its familiarity. Perhaps this wasn't such a good idea.

"That's right. Blame me."

She turned in the doorway of the drawing room and faced him. "You are to blame. If you hadn't gone off with your woman, things would be normal."

She left him still standing next to the front door and made her way into the drawing room, the slingbacks of her high-heeled shoes flapping. He followed her, the flapping of the shoes familiar in a rather sickening way, her small, pert frame swinging and signalling in front of him. Lioness once to his lion. In the cold drawing room, the rose-coloured chintz covers emitted their familiar smell. The house he had been trying to leave for years closed around him, like the bars of the lion's cage.

"Normal, Vera, really ... were things ever normal here?"

"We have three sons," she said quietly.

Alistair stared at her coldly. He could see he would soon be exasperated.

"But, Vera, surely you can't think our relationship was normal. I hoped you'd have had time to think about it all properly. Get some sense into you. Know I really mean business. And you too, Vera," he looked at her with cunning, "you can move on too. I'm no good for you anymore." This was a line he had learned from Arabella - received wisdom from his new partner's therapist. The theme went something like this: "Well, if it's over it's over. She can start to look at her part in the breakdown; she can also have the opportunity to change." It appealed to Alistair, not for altruistic reasons but because it made him suffer less guilt. But now, he wondered. Was this really worth pursuing? He wanted to make it all look good. That he could be said to have done everything possible to ease the suffering of the end of his unsuitable marriage. He also wanted this over, to get back in time to go out with Arabella - dinner with friends.

She said nothing but continued her glassy stare. "I suppose you'll get over it eventually," she said, fondling one of the fine silk lampshades.

"Get over it ... what the hell do you mean?" Alistair felt uneasy.

She looked at him. Her deep brown eyes in which he had so often seen his own reflection seemed smaller and dull looking. She was thinner, but still sultry, still sensual, attractive. The outlines of her face were more bony, but this made them more intense, and the black mane of hair more dramatic. He had lost himself in that hair ... He shook away the memory.

She shrugged, still fixing him with her dull stare. "Well, you won't stay, Alistair. She can't keep you can she?"

"What the hell are you talking about?"

Vera curled up in the armchair that had always been her

favourite in this grand but little-used room. Like a cat, secure in its place.

"Soon she'll find out what you're like, Alistair, and she won't like it. Ladies don't." She played on the word 'ladies.' "And you'll get over her. She's not your sort. It's just that at the moment you are infatuated, under some sort of spell. It's something like a mid-life crisis."

Jesus, he thought, it's all those magazines she reads, she's got some kind of idea of a passage through life that's like shopping at Marks & Spencer and ticking things off a list. If your husband goes off you, it's another woman or a mid-life crisis: get new underwear or start cooking different meals.

"Vera, I'm not going to go off Arabella. This is for real. And you and I were finished years ago, before Luke. We've been through it, you know we have." He sat opposite Vera, in the matching chair, and as he spoke the tone was chill and brutish.

"I'm..." he faltered for some reason he was unaware of, but begun on a course he knew he must continue. To get it over with. He had to. He had to say it again, that it was over, that he had been tired of Vera for a long time. "Arabella and I, we... we are going to be married. It's arranged."

"You're not divorced yet though, are you?" Vera retorted sharply, surprising him. "And I'm not giving you a divorce. That means five years. *Five years.*" She blazed at him from some newly awakened place that surprised herself. She had only just read up on the divorce laws. "If I was into divorce, I'd have given you one years ago, when you first started having affairs. There was Annabel first wasn't there, then Alice, then Andrea, then —"

"Stop it."

"All those fancy upper-class names. Come on, Alistair. You may want to be seen with those smart bitches, but you want to come home and fuck your little bit of northern rough."

He put his head in his hands. He had forgotten how she could talk when pushed. He had forgotten how vulgar she was. Like her mother. Lipsticked mouth set in the same pull, same deep brown eyes narrowed between their black lash frames.

In the moment's silence after her outburst the ticking of the grandfather clock created a background heartbeat. It had once ticked in his grandparents' house and, for an instant, childhood memories rose to soften the moment.

Then he spoke. "Vera, I want a divorce. I've met someone else, and our marriage is over. You are hanging on to something that is dead. You'll get over it, you'll meet someone else."

"Who?"

"You will, you'll meet someone else." He hadn't meant to sound encouraging, to show that he had any interest in Vera's future. He just wanted her out of the way, off his hands, as fast as possible.

"But we've got to be practical, we've got to sort things out. The boys. When and how we tell the boys." Vera flinched. Alistair did not notice, he was intent on getting over his point, on accomplishing his mission.

"They must know before Christmas. I want to take Luke and Dom skiing. Arabella's family have a place in Switzerland." There was no stopping him. He was the same ruthless bull-headed ogre that had gripped the steering wheel while he did 95 miles an hour and told her he was leaving her for someone else. For a second, she hated him.

He pressed on. "And the house. We must agree on the house. It must be sold. You can get a decent place. But this place is much too big now."

"I suppose you want me to get fixed up with that doctor you sent me to."

Alistair was startled. He stared at her as she fingered the skin of her neck, running her nail from her throat to the first button of her blouse. He felt uneasy.

"I sent you to him because I've been worried about you. You're not right, Vera, you're strange, you need sorting out."

Vera stuck to her animal self, to its cunning. "Scared are you that I might go off with Doctor Max," she laughed. "Have a better time with a monk for God's sake. Anyway, he's changing me. I'm going to have a personality change so that you can come back and feel better about everything."

She engaged him with her stare. Then the more pleading side of the animal self emerged. Her brown eyes filled. "Alistair, how can you leave me? How can you leave us? It's you who isn't right. We belong together. We need each other. You may want a bit more class, going into politics, but it's me you really need where it matters most isn't it?"

"And I can do it you know. I can change, and then you won't need her, your upper-class bit, anymore." She was determined, even eager.

"Class, class, you were always fixated on class. It's never made any difference to me." He was angry with himself for being drawn into any feeling or potential argument with her. He also felt bothered by her disjointed thoughts. She was getting worse, whatever it was that was wrong with her. Max should know. Thank God he had thought to send her to Max.

If she remained legally his wife, she could be his responsibility. But he was damned if he was to be expected to live with a nut case or be responsible for one. He must watch out for her with the boys. At least two of them were more like him than her. Got some good genes inside them, from his side of the family. She'd never had much of an intellect. And the sex thing they had got into was a mistake. He didn't want to think about that. But now it seemed she was equating this therapy with some sort of face-lift.

"You can't get me and the boys out of this house, Alistair." She was quite firm. "When there's a divorce, everything is divided." She let her sentences stay solid. "There can be no divorce for five years unless I agree. And this is my home, and the boys' home. And you have to support us. The law says so. The boys need a place to come back to, a place they know, especially after such a shock as their father leaving them. You can't make me leave."

They faced each other from their matching chairs, a million miles apart.

"I can stop paying *all* the bills, Vera." He spoke quietly, with menace. His eyelashes quivered. He sat very still, like a creature waiting outside a hole for its prey.

A deeper silence fell between them. She watched. She watched every inch of him. And those places inside. How they had used each other. It was too strong to give up.

She slid out of the armchair and crossed the room in her stockinged feet, having discarded her shoes under the armchair. As she got nearer Alistair knew what might happen, what he must not allow to happen.

    He felt paralysed, at the same time as desperate to move. He was cornered. Like the addict overwhelmed by the craved substance, that teases with life force but binds its victims nearer to death. The image of a praying mantis rose up before him. With supreme effort he got out of the chair, just as Vera reached him and began undoing her blouse.

# 8

MAX sat in his green brocade chair, hands folded in his lap, resting his attention in the stillness of the room between patients. He kept his awareness of the approach of the next appointment at a slight distance, although his ears were alert to respond to the sound of the doorbell. He also anticipated the click of Vera's impossibly high heels on the hard pavement stones, taking steps toward her two o'clock appointment. Why did women wear shoes like that? It seemed that many women wanted to be taller. Recognition of Vera's slight frame and size pressed something he had been trying to suppress for days. The small, neat, animal body, the feral energy in the dark eyes. The short laugh. The mass of bouncing dark hair.

*A light laugh and the toss of the head, the dark lion mane of hair.*

Max groaned inside. He realised the feeling his stomach had been signalling for days would not let recognition remain buried.

*She was like Little Nutmeg. Margaret.* He swallowed hard.

*Maxwell and Margaret. Twins born within fifteen minutes of each other.*

Vera reminded him of his sister. More than any other patient ever.

But Vera is not Margaret, he told himself firmly. The association was physical, not psychological or emotional. His stomach reacted: was that really true?

Vera had said, "I suppose I sort of lost my own identity, just to keep up with him," meaning that she had suppressed herself in order to be what Alistair wanted.

*Margaret had said: "I have had all these little deaths and now there is nothing left."*

Many people lived in the shadow of their loss, unable to return to life. They went through the motions of living, on automatic, psychologically deadened, passing time until sleep, medication or death released them from the struggle of consciousness. *Some, like Margaret, took their own unbearable lives.*

Max never knew what patients would be able to do with the opportunities psychotherapy offered. He wanted to be optimistic, he wanted it to work. He knew he had to tame his optimism so that it did not push patients into false hope, into believing they could magically transform, rather than learn to make a meaningful relationship with suffering.

*If only I could have saved her!*

That stomach lurch that had been so much his everyday reality before he entered the Order returned now. So fresh.

*If only the skills I have now could have been available to Meg.*

All the 'if onlys'. The regret. The remorse. The guilt.

But to go down that road was to idealise, to make psychotherapy a magic cure-all when it was merely a tool that only worked with four willing hands.

Sitting now, reflecting, he could see that Vera had had to blunt and numb parts of herself in order to survive the neglect of early life with a preoccupied mother and absent, unknown father. The conditional and bullying demands of a husband in a marriage that might have afforded her an opportunity for something different, meant that she had little sense of her own individuality. Who was she without these emotional demands? The question was whether that which had been blunted or numbed could find life again.

Margaret had been too traumatised, too young and too overwhelmingly to find a manageable place inside to live.

And Saxon Pierce? Had she also had to kill some part of herself in order to live?

And now there was Emily, retreating more severely into her illness in anticipation of an unbearable loss she imagined in her distorted mind: "She will take you away from me."

He shook his tired head. The stone Buddha in his bookshelf corner smiled his quiet smile and Max tried to settle. Margaret had not lived long enough to grow into a woman. She had never had the chance to develop Vera Dodds' canny earth wisdom and fierce feral way when protecting her young. A reason to live when all else felt gone. Saxon Pierce had had a skilled enough brain to help her develop into a good doctor and researcher which had, until now, offered her a shield from the storm of emotion not yet practised.

He smoothed the rug under his chair and planted his feet firmly on it, feeling the way in which the soles of his feet met the inside of his shoes. His one extravagance: hand-made good-looking shoes, in leather.

He must keep his feet on the ground. These internal knots revealing yet more emotion connected with past losses. Was there something else he needed to understand about his sister? And the nature of her death?

The Buddha's smile remained when he closed his eyes.

He looked at the clock. Ten past two. Vera had never been late before. He tidied the edge of the rug and picked up a book that had fallen on its side. He did not yet understand her fully, nor what she could work with. He wondered how he would know if something happened to her, if she were to try to harm herself.

*That now familiar lurch in the stomach, the heavy breath, the fear, resignation ...*

The doorbell sounded, a gong calling into the abyss. Relief cleared away the debris of doubt and fear.

"I'm very sorry to be late," she said, staring at him when he opened the door at two-thirty. "I just forgot the time."

The regular hours of therapy slotted into the week, same day, same time, were sometimes the only structure in a patient's life. Often protested at, and rebelled against, these simple routines could be lifelines. They helped in the creation of a safe vessel.

Max signals for her to sit in the chair but she remains standing, looking around like a wild animal startled out of its hole.

"Funny, isn't it. I have just one hour here and it sort of turns the rest of my week upside down."

"Yes, I can understand that," said Max.

She remains standing. Looking around the room.

"How are you getting on with the journal writing?"

"Nothing doing."

"What's been happening?" asks Max. A practical, if superficial question.

"Nothing," she says. Then, "Alistair came to see me. It's

all over."

Max nods. He feels sad with her. He wonders what had happened between them. "Do you want to say more?"

"Nothing to tell," she says in an empty voice. "He's made it final. I'm to be dumped, like any old rubbish."

"You are not rubbish," he says, and means it.

She looks at him, from her standing position, and then sits carefully on the edge of the chair, like someone who feels they won't be staying long. Max can see that she has shut down. During their last session he had seen her open to her own knowledge and understanding and he had allowed himself to hope that this would continue. But he knew therapy was not a linear process; the graph of emotion and understanding always looked like the sheet music of a Scarlatti piano sonata.

Then he remembers his fear as he was waiting for her. His association with her and Margaret. His disproportionate terror at what might have happened to her. He is more upset than is appropriate.

Vera begins speaking after a long silence in which their misery is mutual. She is sniffing and shrugging her shoulders: "I was also late because I thought 'what's the point now, of me coming here? It's not going to get him back, that's for sure'. I just don't know what to do anymore. I have no goal." She pauses, thinking to herself, "Except that of my secret ploy, to keep on trying to get him back where he belongs." But she looks down, concentrating on her hands.

Then, an honest disclosure. "Things are slipping out of my control."

Max is looking at her closely. "How do you experience that, what happens?" he asks.

"I don't think I can tell you."

She couldn't tell him about the videos. She had returned to them after Alistair's visit, when the silence and impossible emptiness offered her no other choices. Screen images of naked stomachs and limbs absorbed in the drama of their own sexual inventions had offered some relief. Camera close-ups of intense faces, eyes closed, mouths open, tongues licking and sucking on the sexual organs of another. Long hair, wet or greasy with effort, rolling eyes or closed swollen lids, the pink of partly aroused flesh. Without sound, the imagined groans and moans, exaggerated for the camera. Body parts red and sweating. Some body parts blotched and spotted, scratched and bleeding. A film without sound. Its watchers could invent their own.

She couldn't tell him that she had given in to Nag.

She wonders if shrinks had X-ray eyes and could see the workings of their patient's minds. She wonders if he might see the marks on her arms under her red sweater, or worse on her backside. She knows he had noticed that she sat down very carefully.

She didn't know if she had cried out, or even if she were capable of crying out anymore. Pleasure was hard to find, however much punishment or pain.

She had played the white evening scarf around herself, trying to replicate the way Alistair had used it. Trying to ignite some feeling, trying to restore to herself their intimate ways.

And in the face of pleasure's failure she had let the Destroyer in, the Grand Nag. He had been wooing her for weeks and she had been staving him off and this had given her some edge, and therefore some pleasure; that she could fend off that last hope for thrill and restoration, promising it to herself, that it would come when she was ready. And then she would be whole.

But the weekend had been impossible. Knowing that Alistair was collecting Dominic from Bristol and going with him to school to see Luke; that he was telling them, introducing them to the woman he was putting in her place. Her pleas, via email and letter, for she had not spoken to him since he visited her, for them to tell the boys together, had been ignored. She had made the first and important visit to Luke by herself, braving that motorway journey with its awful memories of betrayal, and she had decided she would not mention what had happened. She was too shocked over Alistair's visit, too raw and numb, and uncertain. Her only certainty was to make sure her youngest was OK, to touch him and hug him and to carry on as if nothing had changed. He asked her anxiously, "Is everything alright Mum?" He had seen her tired face and the loss of weight. He knew she had objected to him being sent away and had tried to stop it. But now he would find out that she had lied to him. Her only comfort was that because she was so close to him, he would probably realise she had tried to protect him from this obscenity.

So that weekend, knowing that the seeds to the destruction of her family life were being firmly planted and there was absolutely nothing she could do to stop them, she had walked naked through the empty rooms and had relinquished her guard against Nag, letting him woo her. And she had wooed him back, singing lightly to herself and to him as she left doors open in front of mirrors so that he could see her all the time. In fact she had opened herself to anyone who might come in, playing upon her body, inserting into herself, flailing with the whip and baton they had bought in France, using the metal handcuffs, the metal chain.

Grand Nag had finally caught her. A dark figure riding high on his black horse, his pack of hungry hounds sniffing, howling, snarling, grey tongues lolling. Running with the same dead fisheyes as the Great Nag himself as he ordered them forward, pack on pack; the same dead but relentless energy, driven by ghouls from hell. They had fed off each other for the last few days. All locks were sprung, bolts undone. Her body was cut and bruised, the boundaries within the sections of her fragile personality shattered.

Max watches her shake her head as if to fend off some demon in her mind, her eyes shifting to and fro. She was remembering something that made her agitated. Something that had no words. He sat alongside her trying to be within this unimaginable space. As those strong hands pushed the long sleeves of her red sweater up to her elbows, he saw the fresh red marks on her forearms.

He felt relieved that this involuntary gesture had allowed him access to the aggressive feelings turned against herself. If her unconscious was revealing it within the green room there was an opportunity to work with it, to redirect its potentially destructive energies into more useful places.

He had to speak of what he had seen, to help create a bridge between the two of them that would be strong enough to challenge this addictive pull.

"Those marks, on your arms, tell me about them."

Vera looks startled and then shifty. She pulls down the red sleeves and wraps her arms around her quickly.

"It's nothing. I'm getting careless," she says.

"It doesn't look like nothing," says Max gently. "It was an involuntary gesture, wasn't it? Pulling up your sleeves as you were reliving something important. It's allowed us to share it, this compulsion. I'd like to help you feel less alone with it."

"You would just be disgusted," she says quickly, surprised at her words.

"I think that you are harming yourself as a way to cope with the emotional pain you feel."

She is silent. Nag the Destroyer rose up in her mind. Cackling, smirking. Thinks he can talk us out of it, does he?

In her loneliness and desolation Vera welcomed all the dark Nags, for they had come before and she knew them all, the faces, smells, noises, commands. She smiles and speaks like an automaton. "The crack of the whip brings me alive. If I obey the voices, I obey the force and then I have some peace."

"Sleep?" asks Max.

"Yes," she says dully. But it was more than that… They would crush her into unconsciousness. Her body would carry the scars and bruises from these nightly rides and she had sometimes torn herself badly. But she would have had a voyage, and these nights the voyage with Nag and his torturing demons were the nearest she came to feeling alive.

Their chorus, "Go on, why don't you; no one will see; you want it don't you; it's what you want, go for it, only we see, only we matter now, just one little go, just one time, it'll be nice, then there'll be others, you'll want others, and we'll be there. You're not much good for anything else anyway, don't think you can ask for anything nice, nice isn't for you. Just remember you're ours. We've got you and will always have you. You are our slave."

Max thought: wanting to go to sleep, not wanting to feel; but also wanting to be alive, to be awake.

"What do the voices say?" he asks.

She laughs a harsh laugh and spoke, still with the flat robotic tones in a broad northern accent: "Don't think you can have what YOU want, what YOU want will be what I want because I know what's best, and what's right for you. You're not like other people. YOU can't be free, can't have what you want, so don't start thinking about it. You will always be bad because bad came to you early, its there inside you and it will never get out, never get undone. You've known this all along but you haven't remembered it, thinking you could escape by marrying Alistair, escape into a little cosy respectable life, thinking you could be ordinary and that everyone would think there was nothing wrong with you. But we know, we understand the likes of you, we know you." The voice tailed off and she wrapped herself more deeply into her red sweater.

The green room holds a shocked silence. Max is startled, he breathes deeply, staying with her, feeling compassion. He feels the energy of the Guardians draw in close.

"I can't help myself," she says eventually from the confines of the sweater.

"What are the voices making you do?"

Nag would take her hand and cause it to strike against her own body; her now thin emaciated body, lash, hit, scratch. On and on. With or without the television screen to prompt her. Her will was given over.

The relief from this was becoming her own jewel, her precious secret. Founded on the secret she had shared with Alistair. She could hug it to herself. She could hug the idea that this is what he might come back for.

When Nag was there, there was no aching, not knowing how to carry on, how to be. Days and nights roll into one.

Max felt into her silent response. He imagined enough to be right by her without intrusion. "So this week, it has been like this, a blur of harming yourself?"

"It's all I've got," she says in a thick voice.

Max would question this before the end of their session, and he wonders how the voices had originated. Her mother, or her mother's many lovers? Her own self-destructive impulse manifest in finding an edge in sadomasochism. But for now, he asks, "Does it link you with Alistair? Is it something you shared?"

"That's private," she says smartly.

"Yes," he replies. "I respect that. At the moment this harming", he deliberately uses a direct word rather than wrapping it up in something oblique, "brings relief because it carries a close and shared memory. But it must also feel so lonely and painful when you come from it." He pauses, considering how much of his own concern to put in here. "Also, I'm concerned that you are harming yourself and creating a habit that can easily become compulsive and out of control."

She is silent, some remote, unconnected part of her registering his calm acceptance and concern for her. She does not respond directly but reveals something else.

"Sometimes I find myself in places and I don't know how I got there." The voice is clear now, smaller and more refined. Max was startled and another face, another body sat in the chair that was Vera's. *Margaret would go missing and his anxious grandparents would telephone and ask if she had hitched a lift to him at his school. She told him that sometimes she woke up in strange places and that people she had never met seemed to know her and called her Faith. There was also a time when someone referred to her as 'Comfort'.* He had to make himself return to the reality that was Vera's.

"Tell me of an example."

Each night since Alistair's going she had slept in small bursts. It was hard to decide to actually go to bed, or where to try to sleep. The 'play' videos she and Alistair had collected and made of themselves no longer helped her to stimulate any sexual or emotional effect. They no longer kindled the old feelings, which helped her to relax and hope, and allow her to sleep. She would catnap from midnight onward and wake alert around three; the dead, unforgiving time of night. Dark except for London streetlights and only the rumble of the odd lorry to remind her of other human beings. She would lie awake, her heartbeat thumping an adrenaline vigilance throughout her tissues. When she could no longer bear it she would get up and wrap herself in Alistair's black silk kimono embroidered with gold dragons and sit rocking at the kitchen table until it got light.

One morning, instead she had dressed and left the house, and walked in the empty streets. She walked along a dark deserted Victoria Street and up Grosvenor Place. A night bus passed. The cleaners were beginning their shifts in the manicured office buildings. Sharp gusts of wind blew into the seams of her old camel coat. She shivered but carried on. She longed for escape from the pain of being in her body.

Under the underpass at Hyde Park Corner and into Hyde Park. The glow of London lights against the blue-black sky. She looked across through the shrubs of Hyde Park towards South Kensington where she imagined Alistair might be living. She had no address for him except his office. She had tried calling the office number, but all those staff she had so generously entertained had been primed not to give her any information. Even though her body was cold, she could feel herself burning, flaming up inside.

As the cold wind caught her thin face, she imagined him snuggled up asleep or making love to the woman who had taken him away from her. The woman who now had all the power. The woman who had ruined her life.

She wanted the gap inside her to be filled by him, and only him. She wanted him to say "this is all a mistake. I love you, I need you, I want you, I want never to leave your side. I am so sorry to have hurt you." Only he could mend the bruises and fill the emptiness.

She lost contact with a conscious sense of herself. This night, desperate, lost, Vera stopped and the body that housed Vera took itself along the path of plane trees with their piebald trunks, where joggers ran in the early mornings. Without being aware of it she started weeping under the dark night sky in this anonymous park where lonely people came on Sundays and watched couples playing with children or snuggling together in the grass in summer. Where she had once been part of a couple. She burned against her bruises. Tears ran into her mouth and seemed to cover her face without her noticing. The empty well of her being was losing its inside lining.

Something of the dark brown pattern in the rug on Max's floor caught her attention and brought her back to the green room. She caught sight of her hands and played with the ring on her left hand. She remembered then she had not rescued the postcard with the stone circle from the back of the cabinet.

"I found myself at the lion house."

"The lion house?"

"Yes, at the zoo."

She looks at him with a clear and suddenly bright

expression in her dark brown eyes. "But I don't know how I got there."

Max is thoughtful. "What was the last thing you remember before you found yourself at the zoo?"

"I felt so cold," she says. "I can't sleep, and so sometimes I get up and just sit in the kitchen by the Aga."

"What were you wearing when you came to at the zoo."

She looks surprised – "I was wearing an old tracksuit and a camel coat."

"Do you remember putting them on?"

His questions allow her to feel the softness of the familiar worn coat and the way it touched her skin as she put it on in the hall. It was old and not smart, a coat Alistair despised. She remembered the comfort of its familiarity and softness. It was like love.

Max is watching her hands.

She follows his look and says, "It's the warmth I miss. I just can't get any. Nothing warms me up. I am permanently cold."

"What do you most long for now?" he asks.

She trembles and her body arches forward suddenly, tears springing from the corners of her eyes. "It's the love all smashed up. I cannot hold onto what we had. I search and search and there is no trace of it." The chasm she felt inside just seemed to get deeper. Inside her there was no softness into which she could lean or be comforted, no compensation for her loss. "Without it, I'm nothing."

"You are you, and that's not nothing."

She looks as if his words mean nothing. "Have I imagined these last twenty years?" she asks in a high-pitched voice. "Where has all the love gone?" She looks at him directly. The darkness of her brown eyes is flooded with tears, drawing him in.

*The love is all gone, Maxie. Where has the love all gone?* Margaret had said the same thing, had felt the same empty chasm.

"People say 'better to have loved and lost than never to have loved at all' don't they? But why put yourself in love's way if it is to turn into this. I gave him everything. And now, I've got nothing."

"You have yourself. Your boys," Max speaks softly, and firmly.

"Yes," she says quickly, breathing out in relief. "I don't want to sound self-pitying, ungrateful. I love my boys so much. I am so, so lucky to have them. I have my boys." She pauses. "Except ... except that he will try to take them. He will corrupt them. He and his new life. What chance do I have up against all that? What will happen to me?"

*The pleading, the same words: Maxie, what will happen to us now? And later, after he had met Emily: Max, what will happen to me without you?*

He kept control of himself. He said, "Your boys have known you all their lives. You are their mother and from what I can gather you have excellent relationships with all of them. Nothing, no-one can take that away. The boys will need their own live mother to be as she always was."

He should not have used the word 'live'. That was his business, his sorrow. He thinks to correct it but Vera is deep in her own thoughts.

Without being able to shape her identity in response to Alistair's demand she was suffering a loss of self, as if she no longer existed. It was her embodied instinctual self that brought her back.

She pauses with a deep sigh. "I can't think straight."

Max smiles. "It is hard to think straight after trauma," he says. "Our systems go into the survival fight or flight that we looked at when we first met. At the moment our work here is to help you to develop a safe grounded space from which you will in time be able to think things through and see your options."

"Trauma," she says, "I thought that's what happened in accidents. When you get post-traumatic stress."

"Yes, that's right. But it's not only accidents. We can be traumatised by loss, by illness, by change, as well as by accidents. And when our system is traumatised, we are in a state of either high alert or shut down. It seems as if you are experiencing both of these responses. In both these responses we are not able to utilise our objective thinking, we are constantly aroused by our situation."

"Trauma. I suppose it is. Makes it better doesn't it, calling it trauma rather than failure?" She flashes him a rare smile and although professionally it shows him something of her robustness, he wished she wouldn't. Her tone, its surprising objectivity and bleak realisation, was so much like that of Margaret.

"So, what are you saying, Maxie? Just live with two legs cut off and it'll all be OK?"

Max forces himself to continue, to concentrate upon being with Vera. He smiles encouragingly, "Calling it failure is a judgement on it. It comes from the construct you have made in your mind about what is good and what is bad."

Vera returns to her desperation. "I go over and over those early days trying to feel his love again in order to feel me, to feel whole. He was so eager, anything I wanted was granted."

Max decides upon trying to contact the good experience she had shared with Alistair. "What was he like when you first met?"

Her face softens a little, she smiles, "He was so urgent." The image of an earlier Alistair comes into the room. An Alistair Max had first met at Oxford. Tentative, and also, determined.

So he heard from Vera's softened voice how he made careful arrangements for their meetings, checking with her, that the time and place were convenient, that it was what she wanted, and how he was always on time for her. He was so giving and gentle, telling her lovely things about herself. He communicated his desire for her every day, some days every hour. Telephone messages, little notes, a flower, a poem. The way he remembered what she had said, what she had told him about herself and her mother, details of names, places, times, trivial enough, but things he chose to remember and treat as precious. He would speak back to her lovingly, as if he truly wanted to know all about her and rejoice in this knowledge.

There is another silence between them and the green room seems to sigh a little, as if welcoming some softness in the harsh climate.

"This love you experienced, your first love, which was so powerful and so mutual, this no one can take from you. It is something that has helped to define who you are, and it has been there for twenty years. For twenty years you have offered your love, this is a really important part of your life, your history."

"History," she retorts. "That's the problem. I'm just history."

"I didn't mean it like that," says Max. "What I meant was that you have just shared with me an experience of love that was real and mutual. I could feel it as you were speaking. In that moment your face was open and bright, your voice was soft and full, your suffering was secondary. You sound like this when you are speaking of your boys. Those feelings you were communicating to me are yours. They are not Alistair's. He has not taken them away with him. They are in you. This capacity to love and be loved is still there. You might feel bleak at the moment as the love you knew feels as if it has been withdrawn, but you are still you with or without another's love."

She watched him intently. Listening. It was all clever new stuff. She knew somewhere deep inside that he talked sense and she so wanted to connect with what he said. But it was as if there was nowhere inside her that these right sentiments could take root.

"Can you concentrate upon the feelings of love you have just described, that are inside you?"

Some warmth entered her then, at these words.

"There's no point, is there, just loving on your own?"

"Do you feel there always has to be another person?"

"Well it's relative isn't it; mutual give and take, as you said."

She was unable to feel what had once been between her and Alistair.

"He's ruined what we had," she said quietly, and Max felt a slight relief that in that statement she had separated herself from blame.

That old feeling, of being queen. All the things she had never dared to even hope for, were placed before her. She could hardly believe her luck, then.

"It mocks me now all that. Mocking, teasing."

"So there is a mocking voice inside you that would devalue your experience."

"What good is it now that it's gone!" she cried.

Max heard a soft whisper in his left ear. *"Memories are so cold, Maxie. They offer no comfort. They open the chasm deeper. What's the point?"* The only love she had attempted had been blasted away by a drunken motorist, a kid of 18.

The green room listened and watched. Margaret was here. Little Nutmeg in her green-check dress running along the beach. And the young Alistair appearing at the end of Vera's working day, waiting for her in his open-topped Aston Martin, wearing a freshly laundered shirt. And everyone in the department store knew. They knew that he had chosen her and was not ashamed to show it, despite the protests of his parents. That hungry, empty place inside her would be banished forever to the damp misery of childhood, she hoped. She was proud and fit to bursting. She was ready and willing to be filled and satisfied by the ways of this man who had changed her life. She hugged his desire and love for her like a precious jewel. She rewarded him for choosing her by a fierce loyalty, an adoration and servitude. She had easily become his slave.

"I go over and over my memories, to try to make them come alive again, to have something to hold on to, to make them come real again. The Alistair now, is not the Alistair I married."

Now, as the light was fading in this pale green room in South London she moved back into her lost night. She remembered the roar of diesel lorries as they went too fast up Park Lane. She remembered pausing in the darkness of Speaker's Corner, the place where people could shout their views, could find their own voice. What might she say now? What was her voice? Did she have one? Had she ever had one? She had seen a discarded orange box and bent to put it straight, before standing on it to try herself out. How little she knew of life she realised.

Because now, oh what a shock the now was! Before, when she knew he had been with other women, who had held his hand and stroked his thigh, with whom he had allowed himself to be aroused, she could hug to herself the fact that he came home to her. She lived inside his house, was mother to his children, their names were joined together on the cheque books and the account at Harrods. Mrs Alistair Dodds. This was who she was, the person he had helped her become. Most precious of all was the fact that he had chosen her first. She had accepted the hungry, angry adolescent in him and served his need to tame. This, Her Most Secret Knowledge, she had believed would hold them forever.

But after Speakers Corner, she could not remember walking down Oxford Street, passed the darkened windows of the shops she usually eagerly scanned. Workers started to open up inside Burger King, yawning as they switched on lights and separated the papers that would hold fries and buns.

"Your secret?"

She must have spoken.

"Is this the secret that leads you to turn your hand against your own body?"

She blinks. It is hard now for her to stay in the pale green room.

"I can see that this is getting hard for you. We can come back to it next time. For now, let us concentrate on connecting to the stone circle, the safe place."

She was not listening. Her secret knowledge was that she could control the poisonous snakes that lived inside Alistair, that Vera believed had been put there by his mother and confirmed by his nanny. Poisonous snakes that rose up out of him because of his hatred of women, hatred born from being dominated and possessed. Vera thought that Alistair's mother was a spiteful frustrated dragon, and that women like her should not be allowed to be anywhere near boys. They were jealous of power and difference. They tried to punish their sons for making them feel inadequate. They wove an invisible web of love and guilt that would bind their sons to them. The sort of internal web men could not get away from, however many women they tried out or how far they travelled. Vera had never articulated such ideas, but she had taken over the role of Alistair's indispensable 'other' by being prepared to be a container for all his needs, however bizarre, and without question. She could tame the hissing snakes, and their anger and vitriol; she could calm Alistair by taking over what his body demanded. She could submit to the blows he needed to inflict to get the snakes and their poison out of him. She had learned to bear it, to ask her body to allow him to enter her in all the ways he needed to get himself right again. She had learned early, too early, to take what men couldn't control themselves. She accepted his demanding rituals and after the final surrender they could have peace. And then in those moments she could feel that he really did love her, and she could be safe. That was her surest place. The place where she had control. Her Most Secret Knowledge.

She kept going back to this place.

Her body had walked on up Baker Street past the underground where people were emerging into the early morning, and into Regents Park. One or two blackbirds had started singing and the smell of dew on early morning earth rose up with its eternal challenge to what would be a day of London grime and fume. With her body intent on walking as long and as fast as it could, Vera noticed none of this. Now, in the flashes of awareness in the green room she focussed on holding on to Her Most Secret Knowledge and its animal quality. She and Alistair had been the lion cubs in the lion club. But cats also had another game to being kittenish, and it was a game that Alistair had taught her well. She could bite too, and scratch and run. She felt brightened by the thought. She must be alert. She had to be ready with her lion cat self for when Arabella failed to take care of his needs properly.

She spoke into the green room from a hazy sense of time and content. "I had this dream. And then the dream came out to meet me."

The amber eyes of the lioness had glowed and blazed. She stood in complete stillness, a stillness that made Vera catch her breath. The queen of cats. When her jaw opened, she showed a fine mouth that could nuzzle and play with cubs; that could also devour and relish the flesh of prey. She moved silently and smoothly on soft-pawed feet. The queen of cats.

"The queen of cats," says Vera into the room.

Max was finding it hard to keep up with her. On top of concentrating on Vera's lost night, the self-harm, the private secret with Alistair, were his associations with Margaret. How he had held her frightened body in his hand in the similar way he was now being asked to hold the space for the fragmented Vera.

*You and I don't have to be alone in the world, my Maxie. We've got each other. We can be lion and lioness fighting in the prairie together, fending off all the hungry jackals.*

"Would you like to tell me about the dream?"

Vera smiles. There was something in her hand. She looks down and sees that as she has been speaking, she has picked up one of the stones from the basket by the side of her chair. The stone felt smooth and firm and she turns it round and round in the palm of her hand. "I did hope that I would find some actual stones," she said. "I've got the postcard with the stones, to remind me of the safe circle." When she spoke, her voice sounded steadier. The Guardians in the green room and Max's presence was in some curious way facilitating a process of internal gathering. Max knew that something important was going on inside her, but he did not know if words would follow straight away.

"And I have my queen, my champion. Yes, I remember now and it makes me feel better. You don't have to worry."

She looks at him suddenly with intent and focus in her expression. He feels chilled.

*"You don't have to worry, Maxie. All is taken care of," Margaret had said, before she drowned herself in the sea.*

Vera's body tenses and rears up, her back arching.

"What is happening?"

Vera shudders, excited. "I am remembering now."

She had come back into her body as she sat down on the bank near Regents Canal. Dawn was breaking, the canal water still dark and dense. The grass was wet and it was this and the cold that welcomed her back into her body. Looking forward, she followed the line of the canal until she could make out, in the dim light, the high wire netting partitions of the London Zoo where she had taken the boys many times. Her nostrils opened, she breathed in deeply as if for the first time since Alistair had left. She could smell animal, and that loneliness of zoo animals so far from their native pacing ground. The lioness from the dream. She was real, and she had called her! Help was at hand after all! In her new reading she had read that Mother Nature both nourishes and devours and at the time had thought it intellectual rubbish. But now she could see that the lioness had just such capacity, and that it could also be inside her. Such a proud animal, fierce and graceful. She was no victim, imprisoned by having to give in to a mate, to take what was thrown at her and think herself lucky! The thought that she, too, was a mother and could defend her young, primed Vera to defend herself and outwit those who threatened her or her young. The lioness could help her fight for her boys, for her life!

"So, if I connect with her at the zoo in that state I was in, half in and half out of my own body, and if she's already in my dream, then she can be there for me can't she?" she said now to Max "All I have to do is reach out my hand …."

And now, as she reaches out her hand toward the soft green rug Max kept at the back of the chair, the face of the lioness appeared in her imagination. It was a face and body she could learn to stroke, to tame, to set free, so that she could come to live inside her, to conquer the lands where the Destroyer lived. Nag the Destroyer, Snag the Torturer would be replaced.

Max saw how some primitive process inside her was working itself through. Rather than answer his questions verbally it seemed as if a capacity to use image and energy was forming itself inside. He was not sure whether her attachment to the image and energy of the lioness was a delusion to avoid the pain of her loss, or whether she was integrating energy derived from both dream and animal presence which would be useful. It could be a mixture of both. He saw a physical change, in the set of her jaw and the squaring of her shoulders, like an animal survival stirring within her body. She had a hazy sense that fusing herself with the lioness would offer her some great animal strength. She was holding the stone, moving it from one hand to another. When he looked down, he saw that she had slipped off the impossible shoes and was resting her stockinged feet on his rug.

Feeling his rug with her feet Vera realised that she wanted to be free of her need for another's approval that had caged her, like the cage in which her champion was living. She could control of her own life but not through being someone else's servant. Getting the books was a good idea. She could learn. She could study from others.

She knew then, in that session, that Alistair's initial obsession with her had ignited the possibility of being loved, of having a home and a secure respectable life she had never known. And some of this had indeed happened. But it had not been enough to help her feel complete as a person because it was on someone else's terms, and she had had to distort herself to accommodate him.

"I don't really know who I am," she said next, surprising Max.

"Perhaps that's why you're here," he offered, smiling.

# 9

MAX could not concentrate during meditation, his body was restless, and hurting. When sitting with patients he thought about walking on the beach in Suffolk and what delicious meal he would make for himself after braving the North Sea winds. The energies he thought of as his Guardians waited where they could, the half-smile and compassionate gaze solidly present, unchanging. When a space opened, and Max allowed himself to be touched by the silence within it he could recognise the feeling of falling and experience the fearful quality of its blindness. He did not know where it would take him. He had no maps of the way.

For how long had he been afraid?

"Since you were ten years old," said a voice inside him.

But why the falling again now?

"Because it is time," continued the voice.

Then the image of the robin he had tried to revive filled his mind, followed by another of it lying dead on his door step the next morning. And this terrible war in Iraq. The war millions of ordinary British people had marched and campaigned against was started anyway in their name, because of a myth and a lie. His newspapers were full of its hideous murders of civilians. He had never felt so helpless and afraid and as if the contribution of individual conscience and practice counted for nothing.

"I need to follow the images," he thought. "I need to be alone."

His supervisor, with whom he discussed his cases, who had been his wise supporter and challenger for many years, had said, just yesterday, "You have a great deal on your plate right now. These two patients are difficult and at risk. That's always demanding and raises anxiety. You are doing an excellent job with them. And you have a journey of your own to make. I'm on the end of the phone."

He had looked up, his brown eyes intense, brimming. His supervisor's face was full of concern. Max's barren life with Emily and his brutal past was an acknowledged and painful mystery.

He walked home from his meeting, pushing his bicycle.

His body had rejected the effort of pedalling into the wind. Inside the heaviness of his heart a fresh breeze had blown onto a long-smouldering log to ignite impossible feeling. It was not hard to name the emotion as that old chestnut, anger. One word that had been favoured by psychology and social work to explain multiple psychological presentations. But the body experience and the felt sense was individual. Anger could burn, smoulder, and freeze.

He sensed that what was trying to rise from that smouldering log was more than simple anger but rage. That dark, heavy, dangerous substance that hid in impossible crevasses, in the joints between bones, and in those secret chambers of blood inside the heart. It was primitive, it hurt. For Max, it had been, in all its forms, always forbidden.

Having recognised it, he practised with it, breathing in and breathing out.

\* \* \* \*

Saxon waited until the first signs of dawn began to appear and then put on Alma's lead in preparation for taking her into Kensington Gardens. At the sound of the old-fashioned metal lift gates closing, she shivered and kept her eyes fixed on the smooth blue leather of Alma's collar. The previous evening, she was putting her key into her apartment door when she heard the lift arrive and the metallic clanking of the gates opening had stirred her, unusually, to turn. She had never wanted to mix with neighbours. A young man emerged, walking slowly with bliss on his face, his arms full of something wrapped in a pale blue blanket, followed by a young woman carrying a Moses basket. It seemed that this previously faceless couple with a pregnancy she had never noticed lived right next door to her and were bringing their baby home for the first time. They had that flush of joy she had seen on the faces of the couple in Hong Kong. And in that moment the twist in her chest and explosion in her head told her that she would not be able to forget. That right now, here, in sober London, those events she had tried so hard to keep away would come tumbling out.

She had been awake all night, fending off images and thoughts whilst every pore of her listened out for that sound, that particular, eerie cry of a newborn.

Those tiny creatures with pickaxes that lived inside her chest were hammering in earnest. They were opening up all the old wounds – cutting her to the quick.

She knew that she must go somewhere, she must be in the open air and on her own, ready to run if needed or she would be trapped inside her apartment, suffocating.

Sharp frost had stiffened the tips of grasses but there was no sunshine to reflect any sparkle. The brown water of the Serpentine flowed heavily. She sat on one of the frosted benches, her knees firmly together and her back rigid, looking straight ahead, her little dog close by her side, sensing something wrong. She held onto Alma's lead, smoothing the soft leather with her fingers, every now and then bending to touch the hair of her back. Her heart was racing, her body cold. The water of the Serpentine soon began merging with the water of Hong Kong harbour, dark, filthy and fathomless.

*They had offered to let her hold their newborn baby. At three weeks his naked head was vulnerable, the open fontanelle throbbing under mottled skin. The wrinkled face still bore the faint imprint of a tight womb sack. His tiny, perfectly formed hands lay still, the fingernails white and flaky. He had both new, and yet ancient presence. The miracle of new life always irresistible.*

*She had avoided the couple, eager for their child to be held and cooed over, but after she had gone outside for air for the fourth time, they followed her, babe in arms. She knew she was the only guest who had not held him. They thought she looked tired and lonely. In fact the couple had learned from the hosts that the woman doctor had no children and they felt sorry for her. Perhaps she couldn't, they had whispered to themselves. Or perhaps she was the sort who put career and work first, who, in their eyes, failed at relationships. Or the sort who didn't like their house messed up by children. Secretly, the couple despised women who worked too hard and left it too late. They thought, with a smug and patronising logic, that holding their baby would do her good. And they knew he would be quite safe with her, because, after all, she was a doctor.*

*They began moving toward her with their eager faces, offering the sleeping body of their son in his blue quilted wrap for her to hold. A loving balm to soothe a lonely heart? To coo and aah, rock and cluck, to return to Eden's innocent bliss.*

*So she took the child into her arms and held him stiffly, not smiling, which made the couple encourage her more, mistaking her hatred for nerves, joking about newborns making adults clumsy. And even though they knew she was a doctor.*

*Turning away from their faces and the background blur of the frenzy and noise of harbour life, she had looked down.*

*He was warm and still, sleeping soundly. The skin of his face was new pink, the flush of just visible down inviting a stroking finger. His little eyelids with the mottled skin were almost transparent, so small they could fit onto an adult thumb. The long eyelashes quivered. Breathing was deep somewhere in the blue quilting. Once he sighed deeply, a big sigh for a tiny frame, as if he were already old. His mouth was perfectly formed, not yet shaped around words. A mouth not yet set in attitude. Nothing but mother's milk and the odd cry had passed between the lips; some wind perhaps, a little cough. But the vitriol of words, the expressing or holding back of hurt, rage, love, even passion, was yet to come.*

She came out of the memory as Alma strained on her lead, waiting to be friendly to a pair of black poodles whose owners had let them off leashes. The dogs were just puppies, eager for fun at dawn on a Sunday morning, their owners a young French couple absorbed in each other. How fresh and young they looked, how free! She gave Alma enough lead to play.

The image of first taking the child was strong, and vivid. But after this the thread of memory was slight, and exactly what had happened on that boat was obscured. She had, so she understood, blanked it out because it was impossible to bear. She remembered the lightness of her arms, still in the holding pattern, but the child no longer there.

*Even though she could not see it, as the bundle hit the dark water the grip at her neck and chest tightened so sharply, she thought her heart had gone into spasm. The chaotic swirl of the harbour water had risen up outside and had got inside her. She no longer existed. There was just chaos. Her heart beat fast and furiously, pumping chaos into every pore. And at the same* time as being cold a hot dense substance rose up with volcanic charge, flooding every tissue to make each nerve ending come on fire.

\* \* \* \*

When Dr Max opened the door to her the following day she remembered that when she had first stepped into his room she had seen the figure of a man in a crumpled suit. The same figure that she had seen by the steps on the Chinese junk and after she had found her arms empty.

*The figure of the man in the crumpled suit flashed incongruously and was followed by a curious inevitability and acceptance. She did not know exactly what had happened, or how it had happened. She had done something irrevocable and there was the resigned feeling that it had been long coming. Now it was out, and she had changed the pattern.*

She sat in the green chair, alert and on edge, for the memory of that day would not stop. Now that the man in the crumpled suit was somehow Dr Max the other pieces started coming into the room. She held onto the arms of the chair. Max saw that she was swaying slightly and from time to time a strangled sound came from her throat.

*She heard the mother of the child start screaming and soon panic and chaos broke loose around her. Saxon remained standing rigid, rooted to the spot where it had happened, next to the narrow rail, bent over. Someone moved her all of a piece and helped her to sit. Some people tried to get off the boat and into the water. The natural clumsiness of physical fear created slowness. Shoes and sweaters took time to pull off; no one seemed to know quite what to do. Someone was yelling orders, but no one was listening. The screams of the mother of the child gave way to primitive grief reactions, keening over the rail and water whilst wringing her hands in the air.*

*The red-faced father looked confused not taking it in. Guests appeared and started yelling to passengers on other boats, pointing frantically. These passengers stared looking puzzled, or they shrugged, not understanding, not wanting to get involved, maybe not even wondering what all the fuss was about. Oh, the English!*

*The skipper, unaware of the drama, was motoring on, in*

*charge of his junk, needing to be back at the pier by five o'clock to get the junk ready for the evening. The blue bundle was being left behind. And although at first it had floated, the blue wrap, full of air and light, it had now begun to darken, and seemed to be disappearing.*

The day before she had found herself by the Serpentine in that same fixed position, her hands at chest height as if still on the ships rail. Alma was again whining anxiously, pulling on the lead. A flock of geese had glided across the water toward some early Japanese tourists and were squawking at the feeding gulls. Her heart fluttered inside her chest, those homunculi with pickaxes drumming in staccato rhythm. The wound was growing, bleeding, raw. She felt surrounded by the smell of disturbed water and debris, the same as in the cacophony of Hong Kong harbour. She was being torn in two on this ordinary dull grey December Sunday morning, with the hum of London traffic just beginning.

Saxon could not move. She sat, the Hong Kong events like a hideous dream closing in on her when she had tried to distance herself. What had she done? And why?

It was unbearable. She could not speak of the unspeakable.

The green room waited for her, its green chair welcoming her body in recognition. Dr Max became Dr Max again, impassive and serious, solid in his green corduroys, the image of the slender man in the crumpled cotton suit, gone. He was looking at her intently, noticing the energy around her and wondering what she had brought with her. For a few seconds his mind's eye had glimpsed the red and gold of the Chinese junk and his inner ear was split by the sharp, shrill cacophony of China's tonal sound.

"Why do you watch me?" she says hotly.

"I am wondering what you have brought with you. It feels as if you are very full today."

She glowers. How could he know? She didn't want any psychic stuff.

Somewhere within the hammering chest was the feeling of an animal's tail thumping and she is taken back to the way Alma uses her strong tail when something needs her attention. She braces herself to speak the unspeakable as she presumes she must.

Her mouth opens with intention to speak but the words will not form themselves around what she had experienced the day before. Yesterday she had been on the edge of panic, imbedded in those images and body feelings with no space for thought. Now with another person ready to listen and sitting right in front of her there is a glass partition that separates her personal horror from its sharing. Whatever words she might speak are silent and hollow and the memory is fast becoming insubstantial, slipping through her like a ghost. It was easy to imagine that the nightmare belonged to someone else and that the pickaxe people inside her chest were signs of chronic indigestion.

So, in this green room, and with Dr Max ready to receive, she cannot speak of what she has started remembering.

Max had returned from his usual Suffolk weekend still tired, unrefreshed by his beach walks, unable to find peace of mind or a point of stillness despite his increase of meditation practice. Emily had withdrawn into her own thoughts and into frenzied lace making. As he heard the click of the bobbins and from his peripheral vision saw those slender white fingers dextrously weaving the threads back and forth across the blue box, his inertia solidified. He was becoming more detached about her. He did not know what to do.

He can feel the activity in Saxon's energy and knows that something is moving toward the surface of her recognition, but she is not speaking of it. He senses that her hostility to his noticing and his gentle questioning would be counterproductive. He tries making a link with the last session and says: "The last time you were here, you left saying what queer things you remember here."

Saxon, ready to fight him again, is taken off guard. Had she? Or had he made it up, to trick her?

"I don't want to remember anything," she says firmly. Max notices her hand pushing away something like a small animal beside her. Her body mask wraps itself around Hong Kong and closes it off and the glass partition intensifies.

"What are the queer things you remember here?"

Then unexpectedly she says, "I know that there's a

distance between me and other people."

Max looks interested.

"There's glass."

"Yes," he says simply, "it does feel like that, between you and me, right now."

She breathes in deeply, having no idea where she is going with all of this: "You try to invite me in and I don't know how to do it."

"Yes," Max smiles. "It does feel that way."

They sit with this understanding together. So, he does not judge her or think her odd. that she has this glass. And he seems in no hurry to smash it. Saxon wonders what might happen next. At least Hong Kong horror is off the agenda for now.

"Don't know what good knowing about it will do me!"

"Actually, it's really insightful you have noticed." He is trying to decide how to make the steps with her.

"So, we have the understanding that there's a part of you that recognises invitations to move closer, and a part of you that feels unable to respond. This might be because of fear of closeness, or what happens if feelings are involved. There is also the part of you that has been able to notice each of the two parts, and the habit of distancing."

She wants to say, "I'm not stupid you know," something her mother used to say over and over to her clever father. But she thinks it petulant and actually, as a good scientist she is interested. She likes the jigsaw piece approach. But her sarcasm is not far away.

"You mean that I am composed of parts like a clock?"

"It's one way of understanding the whole —"

She interrupts him: "Oh God, not multiple personality crap!"

Max says firmly through his exhaustion and recognising the rise of his anger, "No, not multiple personality crap."

He continues, breathing in to and softening his own irritation: "Let's look at it scientifically, seriously. Part of you defends yourself from other people and the glass is an image of that defence; but part of you senses not everyone has this glass; and part of you sees both these ways of being."

She felt chastened by his clarity.

Looking down at her hands, she says: "There was this family who brought me flowers and chocolates following their father's successful operation. They were so, so ... warm toward me – what some of my psych colleagues would call "emotionally available". She pauses and Max notes her reference to having 'psych' colleagues. "I felt like someone from another planet. They had made me into a sort of hero, but someone untouchable." She is thinking as she goes along. "They were not afraid to show me their feelings and open to me, not afraid of looking ..." she wanted to say 'stupid'. She pauses again, clearly reflecting in a way he had not seen her do before. Relief that she might be able to use her insight stirs in him.

"It was more than admiration. I get lots of that. As a family, together, they were so ... accepting, so warm and kind. It was something genuine. They really loved each other I suppose." Her voice was starting to choke, and her hand was on her chest.

Max feels he must hold this thread that is being offered as gently but firmly as possible.

"So that quality, of love, is something you recognise, and it moves you – you have the words for it and you can also feel the body response. So actually, you also are connecting with it. If you weren't you wouldn't feel it."

"Not sure I want to feel it ..."

Max ignores her protest. "Can you just follow that connection to feeling now, perhaps starting with how it feels under your right hand and feel free to allow whatever wants to arise, as we sit here together?"

She is having a different experience in her chest. The hammering of the pickaxe people is receding, and there is a growing feeling of something softening and opening. She thinks, "Oh well, party games" and leans back in the chair, her hand still on her chest, as instructed.

Her ears tickle. The softening inside her chest increases and there is the sense of a small terrier not unlike Alma waiting nearby, alert. Then there is the faint sound of a Spanish lullaby as if it were emerging from a faraway mist. And also, from the mist the image of a pair of deep brown eyes. The sound and the brown eyes hold her in a new space, whilst the choking sensation in her throat continues.

She starts humming, something about Spain. Max leans quite close to her in order to hear.

"Spain," he repeats softly to help her stay with whatever association or memory is arising. He imagines that this is something from her early life and could be connected to the experience of feeling love. "What is it about Spain?"

She does not open her eyes but answers automatically, so well trained at reportage, but remains deep in a memory from her past. "It's where we lived when I was a child. I can hear the songs, the music ... I feel a bit ... small."

Max hears curiosity in her voice. Her own curiosity to her inner processes would have its own authority and control. Maybe in time this would be strong enough to challenge the glass. He sees her as small and curious rather than small and afraid and defensive. He invites her to continue.

"Perhaps we can be curious together, about those sounds and the connection with the time in Spain, just follow what you are noticing and see what happens".

*Spain, and Begonia. Begonia singing, always, and dancing. The sound of her sweet voice, and the swish of her skirts; Begonia, always full of petticoat and laughter. The glint of the gold earring, and the red of the flower behind the ear and the rich red skirt. Begonia smelling of garlic and Naja. Begonia's deep black eyes, pools with love in them. The life, the fun, the ecstasy! Begonia who showed her how to click her heels in the way of the flamenco. The click, click.*

*Begonia, courted by Gabriel in his tightest trousers, in the style of Spanish matadors. With Begonia and Gabriel, sharing their love with her, in walks in the pine forests, those whispered secrets, the play, the joy. The... was it love?*

So much movement in her chest. Dancing, playful, softening.

Her rational sardonic mind rises at one point to witness the play with memory. "If I were not in a shrink's office, I would think I was having some sort of event," she thinks. But she is intrigued by the reality of the body experience. The iron tightness softening into a light and expansive feeling. And to remember Begonia, her Spanish nanny, of whom she had not thought for years. And Spain itself, that country of grace and magic, and Andalucia, Lorca country, full of passion and ... something else, darker, violent ...

*The house in Spain. Dark wood and large cold floors, white walls. She was too small to open the large carved doors. Being loved. Yes, she was loved, then.*

*Something darker.*

*The special dance shoes Begonia had bought with her own money at the market in Rhonda. Saxon, Saskia then, learning to dance, to click, to tap, then twirl.*

*And then one day she could not find her shoes. Mother had burned them, said she was not to take herself 'down to that level'.*

*Darker still. Begonia turning the black and amber beads she kept in the deep pit of her pocket, crossing herself, covering her head in black lace.*

*Noises in the night. Shouting. Going out along the corridor. Mother fallen against the dark doorway. Father coming to block her view and turning her into her room firmly. His strong aftershave, clean smelling compared to Mother. The glint of the handmade silk suit, trouser creases, even in the middle of the night.*

*What is the matter with Mother?*

*Father's large hands reassuring her, gently turning her and leading her back into her room, tucking her up in bed, his cufflinks glinting, silver hearts, the wind blowing a curtain aside to reveal the light of the moon.*

She opens her eyes. Max is sitting with her, alert.

"Just now you looked as if something was opening, a part of you that wanted to speak. And now it looks as if—"

She interrupts him, blazing. "Why do you interrupt me. Who do you think you are!"

"It's just one of her turns, nothing to worry your pretty little head about."

She would lie waiting for the curtain to part again and for the moon to shine in on her, visit her with its magic. Begonia had told her that magic happened in moonlight.

*Begonia muttering and crossing herself. Tossing the black hair.*

The green room feels intense, waiting for the memory to be revealed in the present moment.

Max keeps his patience. "Let me know what is happening when you are ready."

She moves in the chair and settles her hands on her lap. Her breathing is steady and coming from the bottom of her lungs.

"I was remembering Begonia, my Spanish nanny. I think she loved me." No sign of the previous flash of anger. Her blue eyes are filled with wonder and also with sadness. The energy of the room is beginning to gather around her like a company of kind hands.

Then suddenly it is cut off.

"My poor mother," she says suddenly.

More images. Unpleasant.

*Mother's long thin legs hanging over the edge of the bed looking lifeless, the pale skin, the reddish freckles, the pink edged toenails, the fingers round the cut crystal glass. The stomach starting to become bloated early, after childbirth and then with the effects of alcohol. Not the graceful slender mother with dancing freckles on her pale skin and the swing of red hair when she had danced and skipped, who had once made Saxon laugh and skip, the mother with whom Saxon had once been able to be a child. That mother had gone after her brother Tom had been born.*

Saxon longed for a cigarette. Out loud she said: "Begonia said it was a curse. It was a curse because of mother's behaviour. She started crossing herself and muttering, she kept taking me to church to convince herself that I would be free of whatever were the evil spirits she felt had created Tom's death."

"Tom?"

"My mother had a son who was born prematurely and died."

Max is watching her hands twist tightly, over each other, over and over.

Saxon closes her eyes again.

*The sour breath smell, the unsteady walk, the high-pitched snigger; the bottles, fits, the grim face of her father, the hushing up, the sudden moods, the unpredictability.*

"What's happening with your hands?"

She is wringing them together as if they had suddenly become sticky.

She looks down. The hands stop moving immediately. "I didn't realise I was doing that. It's Begonia – she does that."

Max notes the present tense.

"If you were to just concentrate on your hands, what does the movement feel like now?"

Saxon watches her hands in fascination, but looking, not feeling into.

She interprets. "As if I'm trying to get something off that won't come off?"

She grimaces and is quick to associate.

"Lady Macbeth... wrong way round..."

Then she looked serious as if something was trying to form itself in her mind.

And Max was thinking too, the reference to Macbeth was not empty. Her child's hurt and rage toward the experience of rejection and neglect was mixed up with her mother's inadequacies and hidden for fear of losing what little she has of her. It may well have had – still have - a murderous take on it. Her hands might be expressing the stain of guilt induced by such rage. Worse might be the burden of guilt if she had magically taken the blame for her brother's death, which often happened if children were not told of all the circumstances. It seemed as if she had unconsciously chosen to identify more with the clever admired father than the depressed and needy mother which would explain her arrogance and her fury toward anything vulnerable or fragile, such as tender feelings or a newborn child.

But Max judges it too early to introduce these complex understandings. He is beginning to understand her more clearly, that her need for tight control in everything is a learned way of protecting herself from the mess of feelings such as guilt, and rage, and to being vulnerable to loss and fear, to emptiness itself. The glass was her protection against feeling but also her prison.

"What is your earliest memory of your mother?"

Images were coming more fully now. Images she had not thought about for forty years.

"The earliest..."

*In the pale green room, a flash of red hair.*

She looks at Max and smiles a rare smile. "I've just got a picture of my mother smiling. Her red hair all brushed and falling down her back. I used to play with her hair. I loved it."

"That sounds like a good memory."

"She used to sing to me and read stories with funny accents. There is this one picture of her still around. Laughing. She's so young and light-hearted."

This memory is relished between them. Then she says, wistfully: "I was Saskia then." She looks at Max and there is something tentative in her look. She is gathering information from long ago.

"My mother was studying Rembrandt when she met my father, in Holland. They were evidently very much in love then. She vowed that if she ever had a daughter, she would be called Saskia, the name of Rembrandt's wife."

Max listens deeply, knowing that he is being told much more than the shift of a name.

"Romantic I suppose. But that didn't last long."

"How long were you Saskia, with the happy, playful mother around?"

"I don't know." She spoke quickly, Max's door has become blue.

*Who was doing this, changing the colours of the room?*

*The chauffeur, the gold rope around his blue hat, bringing me home from nursery. If the blue door was shut, she was sleeping it off. Relief. I would play by myself or with Begonia. If it were ajar, she would be waiting for me and she'd call me in. She'd be in her underwear with a dressing gown over.*

Saxon pauses from her memory, biting her lip, and whispers inside herself like a small child so that Max cannot hear.

*"Something very wrong happened between Mother and me, something bad which meant Mother couldn't live properly like other mothers. She said I had drained her strength by being born; she had nothing left when it was Tom's turn. He was born without any juice, so he could not live. She said I was greedy.*

*After Tom she did not want to dance any more or hug me like a mother, like she used to. And because she'd had all the stuffing taken out of her she was always hungry and thirsty which is why she needed the bottles all the time."*

Saxon speaks: "What I can remember is that in the mornings she would be behind the blue door, and it would be shut, nursing a hangover I expect. Breakfast was a silent formal affair with me and my father and the maid serving us. I always spilt something."

Max felt sad. "And how did that affect you do you think?"

"I learned not to bother her." Her voice has gone very flat. "And I became my father's stalwart little Anglo-Saxon."

Max is listening.

"That's what my father started to call me after I was hit by the boom on a sailing boat. I didn't cry. That holiday was meant to mend us as a family. He was proud of me, said I was his good little strong Anglo-Saxon. That's when I became Saxon."

Max nodded slowly. After her brother had died, her playful feelingful childhood had ended abruptly. She believed that it was all somehow her fault, and that, to make up for this, she had to become a little grown-up who made no emotional or other demands, taking on adult responsibilities way before her time. As her academic and intellectual skills grew, so did the glass which protected her vulnerable childlike self but held her prisoner at the same time. The everyday flesh and blood of ordinary relaxed response, the right to ordinary emotional need, to give and take, which might assist intimacy, was shut out. Anything that could be messy or 'bad' had to be kept out. In Hong Kong, maybe the reality of holding the newborn son in her arms, right next to her heart, had shattered the glass, and flooded her with unbearable feeling. She would have had no way of relating these feelings to herself, either the hidden rage at the infant brother for dying and taking the loving mother with him or the grief at her own lost innocent childhood.

There was not much time left of the session. Max knew that there were many more images and memories.

"Do you think it was during that time that the glass first appeared, as a sort of protection against what felt really painful?"

The pale blue eyes focus on him. She held her scorn at the word 'painful'. "Possibly."

"What about now?" asks Max.

"Now?"

"Do you still feel as if you have to cope on your own behind the glass?"

"I've never known anything else." She is thoughtful. "Perhaps it's not as positive as you wish to make it. Perhaps I built the glass after Tom so I could never suck anyone dry again."

Max is startled by her use of words for she has not mentioned what she feared as a child, that she was responsible for her brother's death. Only the green room and the Guardians have heard those whispers. He wants the flow of her connections to continue as long as possible although he knows he cannot go over the session time. And he wants her to connect with what was positive in her relationships, both with others and with herself.

"Is there anyone with whom the glass doesn't happen?"

She smiles. "Alma," she says easily, and proudly.

"Alma?"

"My dog. My little terrier." She laughs, an easy laugh after all the tension and pain. "You're surprised!"

Max says, "Yes, I guess I am. I did not imagine that you might have a dog."

"She's a white short-haired terrier. My companion. Not too cuddly but warm. Intelligent eyes." Then she adds, "I share her with Lewis."

Max waits. He is aware of her discomfort.

Her voice drops. "We have known each other for a number of years. We live at each end of the park and we meet in the park when we take Alma out."

Max listens.

"I suppose you think that this is odd."

Max waits whilst their eyes met.

"That I have a man friend, but we don't live together." She pauses. "We did try it. But it didn't work."

"I'm sorry," says Max, and means it.

Their time is nearly up.

"It was me," she says suddenly. "He is a good kind man. He did everything he could. I just couldn't do it, the intimacy thing."

They sit together in a companionable silence, sharing the sadness, the clear despair of her world.

"Does he call you Saskia?"

She breathes out heavily. "Sometimes yes, he does. And," she remembers, "so does Daniel."

"Would you like to be Saskia here, and for me to call you Saskia?"

Saxon feels her heart begin to race. "I... I... don't know."

"Think about it. Experiment with it and see how it feels. For now, can you see the pattern we are getting closer to? That you have divided your inner world into two extremes? It's as if you have to be either in perfect control or you fear a terrible mess. Perfect control seems to involve strict discipline at all cost, no intimacy or feeling and getting things exactly right. The mess seems to involve anything fragile, unknown, small or vulnerable, which is despised. The glass separates the two. The illusion of the glass is that it keeps mess at bay, but another way of looking at it is that is keeps you in prison. It's as if nothing is allowed to touch you or you it because of the fear of the consequences of mess, or disaster. But now an event has occurred that challenges these two extreme absolutes. Perhaps inviting you to find a third position, one that is not so polarised."

She listens to him in silence.

"I am feeling that it is going to be important for you to find a way of being that values your own feeling, which is quite different from your mother's, or your father's. You are not like your mother, nor your father. You are yourself. Unique. And from what you have told me all your feeling, compassion and softness is saved for your patients, not yourself. Is that correct?"

She looks down.

"Perhaps it's time for you to find some care and compassion for yourself."

Then, as she is leaving, she puts her hand on the green brocade curtain and turns to face him saying: "Guilt's pretty messy don't you think? Do you suppose that this baby boy going into the water is connected to my brother's death all those years ago?"

Max feels cornered, with no time to answer fully. Before he could speak, she continues, opening the door with her strong doctor's hand: "Shrinks usually think that everything is to do with guilt, don't they. So I suppose I feel guilty about my little brother and for my mother's ruined life for which I could never make amends no matter how clever I tried to be. But why I should try to throw…" she stops abruptly. It was the closest she had got to speaking of Hong Kong and using the active word "to throw" …

They are both standing on the threshold of the green room and the words hang between them.

Max realises that she is going to have to leave on this note.

"You have just said some really important things right at the end of our time together," he starts.

"I know," she says quickly. "I need to get out of here, now."

"We will come back to this next time," says Max firmly.

\* \* \* \*

Max returns into the pale green room relishing its silence and its energy. He thinks about Saskia and the burden of intolerable unconscious guilt possibly triggered by holding the new baby. She had not been shown how to care for her own responses and feelings, she can only judge, loathe and dismiss. He remembers that Rembrandt was the first painter to paint light in darkness. He feels a stir of hope. But also, Emily's words, "She will take you away from me."

\* \* \* \*

As Saxon walked back to her car she remembered the four miserable months with Lewis and the terrible sense of failure. Not being able to sleep for fear of his watching her. Her fear of his dirty laundry even though he was immaculate and used to looking after himself as a long-term bachelor.

She had gone off sex. She had stopped talking to him.

She paused by the door of her car and a new thought lodged itself straight into her chest like an poisoned arrow: Maybe it really was true that she had drained her mother of life and that in any closeness she could only turn everything and everyone bad.

She unlocked her car and sat on the leather seat clutching her keys. She was either behind glass or poison. Her mother, Lewis, and before him ... Kim. And, yes, there was indeed one more thing she had killed off.

Kim Reynolds. She hadn't thought of Kim Reynolds for years. His dark body hair, his sensuality. He too smelled of Naja. He too seemed like Gabriel. He never saw the glass and got through before she could make sure she created it. He was a real hope for her in her barren late twenties—

She would not go there.

She remained sitting, very still, her keys cutting into her hand.

The list of her attempted killings was growing. The most recent, lest she forget, indeed as if she could forget, the child in Hong Kong. So maybe it was true, she was a killer to new life. A murderer.

She saw the next person arrive in a red BMW and park unevenly. A petite woman in a red suit with a lot of black hair got out and walked toward Max's rooms. For a moment Saxon imagined that it was Begonia, looking for her, far from Spain and Andalucia, waiting to sing her a Lorca song. Had she too come to haunt her, here in South London?

Pull yourself together, Saskia, she thought, be Saxon. She watched the woman ring the doorbell and saw Max hold the door open, so that the woman in red might be swallowed up by the green room.

She was just another patient and Saxon was just another patient, someone to be deciphered, diagnosed, discussed in supervision. To Max she was only a means through which he did his job.

The chemistry, Sax, it matters, Daniel had said. Did it? Did it matter? It was true the man needed to be clever, and he was in a way, or Saxon would have left ages ago. But there was no chemistry between them. What had he said? "Yes, I can feel it here between you and me." Meaning the glass. He could feel it. Well, where was the use in that? Perfect control or perfect mess. Yes, that was true, she could see that, but that was her choice. A third, middle position sounded vague.

\* \* \* \*

Max felt as if his life energy was being drained from him by a mysterious force, as if some plug within his being was being pulled ruthlessly out, without thought for what would drain away. For the first time he wondered whether he was fit to work, to listen properly, to be thorough, to offer people the service they were paying for. He shook himself. Could he use this new powerless feeling creatively, as he would be inviting Saxon Pierce to do? Could he uncover and work with his own fragility and vulnerability alongside being there for others. He thought of one of his Buddhist teachers who spoke of "shaky tenderness" being the living water within all humans, which linked them in their humanity, without the distortion of the habitual mask.

Could he be fragile and still ask the questions and give the answers needed?

As he opened the door for Vera, he noticed his fear that he would have no strength for her, and her disorganised, dishevelled look brought Margaret right into his room.

"Christmas is going to be awful," she began.

Max is startled. Had they had half-term yet? Had he missed something? Had Vera already seen her sons? Did they know? He felt confused and as if he had missed the last two months, that his listening had been empty.

"I imagine it will be a very hard time for you."

"My mother's found out now and she's furious. Phoning me all hours, blaming me, ranting and raving. Says she's going to go right into Alistair's office and demand he return to his wife and family ..." Vera looks terrified. Then she says, her basic common sense emerging: "Except she doesn't know where he is."

Vera has not seen her mother since a rather dismal Easter weekend they had all had in a hotel in the Lake District year. Alistair had been brooding and snappy, complaining about the hotel service and its cost. Leo was worrying about his 'A' levels and had taken to biting his nails. Luke had become clingy toward his mother which increased Alistair's petulant aggression. Dominic hadn't come, preferring to spend the weekend with his new girlfriend's family. Vera had worked hard to try to make the weekend a success, planning good walks, but it rained most of the time, her mother got wet, muddy and constipated and Alistair kept disappearing to answer his mobile. Vera's sick stomach told her there was someone else on the scene. She prayed that it would not last long and that her mother would never know. She dreaded her mother's crowing criticism.

Tears run down Vera's cheek, mascara with them. She has lost her initial formal way of speaking. She is no longer trying to keep up appearances. She gets up out of the chair and walks around. Max feels alarmed, wondering what she might do next.

"All because I forgot her damn birthday – her *damn* birthday. Scorpio – we've gone into Scorpio … don't expect you have anything to do with the stars, do you? But for the first time in my life I've got something else to think about other than my mother's fucking birthday …"

Her face is wet with tears, and she does nothing to tidy up the mask of makeup she always wore. Max watches this life in her, fascinated. Something real was happening as she prowled around like the lioness of the zoo. He starts to feel more in charge of himself.

"Funny isn't it," she says suddenly, "all these weeks with Alistair gone… me coming here trying to get to grips… trying to change myself so I would get him back – wanting you to change me." This is new to Max. He has to work hard to keep up. "My obsession all haywire, cutting and scratching, not eating, letting myself go to the dogs … all this. Then him visiting me and us getting nowhere, only making things worse, the solicitors… Then just now I find that Luke... he knows, he knows before I could tell him face to face… Dominic and Leo… they know too. Bloody email. So quick. They've all got it. I'm not that good at it yet, takes me ages, silly me, I resisted it. Now it's all endless emails, smart letters and presents… all this and in all these hideous months, September, October and now we're in Scorpio time… all this, I haven't cried properly. My face has gone wet like that last time here and the walk in the night to the zoo. Tears have come I suppose. But I haven't had a proper cry."

She sits down and howls, pulling out tissues and mopping her whole face like a man. Max finds himself thrilled at the emergence of this energy, fresh and uncontrolled, something robust and appropriate and not restricted by the artificial over-refined self.

They sit quietly for a while as her sobbing slows to a whimper and quiet hiccup at the back of the throat.

"All these books you've got," she says quietly, looking around. Max smiles. "I've been trying to read things. I've got all these books on self-help. I've actually had them for a while and had a go at one or two ... Never thought I would need such things..." she trails off, then brightens herself, the quiet sobs still breaking through from time to time.

"Actually, when I can concentrate, some of them are quite good. The stuff about the rhythms of life and it always changing, and that change can be opportunity, crisis can be too. I can see that there is a way you can help yourself make the best of yourself – not through looks and things like that, or sex," she looks at him warily and he tenses slightly, "but behaviour patterns and all that, learning what you've got used to as a way of being."

Max is surprised.

"It's quite interesting. But it's doing the job you do I suppose."

"What have you found out so far?"

"Well, I have got my champion, haven't I? The lioness. I've been to see her a few times." Vera sniffs. Max was not sure yet how to work with this. "From the books – oh yes, that there's something we all are born with that is always OK. I really like that idea. One book called it the healthy self and that we can have a healthy island, whatever's happened to us. I think that's probably what you were suggesting in a way when you helped me find the stone circle. But our proper self, or whatever its called, it's just that it's how we distort it that gets us into trouble," she pauses "and we distort ourselves because we have no choice... it's a way of surviving. Like me with no dad. I sort of, had to make him up but that meant I got a bit fanciful. I allowed Alistair to sort of rescue me like you might want a dad to when you're a little girl. But I ended up in a prison."

Max is impressed, and amazed.

They sit together in companionable silence.

"Getting cross with your mother has done you good," says Max.

She laughs. "Yes, talk about getting the juices running."

Then her wailing begins again, suddenly, and forcefully. Through the keening she said, "I couldn't get cross with Alistair, could I? I want, I want, him back…" Her voice trails off and she begins wailing again.

Max sits, thoughtful. "I guess that your feelings will swing from one extreme to another for a while. Just now there was the recognition that feeling appropriately cross with your mother gave you a sort of freedom. But then you recognised that you could not feel that way with Alistair and this perhaps made you feel helpless again. Victim to his power – rescuer, or bully even." He wondered if he might have said too much. But much needs to be said to help Vera get hold of her own strengths.

She is clutching her sides with her thin arms. "I've got to try to say it haven't I? Or I stay in fantasy land." She paused, took a deep breath and said loudly, "He's not coming back. It's done and dusted." The wailing began again in earnest.

*They're dead, Maxie, dead, dead, dead … they are never coming back… do you see it, do you? Never, never, never, and I can't stand it Maxie, I can't stand it… I can't live without them…"*

Max steadies his breathing. Vera and Margaret were merging on his sofa. He has to take charge. He has to be in the present moment.

He concentrates on the person before him being Vera. Vera with the three sons, abandoned by Alistair. The Guardians get in close, and he feels the strength of their presence. He relaxes and he and Vera sit with the painful truth of Alistair's going.

Vera settles then and leans back onto the back of the sofa. "I don't mind being here anymore," she flashes a smile at him.

"How are your nights?"

She shrugs.

Is she still wandering about the streets asks Max to himself. And the self-harm?

"I don't sleep much, and I still sleep on the sofa. No point going up to the bed." There is a pause. "I've seen my champion again." Max is mystified.

"You know the lioness, at the zoo. I went again and stood and watched her. All these kids around and me with none. I wanted to tell someone. Look at me, I've got three sons and they're all away." Her voice begins to rise. "I wanted my Luke to be there, to look at the lioness with him. I wanted to say to those mothers 'Don't let them take your sons away'."

Max can see that her mood is unstable, and that hysteria could escalate. He wants to keep her with the positive energy of the lioness and ground it in her experience.

"What do you feel when you see your champion, the lioness?"

Vera smiles, and there is a slight glow in her eyes. "Better, as if she could help me find my spirit again."

"You do have good spirits. And from what you said earlier you've also found your healthy island. Are these feelings similar?"

"I hadn't thought of that. You mean what I feel when I see the lioness links in with my healthy self and island?"

"Something like that."

"Funny I've got a healthy island at all!" She pauses. "I suppose you have to have something to make it through a really tough background, don't you?"

"That's really positive thinking."

"Thanks. Something anyway. But I have to keep it up. When I'm not in here," she looks around the green room. "It's much harder when you're on your own with all your old habits ready to grab you." Tears emerge again.

She looks up. "Alistair and her. That bitch with the posh name. They went to the school." She has forgotten that she has spoken of this before. "They told Luke. They did it without me. I had him on the phone crying, asking me if it was true. I saw him the week before of course, for his first exeat, but I couldn't tell him. I told him his dad was away. So now he knows I've lied to him. He won't know who he can trust anymore."

"I am so sorry," says Max for the second time that morning. "But I also remember you saying that you thought Luke would realise you had been trying to protect him."

"Yes. Oh yes," she says thoughtfully. "I did say that. Well thank God you remember what I say!" She breathes out a big sigh. Then she is tearful again.

"He's going to win, isn't he? He's got it all sorted, what to say, what to give them, what to do, even got the masters on his side because of course he's an old boy and I just don't know my way around that system do I. Public bloody school."

Max feels encouraged by the fight in her voice, even though for now it is in protest against? He hopes she will use it for herself.

He forces himself to ask about her self-harm.

A sly look he had not seen on her face before reminded him of that same look on another's, on Margaret's face when she started evading his questions about what she was doing when she skipped school.

*"It's nothing, Maxie, nothing to worry about... I just go off to play by myself...."*

"I know it's bad but sometimes there is nothing else for it."

"Will you let me see your arms."

"No," she says. "They're bad, but I put cream on them."

"And when you do the yoga stretches, what then, how do they feel?"

Vera slumps in the chair feeling found out. He was supposed to be helping her, so she supposed he had to probe. But how could he understand?

She sighs. "Yes, they hurt. But that reminds me, helps me to actually feel something. I'm so numb most of the time, so dead, so not there. The blood flowing, the pain, it brings me to. I make tea then and I've even called my friend Coral."

"Would you be open to experiment with something else to take the place of the cutting?"

So, he wasn't going to disapprove, to read her the riot act.

"OK then."

Max teaches her how to concentrate her mind on the in-breath and out-breath. He teaches her to focus on the actual physical location of the emotional pain inside and to put her hand there. Under the hand her mind could direct the breath in a calming or soothing way.

"What if its everywhere?" she asks.

"Then it's even more important to find the lioness energy again. To picture her, as you remember her at the zoo. To notice what you feel and where, when this energy arises. You can also hold the stone you found last time. Hold the stone as a representation of all that is strong inside you and outside you just waiting to help you. Direct your attention to the stone or to the image of the lioness as a source of strength."

"Yes, I can do that," she says.

"Then sometimes you can use an image. Do you have an image for the pain you are carrying?"

"Like being hit by a truck."

"And the pain of being hit. Where do you feel it?"

She touches the left side of her chest, near the heart.

She looks sad and tears roll down the now red and swollen cheeks. There is real feeling in her voice: "It is so sore here. And there's a crushed feeling, as if it's been crushed by a truck load of stones and some of them have got inside."

Max smiles gently. How he knows those inside stones!

*"Too much pain, Maxie. It's too awful, I can't bear it, I can't do it anymore, I don't want to..."*

"So, stones are inside and outside. OK, so you stay with feeling of being crushed and the stones inside and just keep on noticing it. Find out as much as possible about it, all the words you can to describe it."

They sit together, each breathing in and breathing out of the sore heart.

"I was wondering," says Max "whether you could now bring in your connection with the healthy island."

Vera gasps. "Oh, it's here" she said. "I can see it."

"What's it like?"

She smiles and describes the space.

"Would it be possible to bring some of the pain in your heart into the healthy island to take care of it?"

She smiles and sits in silence for a while.

When she opens her eyes the session time is almost up. Max says there is another bit of 'self-help' you might like to try in between sessions.

He told her how to breathe in to the painful feeling then to breathe out tension and pain out into the earth.

"The earth can take it," he says.

"Thank you," says Vera. "I like this, I remember the first time you told me that. The earth's always there isn't it. It's a practical approach, that you can work with your body to get a sort of mastery."

As she is leaving, she says, "Thank you for today. I feel as if you've given me a lot to practise and think about. I just hope I can do it in between coming here." She looks wistful. "I want to get stronger, don't I?"

The Guardians stand right beside them, and Max closes the door feeling for the first time in a while that he is able to settle his thoughts and his feeling.

## 10

VERA had avoided thinking about Christmas until Luke had asked her what sort of tree they would be getting. "Dillon's getting lights like candles on his tree." His voice on the phone was strained and high. He had started stuttering again. The end of term was in just a week and she knew that he was miserable and worried about her and that Christmas was something he looked forward to. She wanted to make it good for him. She had spoken to Dom, who was to return soon from his first term at Bristol. He sounded awkward, and avoided the subject he dubbed 'parent probs' to his friends. He said, "Don't worry, Mum. Luke'll get over it all. Everything's *all right*."

She knew that Dom had already been taken to Alistair's new home with Francesca, but he did not speak of it and Vera was glad. Leo was in Africa, so just the two boys would be with her and her mother for Christmas itself and then Alistair and Arabella were taking them skiing. Skiing of all things, thought Vera in exasperation. Alistair had never ever wanted to go skiing. He hated the idea of learning something new and of getting cold. She wondered how he would cope, whether Francesca knew he had never been skiing. Unless that also was something he had kept secret. That as well as having a mistress he had learned to ski.

She finds herself saying to Max at their penultimate session before the Christmas break: "God I hope he breaks both legs!" before checking herself.

"Go on," encourages Max.

"I have these images of Arabella, pale, fragile, immaculate and elegant, holding a pee bottle and having to empty it! That'd sort her out!" Vera smiles for an instant.

In previous years she had planned the decoration and cooking for Christmas all year round, buying from mail order catalogues and markets, and her favourite stores. But this year she had not felt in any way anticipatory about the festivities, as if some premonition indicated that this Christmas would be the one from Hell.

Today she feels as if she could come apart, her stamina is gone, her fight subdued. She says dully, "I dragged myself off to Harrods. I thought I had better get something organised for when the boys get home," she sighs heavily. "It was really awful. Not at all like it used to be. I used to love going there, being Mrs Alistair Dodds with my own card, you know." She looks at Max wondering if he ever went to Harrods.

*In the carved and gold-embossed lift she had been pressed behind two confident young women dressed in expensive beige and smelling of Joy. On the fourth floor, Christmas shopping was in full swing. Each of the designer Christmas trees had a 'theme': tartan bows and red hearts; pink angels and glittering white moons; blue dinosaurs and turquoise trolls. Most were made in China and cost over £5.*

"I looked at all the stuff there and it, sort of made me feel sick." She had wondered if these goods would please her young son more than the hand-made objects she had collected since her own childhood, around which she wove stories that had once thrilled them all. *Her grandmother's knitted angel doll in scraps of muslin with thin paper wings and pipe cleaner halo, most of the old glitter rubbed off, much of the needlework faded and worn. Vera had watched her being created before hanging her at the top of their artificial tree. Then there were paper lanterns with cut out fringes; papier mâché balls painted in red and green poster paint; an old wooden rocking horse made in Poland.* In the past the boys had pulled them out, wanting to hear again their history in their mother's life. But perhaps even Luke would now find them 'naff', not in keeping with what would be found in the homes of other boys.

"I spent £165 on Christmas decorations, new lights, crackers, chocolate santas and foil wrapping paper covered in green Christmas trees. Then I went to the food hall and ordered turkey, smoked salmon, quail eggs, breads of different kinds, stilton and cream cheese." She reels off her list of goods, wondering if these details might be boring for Max, but she has become used now to sitting in the patient's chair, she feels no pressure to be social, to ask Max what he might be doing at Christmas.

"You see it used to be my favourite store and I thought it would make me feel better. But I was wrong."

*The energy of the lioness had seemed far away in that*

hot, cluttered store, and unavailable to her. She had felt choked by the rush and intensity of breathy bodies. Every pillar had had a plastic tree strapped onto its ribbed column and the pink eyes of pink-haloed glitter pigs blinked and flashed.

"What I want to tell you was that I had this queer thing happen. I started to feel faint, and you can't really faint in Harrods, can you?"

He wonders whether she had ever read *The Pumpkin Eater.*

"I took the Egyptian escalator," she looks at Max to see if he knows what she is talking about. "You know, it's the one decorated with Pharaohs and stained glass." It sounds grotesque to Max, but he senses the slight awe in her voice and wonders where she is going with this. "Well, I remembered the memorial to Princess Diana and Dodi Fayed. It struck me, she was a woman who had married above herself and then was betrayed by a man who never realised that she really loved him."

She had, like millions of others who had mourned Diana's death, had left flowers outside Kensington Palace. "She was cast out.. It was all so public. Where could she go to?"

"Do you think of yourself as being like Diana?"

Vera is quiet. "Not as beautiful or well-connected of course. But I suppose she trusted didn't she, she was naive and yes that's what I think I am – naive." They are quiet together. "How do you get over that without being cynical and shut down. Or dead in a tunnel in France?"

"It was a dramatic and shocking end wasn't it?" Max is interested in Vera's choice of words. "But to return to your main point. It's a really good question, how do we not become cynical or bitter when our ideals fail?" Vera noticed the we and thought it quaint. He couldn't be talking about himself, could he?

"I think that finding a middle ground takes some practice. And the middle ground I see as something to do with being aware and mature – which comes from knowing realistically what can happen and trusting your own assessment of other people. You seem to me to be naturally quite shrewd. Do you think that Diana became cynical?"

Vera is thoughtful. "Well, she wanted revenge didn't she! The *Panorama* interview and all that going in among land mines! Getting herself an Arab boyfriend! That must have made royalty sweat, if they do sweat."

Max warms to her. "Perhaps she had no vehicle for expressing her anger at what felt so unfair."

"Like me then. I've no vehicle, have I?"

"We've looked at this and discussed that as long as you are trying not to be appropriately angry toward Alistair, because you want him back and want to preserve your ideal of him, then your anger gets turned onto yourself. The cutting."

She looks up sharply. "Yes, yes I see."

"The fact that you are now conscious of this gives you choices. You are already monitoring the times when you turn your hand in anger against yourself and are starting to feel it inside you and attend to it directly. Then there's the writing, speaking here, using the breathing and feeling into what is under the anger, like the hurt," she is close to tears.

"Yes," she says quietly, "yes I have been trying that."

"Yes, I know. You are doing really well you know, Vera, really well."

"Thank you," she says.

"You can in time free yourself from the attachment to the Alistair who is no longer the person you married. Then you are freer to step into your own individual life."

They sit together thoughtfully.

"Do you think that she was self-destructive?"

"Diana? I don't think I can comment on her really, I didn't know her and there is only what one reads."

"Yes I know, but she did seem to court danger didn't she. She was that cross." .

"Do you feel as if you might do that, court danger?"

She draws in her breath.

"Well I did tell you at the beginning, didn't I, that I wouldn't harm myself because of my boys. And it's the same now. Only, recently, I do have queer things go on. Things I cannot account for, like finding myself at the zoo that time."

Max knows of her fragmented selves and how they hang together by threads of her common sense, by her motherhood and by uniformity and routine.

"You see, in that store, I suddenly thought I'm no better

off now than a single parent. That's what I am to become. And a divorced one at that. No better than girls I knew at school who had babies without fathers and live on welfare. I know it sounds snobby but..." She breaks off.

"Are there any role models of women who have survived their divorces and grown stronger through them, finding aspects of themselves that were hidden perhaps by the adaptation required to be married? Can you think of any?"

"Well... I suppose there's Coral, there's my neighbour Michaela, she's had three husbands and right now she's on her way to another." Vera is thinking hard. But these examples were of women who were hard-bitten, and cynical about men.

"What I wanted to tell you was that, after I felt faint, I had to find the Ladies, and well I sort of... I heard these two women talking. I thought one of them must be Arabella... and... I followed them."

*In Harrods the sick feeling and dizziness increased. She had to get out. She almost fell from behind the mass of travelling bodies and into the rug department. She used to know which exits were where, but her panic rose, she felt trapped, unable to find the way out, 'in Harrods of all places," and in life. Eventually she found the stairs and leant into the cold emptiness with some relief. She was retching inwardly, her empty stomach holding nothing to bring out. As she reached the first floor staircase, she remembered the new Ladies Powder Room that you paid for with your account card, and the pink interior with cool marble and soft lighting comforted her. She clutched the bags of things she had bought and locked herself in one of the beige cubicles. She sat on the toilet seat feeling sick and confused, feeling she could disintegrate. She was falling apart. She used to be so proud, of whom people said "you've done well for yourself, love." She who thought she had made something of her life, changed herself, gone up in the world. She thought she knew how to play to the rules and be in control.*

She tells Max, "So there I was, less than eleven days to go before Christmas with no preparation, half crazed, dishevelled and alone in a lavatory in Harrods. I thought, I'm no better, I can't cope. Coming to Dr Max for two months now, every week, sometimes twice a week, and I just can't do it, all the things I'm supposed to do to get stronger."

In that Harrods lavatory any remaining hope had been dashed. The hope that Alistair would by now have found out that he needed her in the private way she knew him. Her hope that he wouldn't really stay away for Christmas when she had always made it so perfect. But now she really did have to face that whatever she did it would make no difference to Alistair. In past time when she suspected her influence over him was waning she had been able to fix it. Being with him in whatever way he wanted. Letting him take out his rage on her so that he could be rid of it. The belts and ropes, the white silk evening scarves. Controlling the boys in the way of his image, so that, for the moment, they were the sons he imagined he wanted, the sons she had produced and made perfect for him in the way he wanted. Arranging parties where he could show off his home, his family, his success. Spoiling him as she had seen his mother spoil him.

It must be nearly a year since she had been sure of the old ways. Nearly a year since he had started coming in late smelling of another woman's perfume. Femme. Hardly a perfume for an innocent. She could smell it now, that musky, woody, heavy perfume that clung remorselessly to whatever it touched and spread itself about. Like ivy onto a tree, like this woman Arabella had clung to someone else's husband in order to claim him for herself. Poison ivy, taking over, to prise Alistair away and suck out the juices of Vera's life.

Before this Vera could come down at one, two in the morning and watch her husband standing in the kitchen drinking milk direct from the bottle and reading the still laundered Times or her Daily Mail, his crumpled shirt, probably worn by the girl in a spirit of romance after her stolen moments, reeking of Femme. She would watch him quietly for some time before he saw her, or sensed her on the stairs, like a still dark cat watching from in between the banisters. In the beginning he would look startled, awkward, guilty, and she knew then that she could fix it. Sometimes she would go down to him, her pink silk dressing gown over her naked body coming undone as she walked, and she would just take him in the state he was in. Sometimes she would remain on the stairs holding her breasts in the thin silk, *stroking herself with her slender fingers, opening her legs and fingering there in between as he watched her. Until he was unable to contain himself and would stand at the foot of the stairs in silence watching her masturbate, drinking his milk, his erection rising; or he would join her and take her there on the stairs, or from behind as she made the pretence of escape. And Luke asleep in the room at the top.*

    She says none of this to Max. He is sitting with her very still. The green room steadies some of the craziness of that day in Harrods.

    "It was when I got out of that cubicle that I saw these two women I'd seen earlier in the lift. They were powdering their faces with fluffy brushes out of gold cases, Chanel on their shoulders, Gucci on their feet. They were whispering. And I thought I heard them say "Alistair", and "taking us to Gstaad". I thought they sniggered at me in my red suit.

    Vera takes a deep breath. "You see, it was then that this croaky old common voice started up... the sort of voice me and my friends used to put on when we went down into the town on a Saturday night when we were kids... well bit older than kids... fourteen or so." She begins to mimic, her Northern accent stronger than ever now, "Look at them, those posh bitches. All fur coat 'n no knickers here. Lanky swanky, could be boys, so flat-chested." Then more harshly, 'They've got sommat you'll never 'ave lass, however 'ard you work, or get yourself fancy fashions or plastic surgery."

    The green room experiences a kind of thrill.

    *These beige women had breeding emanating from their skin, they breathed it in and out of their lungs.*

    "I was doing my lipstick," she remembers how her face had swum in the mirror, her mouth already over-lipsticked in the matching red of her suit, her eyes above heavily made up in black and the deep shadows underneath gave her a hunted, dark, Spanish dancer's look. The eyes stared back at her from the mirror with no expression. *It was then that she thought she smelled Femme.*

    Max is following her closely, noting her slide into dissociation, sensing her desperation and the panic as she struggles to cope with the onslaught of so many thoughts and influences.

"So I followed them, didn't I? Got in a taxi like James bloody Bond." Her eyes roll and then fill with tears. "But first I saw them in the children's department, where things cost a hundred pounds. I thought one of the women fingered a little baby dress, one with all the smocking back and front ... and it made my blood boil! If she's having a baby and it's a girl. I'll kill her and him! It was then that something like a switch clicked inside my head."

*She had been hearing the familiar scratchy voice start inside her for several weeks, the voice she had first used at school when she and her girlfriends walked out together on Saturday evenings. A high-pitched voice and 'right Northern'. It was the voice she had used to describe the lost weekend with Nag the Destroyer. The voice was saying "And here are those two beige bitches who think they're God's gift, with their long silky hair and chic fashions. Think they can have anything. Think they can get away with anything. They can just flick their little fingers and it can all be theirs. Even think babies come that way, gift packaged, ready wrapped. No good sneerin' at me, my luvvies, I know yer game. I know what yer up to. An' yer not gonna win." She had watched one of the women press a five pound note into the hand of the uniformed doorman as he held open the door of a black cab. She copied their exact movements and found herself being dropped by a taxi in a street of Georgian houses in West London. She stood amongst the shadows of large willow trees and watched the beige girls let themselves in, watched as the first-floor lights came on and the expensive curtains closed. She noted the window boxes, with their lions heads. One of the slender branch ends of the willow bent gracefully toward one of the long sash windows, as if spraying its panes with kisses.*

"So, this is where she brings him. This is where my husband betrays his family," *thought Vera, fully in herself. She stood in the street feeling very alone, the winter wind biting her legs in their sheer stockings, her thin knuckles on her bare hands open to the chill. The energy of the earlier heat had drained out of her. She did not know what to do next.*

\* \* \* \*

Saxon thought about her mother as she drove from the hospital, to her appointment south of the river. Whilst she was irritated that she had found herself responding to the cliché about mothers for which shrinks were famous, she could not deny the feelings and images that came unbidden when she sat in that pale green room. Since their conversations about her mother's loss of a son and her subsequent drinking, Saxon had a recurrent horror that she had killed something or someone and that these murders were about to be discovered. Her victims had lain wherever she had buried them for many years and now were about to be uncovered. What happened in Hong Kong was just the beginning. Maybe the dark man who watched her every move as she left her apartment and her workplace was just waiting and watching for her to make another mistake?

She was persecuted by the idea that it might have been her fault that her mother's baby had died all those years ago. Could it be true? Had she done something that no one had ever told her about? Had this event also been following her like a malevolent stalker only to be revealed now, when she was in her forties? And if it were true who would tell her? How could she even speak of such a thing, here in this green room with this mild man? And would speaking of it make it all worse as she had feared from the beginning?

Her thoughts wandered from the unbearable idea that she had killed unknowingly, to thoughts of her early childhood with her mother. What had made her mother fester in the self-imposed prison of grief where she had lived since Tom had died? For the first time she wondered why she had never been able to find solace?

There were all these thoughts as well as the now returning images of the boat and harbour of Hong Kong. Her heart heavy, the feeling of sickness her constant companion, she tried to rehearse what to say so that she could get it over with.

But once in the green room the words died immediately. The room was always waiting for her in the same way. She was torn between an initial relief and by thoughts about it all being sinister. As she sat in the familiar green chair and leaned back for this December session she was aware for the first time of something in her that felt broken. Not a break to be fixed by splint or steel but something quite unfathomable she could neither see nor touch that had left an indelible mark.

"There is something wrong with me isn't there?" she asks plainly.

Max looks at her fully. He is more open to the vulnerability of these places.

"It's hard to feel connected to others if you have had to put away feeling because in some way you've learned not to trust it. It's hard to distinguish the value of simple feeling." He pauses, wondering if she is listening. Her head is bent and her hair has fallen forward. "It's as if from the time you were very small you have had to be very grown up and not allow your own feelings to be seen. Perhaps because of the very sad loss of your brother, which seems to have dominated the family. You've had all the external supports, education, food, shelter, but it feels as if the happy playful child you have described being with Begonia was parted from the smiling mother, creating a feeling of glass between you and others to whom you might be close."

"Yes. That's right. I can't feel properly," she replies. "I can see others doing the feeling thing, but not me." The she adds. "My mother is all feeling."

After mother had lost her son she had become bitter. It was as if she decided that life or fate was against her and all she could do was rail against it. How often mother said how unlucky she was and lamented her fate; how often she looked at others and said "Well, it's alright for some" . How often she had said to Saxon, "You've been lucky. You've got a good career, you've been able to make something of yourself. Just as well you haven't bothered with marriage or the burden of children." She said it as if it were fact, unaware of the impact of her words upon her own child. She wondered now if her mother were spiteful, and she felt a stabbing sensation in her chest. She would have said before that she never felt guilt, it was an indulgence for immature people. But she could see now that it was guilt that was behind the way she had tried to make up for what she perceived as her mother's dreadful life in whatever way she could. Presents, time spent listening to her, then doing well at school, making something of herself for which her mother could feel proud. Although she never did feel proud. Saxon realised from the safety of the green chair that her mother had never shown the slightest interest in her career, her life; she was not someone in whom Saxon had ever confided.

She breathes out deeply, longing for a cigarette again. She wonders if Max ever smoked. Not the type. What had he said, or had she said it? "Does it feel as if you've had to make up for the lost son in some way?"

It had not occurred to her as she grew up that she had had to be very, very good because deep down she believed she was very, very bad. The space around her heart felt lumpy, churning. She had no idea that her body could be so expressive, so demanding. In that green room she was being asked to look at her body symptoms in a completely new way. Not to be a doctor anymore, who interpreted symptoms, but to be a voyager inside the body's sensations. Quite novel and quite disgusting.

If her mother's son had lived, would Mother's life have been transformed? Would Father have loved her more, not had affairs? Would he have been there for her in the way she thought she wanted? Would the son have been a better child to her than Saxon? Then a new thought arrived. Mother could, had she chosen, have spent all her love on her one remaining child, but she did not. She retreated further into alcoholic denial of what was real and the glass grew and grew.

"Tell me more about the glass," says Max.

Saxon grips the arms of the chair. She looks pale.

"I can't feel it. It's just there."

"Can you feel it now, here, between you and me?"

Saxon looks down. "I don't know. You don't know me do you?"

"I'd like to try."

She blurts out, "I could be a murderer." Then she looks away, horrified.

Max looks concerned, surprised.

"A murderer. Where has that come from?"

"There's something not right with me. Things happen around me. Bad things. And I don't know how they've happened. I can't account for them."

The room feels heavy, and the Guardians gather in close. Max feels deeply sad and alerted. It is time perhaps, after eight sessions, for her to speak of what had happened. He is relieved that she has at last spoken of her fear, but it feels a heavy sentence that would be hard to shift.

"Are you referring to what happened in Hong Kong?"

She is silent; the images that had started arriving were right in front of her.

Max says, "Are you able to tell me now about what happened in Hong Kong?" She looks down at the rug. Could she? She has already told him the worst. He can think what he likes now. So, she supposed she must. The green room held Hong Kong in its breath.

*She had taken the child into her aching arms and held him stiffly, not smiling, which made the couple encourage her more, mistaking her hatred for nerves, joking about newborns making adults clumsy. And even though they knew she was a doctor.*

*Turning away from their swollen faces and the background blur of the frenzy and noise of harbour life, she had looked down. He was warm and still, sleeping soundly. The skin of his face was new pink, the flush of just visible down inviting a stroking finger. His little eyelids with the mottled skin were almost transparent, so small they could fit onto an adult thumb. The long eyelashes quivered. Breathing was deep somewhere in the blue quilting. Once he sighed deeply, a big sigh for a tiny frame, as if he were already old. His mouth was perfectly formed, not yet shaped around words. A mouth not yet set in attitude. Nothing but mother's milk and the odd cry had passed between the lips; some wind perhaps, a little cough. But the vitriol of words, the expressing or holding back of hurt, rage, love, even passion, was yet to come.*

*It was when she pressed her face closer, in an instinct never forgotten, that the power of a new baby's smell reached right inside her. That unmanufactured fragrance became an unseen hand that rose up to turn her stomach and prick at her throat, the sting of tears surrounding her eyes. She had gasped, and her body compacted. The fragile newborn life became leaden against her aching chest, an aching that, dammed up for years, had never had the right to speak. A wordless place holding molten feelings of an intolerable searing pain. Fear. Dread. Hate. Rage. And somewhere far off, pity, pity for a small thing.*

The father of the child was discussing purchasing orders at the other end of the junk. The mother was not looking. She had seen that look on Saxon's face. The closed eyes, the shiny drop of a tear, and mistaken these for bliss. The bliss she was so cosy with in her new motherhood. She thought it right to let this unhappy woman have her private moment. She turned to freshen her red lipstick. A lone gull flew down closely over the junk, circling the cramped body of the English doctor with the baby, over which she was now bent nearly double on the increasingly swaying deck.

Saxon could hardly breathe; she did not know where she began or ended. The weight that pulled her down became more deadly, an intolerable burden. It took over. The harbour water swirled darkly. The junk swayed, the floor rose up to meet her, the wake from the energetic start of the Macao ferry caused a violent pull.

The baby was flung wide into the harbour water.

Her hands and arms were empty. The baby had left her. She couldn't see him. She couldn't see or feel anything.

Max is listening. He feels the weight of the child, the horror, the not knowing.

They sit together in silence.

Saxon takes some water from the small flask beside the chair and continues in a flat, low voice. Much of what she has said is garbled and jumbled up in sequence, but the scene is right before them in the green room. Saxon is staring ahead, not speaking, but remembering. On that Chinese junk all those months ago she had not looked beyond the swell of the harbour water. The scene Max imagined came from what had happened next.

*The child seemed to hang in mid-air, a quilted bundle. He could have been a miniature parcel offloaded by stevedores and now suspended over the dark and churning water. On an intake of breath, it was an image that would forever haunt those who witnessed it. A still life still alive in frame but hovering. What might happen now? Will he be saved? If not, who might he have become had he been given the chance?*

*What might we all have become had we had a different*

start?

*The mother on deck stood still, her bright red lips freshly glossed. The lipstick fell from her hand and bloodied the deck with its vivid colour. Shock. Frozen.*

*Even though she could not see it, as the bundle hit the dark water the grip at Saxon's neck and chest tightened so sharply she thought her heart had gone into spasm.*

She spoke of what she remembered next.

*The chaotic swirl of the harbour water had risen up and had got inside her. She no longer existed. There was just chaos. Her heart beat fast and furiously, pumping chaos into every pore. And at the same time as being cold a hot dense substance rose up from her belly with volcanic charge, flooding every tissue to make each nerve ending come on fire.*

Just before she sat up she saw once again the young man in the crumpled cotton suit sitting in Max's chair. She blinked and he was gone. She took more sips of water.

"Now you know," she says. "Now you can do away with me."

Max smiles "I'm certainly not going to do that," he says firmly. "Thank you for telling me what happened. It is very brave of you. I can see it all very clearly. And I can see how confusing it all is for you."

Max does not know whether it was the lurch of the boat that caused the baby to fall into the water or if she had unconsciously thrown the child. He had read the reports and knew she had been thoroughly examined and it was unlikely she had suffered a petit mal. Perhaps no one would ever know what had happened for sure. But there was much work to be done with her sense of herself and her badness.

"How do you feel now, having told me of this?"

"Numb." Her voice is thick, and small. She dares not look at him. "Glad of the glass," she whispers finally.

"Do you have any sense of how it all happened?"

"No," she says, still dully.

"I can see now why that question I asked you on our very first meeting was so alarming."

"I don't remember."

"You told me a little about the boat, the baby and parents,

and I asked you "What was it like holding it?"

She is completely silent and Max senses she has closed down. He understands now the relationship between the glass and her irrational fear of being bad, even a potential murderer. And now that she has revealed her crime to him, she is like a child just waiting to be punished, and by him.

"Are you expecting me to judge you?"

"Yes," she says simply. Then she looks up. "How can you hear all this and not judge me?"

"I'm not here to judge."

"You've got to make a clinical judgement haven't you and you might decide I am dangerous." That lethal combination of her highly developed adult critical awareness and her frozen child self. There was no interface between these two parts of her, in which new ideas might be explored or reflected upon.

"I'd like us to work together to unpick the belief behind your thinking that you are intrinsically bad and guilty. It seems that the glass wall is made of this belief. There's something in psychology we refer to as 'magical' guilt. It's magical because it's guilt for something we could not possibly be responsible for. It's quite a difficult concept to understand and we start by noticing that we have an inner saboteur who tries to stop us having a happy life."

She is not really listening.

"What happened to the child?" He knows, but he wants to hear it from her for she has not mentioned it in any session.

She looks surprised. "Oh, they rescued it of course." She says this vital fact without feeling of any kind.

"So you are not a murderer."

"No. But I might have been."

"How was he rescued?"

"Those cleaning junks. Their booms had webs on the end for collecting rubbish and they just picked him out of the water."

"Was that a relief to you?"

She is quiet. "I don't suppose I felt anything." She looks surprised. "You'd think I would, wouldn't you, that it would be a relief he was saved? You see, I just don't do feelings."

"So, the fact that the child lived offered no relief from

the thought that you are bad. Did you speak to the parents?"

"Oh God," she shuddered and looked as if she might faint. "They were completely hysterical. They kept wailing, calling his name" she pauses, whispering, "Gabriel, Gabriel." She looks at Max. "They were, so, so furious, they were beside themselves."

Max is quiet. He wonders whether she heard his name before she held him, whether the name was the trigger…

"Have you ever wanted to visit them, or to see the child again with your own eyes?"

She looks up sharply. "What on earth for? To get punished even more!"

He realises that his question is much too early. But he holds it near, as something she might want to do in the future, as a form of reconciliation and forgiveness. He returns to the links they are making together.

"What I'm thinking is that your unchallenged thought that you were a bad girl early on in your life seems to be connected to the way your mother and father acted over the death of your infant brother, which was not your responsibility. I do feel very sad indeed that no one relieved you of that thought."

The thump of Alma's tail is back. If she had had Max as a parent she might never have believed that everything bad that happened was her fault and that she must make up for it with hard work, never asking for anything for herself. But it was too late now. She suddenly felt very tired, to her core.

"What are you thinking?" asks Max.

"Perhaps I am bad," she says. "Perhaps I'm like that child in *The Omen*."

Max is surprised she knows such films. But time is running out and there are things he wants to say to her.

"Magical guilt" I spoke of earlier. It can really take hold of us because it gets imbedded. It becomes a hidden truth we believe, and we don't question the beliefs because we don't know they are there. Only the results of those beliefs. Sometimes it results in self-sabotage, in not being allowed to be happy or have good things. We feel as if we are on trial, as if we have to pay for something we haven't done."

He speaks from his own experience and looks toward

her, wondering if she has heard him. He is alarmed at how vulnerable she is suddenly and how little he knows her. He is not at his best, but he draws strength from the Guardians as he feels their presence in the room. "Does this make any sense to you?"

She nods numbly. "I guess so."

"I'd like to say a few things. Neither of us knows what exactly happened in Hong Kong and we must try to keep an open mind. You have done really well to speak to me of it and I am aware that it has made you feel sad, and afraid. I'd like to think that you had people around you over the next few days, can you arrange this?"

She is not really listening. She replies on automatic.

"Lewis is away."

"Do you have anyone with whom you can discuss these things?"

"Good God no."

But she had told him about Hong Kong, she had painted the picture here graphically in a way that she had been unable to tell anyone else. With Lewis she had said she'd had a bit of an accident and that it would all get cleared up. He had tried to ask for more and she knew he really cared but she had buttoned up. She knew that Lewis had told Daniel. If he knew about this badness, what would he think? She was surprised that she cared what he thought. Her next thought came in a rush. She was terrified Lewis would leave her and she would lose the only link she had with kindness. She felt just then as if she would break in two.

"I wondered, what about Daniel?" Max smiles and Saxon looks startled.

"You were reading my mind," she says.

"Daniel might be a good person to speak to. I wondered if you might also think about what I've just said about magical guilt. Write down in your notebook any thoughts that come to you, and any more flashbacks from Hong Kong. We can talk about them when we meet early next week, before Christmas."

At the word Christmas she feels dismal. She is about to fly to Florida to visit the parents she has been talking about in this green room. Those parents to whom she was the unwanted leftover, the child who perhaps should have died so that they could have their son. She shook herself, hating the self-pity.

She says dully, "I'm supposed to go to Florida for three days for the annual visit to my parents. They live in a house made all of glass." She looks up at him. "All white, silver and glass... fits, doesn't it?"

"Do you have to go?" says Max.

"I certainly do.'

"Will you think about what we've talked about today, please?"

She is silent.

"Daniel, he came to see me. I think he was trying to encourage me to, to open up more, to trust you, to trust myself in the end, and to go on with this work. He told me about his experience here." She looks at him and he says nothing.

"I can see you are keen for me to have support and I am grateful for your professional concern." Her voice seemed icy. "But, for me to talk to Daniel, then where would his respect for me be, let alone our friendship?'

"You would find out," says Max.

## 11

HIS sense of equilibrium was short-lived. Max struggled on with the rest of his week's work, his body longing for the open skies over the Suffolk marshes, the call of the curlew soft on his ear. The demands of his mood changes restricted his emotional energy and dominated his meditation practice. He was not clear what was happening within him, but clear that he had to ride the roller-coaster as best he could. Much of it was expressed through the heavy uncoordination of his body. His leg hurt and his limp seemed more pronounced. He noticed an urgent grip at the back of his throat when he could not replace the toothpaste top properly, when he spilt milk on the floor, when the computer locked up, he wanted to swear, kick and shout.

He noticed the sour taste in his mouth and the clenching of his jaw when he glimpsed Emily's silent white frame and knew it as resentment at her neediness. He noticed how often he called himself a fool for marrying her; for indulging in the fantasy that by doing so he would be safe from the demands of his own need and desire. He cursed his collusion with his self-righteousness.

Sometimes he gave in to feeling small and helpless, personally abandoned, wanting the arms of beneficent others to take care of him, to fall into the regressive pull back to some idealised past. He longed to feel strong arms around him, to be held by another like a child in blissful unconsciousness. He feared that the carefully developed spacious mind he needed for the tumultuous goings-on in his life had deserted him.

The experience of falling was everywhere, especially in relation to the process of his mind as he watched it tearing into so much of what he held dear. This chiselling voice he named Screwtape; it questioned his beliefs, his commitments, his professional code, even the living presence of the energies he called Guardians who had accompanied him every day since they first appeared on that hillside walk outside Thimpu. His scientific self told him he was in for a period of 'reality testing'.

He knew that his constant search for meaning was both a strength and a weakness. Just now he could see no meaning, but a void he was at risk of filling with sentimental longing for a past that was long gone and with craving for the impossible ideal. His life of caring for others, based on service and on philosophical principles, mocked him. His failure at intimacy. His barren relationship...

Emily watched him in a new silence. They spoke little. He did not want to ask her how she was or tell her about his day. He did not want to talk to her at all. In the past when he had tried to tell her something about himself and his feelings, she had found it threatening; had presumed it was something to do with her, that she was to blame and about to be abandoned, and she would become agitated and sullen.

His fists clenched of their own accord. His jaw was tight. He wanted to make sarcastic remarks. He even wanted to smash the blue-covered lace making box with its pristine white linen, and crush the delicate claws through which the yarn was woven, around which Emily's fingers would spin. And his mocking Screwtape companion sneered: "The only creative activity in this silent house is bloody lace." Its silent fuss sat as witness and rebuke to his patience. But Screwtape again. "What else did you expect from this marriage?'

He remembered that his first analyst had asked him frequently about angry feelings and how they might be held within his body. He had also named his tendency to depression, but these observations had never touched the spot of recognition. The words came back to him now, in these uncertain winter days, when he was less able to maintain a continuous stable emotional way of being.

He had probably been depressed for years but found a way to manage it through the action of looking after other people and taking on their depression. His marriage to Emily was an illusion based upon his need to idealise. Why not admit it? Why not admit that this is how he had managed his emotional life so far, and some of it had worked well.

The call to change had been sounding slowly for this last year. The fatigue and sense of falling, the tuning out at meetings, the heavy heart, women's legs, the reminiscing. Vera Dodds and her uncanny resemblance to Margaret. The call, with its accompanying fear and chaos, was best described by the poets and artists. Dante, waking to find himself in a dark wood, wholly lost and gone. Picasso in his blue period. And in spiritual traditions the lure of comfort and safety was always under scrutiny: Christ in the wilderness; Buddha tempted by Mara.

Max could see that he was now crossing the wasteland and the outcome would be the result of the trials along the way. He would need the stories of those who had trodden this path before. He would need all the equanimity and compassion he had learned and practised as a Buddhist.

He was uncomfortable and inexperienced in being with this new, more conscious anger. He had been angry in ordinary ways, snarled, got cross, exploded. When he held his breath or smiled more than usual, arrived a little late, his analyst would interpret it as being to do with some perceived deprivation; because the summer break was coming up, because the analyst had had to cancel, or some other analytic interpretation. And Max had smiled to himself understanding the theory and quite liking the permission for indulgence, but the interpretations never connected inside. Even when on the subject of his parents. That had remained a complete void.

He sat cross-legged in front of the stone Buddha that was always seated on a small table under the bookshelf in the corner of his room. Many patients never noticed it or if they did, said nothing. It was a Buddha he had watched emerging as it was being carved, during a pilgrimage to Bhutan where he had gone after graduating, and which had changed his life. Now, in his small green room in South London, he was able to recognise the Buddha's half smile and just sit.

This stone Buddha also carried with it the embrace of the green valleys surrounded by snow-capped mountains where he had had his first conscious experience of unconditional love. It was from the ordinary Bhutanese people; women, men and children, with brown polished faces and real, white-toothed smiles, going about their everyday tasks in their national dress. It was from inside the clean air of the cypress-covered mountains of this Buddhist kingdom where love was the main currency and happiness the gross national product. In this Shangri-la, every person was steeped in the Buddhist dharma. It was woven into each action, every moment. After so many sudden and violent deaths, the cynicism of his adolescence and harsh undergraduate experience at Oxford, this openness, this living joy and peace, filled the cracks in his broken heart. He learned the true meaning of being in the present moment. His experience in those green patchwork valleys engaged his whole being.

It was during a climb on a hillside just outside the capital, Thimpu, when he had fallen behind the group and become prey to self-pitying rumination, that he started to realise it was possible for the human mind and body to experience happiness. He had been wholly self-absorbed, dominated by his own emotional suffering, as well as by the lameness of his leg. It was only when he was nearing the hilltop, with his lungs close to bursting, that he became aware one of the guides had stayed with him, walking silently by his side. This recognition caused his heart to swell and his rumination to dissolve. In gratitude he turned toward the guide, offering a rush of joyous thanks, ashamed of his self-preoccupation. "The door is always open to you, Max.'

The lightness of being, the depth of understanding in those words was carved inside him as keenly as the carvings of the stone Buddha.

Bhutan was where he had decided to return to Switzerland and begin his monastic training with the Order.

It was in Bhutan that the Guardians came to be a living presence constantly by his side, however steep the slopes, however deep the ravine, however challenged the path of love.

Until now.

He had not thought ahead to the possibility of Emily being unable to sustain an adult partnership. He had not seen that she was unlikely to be able to develop a robust self where she could relate equally, which would have meant that he would receive. In the thrall of his idealisation he believed he had enough love for both of them and that this love would conquer all, including, fantastically, her mental illness. The omnipotence! The arrogance! But there, he had thought it. No longer the bland excuses or euphemisms of trauma, personality disorder, fragile personality, but actual mental illness. Fired up as he had been by his idealism it did not occur to him that his own emotional needs, remaining unmet, might fester and lead to his becoming unhappy, and angry.

His new-found anger nudged him to think that Emily was just waiting for the day he would leave her so that she could properly surrender to her illness and never have to try much at life again.

Did he want to leave? Did he want to be relieved of the burden he had so joyously, 'blithely' said Screwtape, taken on? Or was he now having to face what he had been unable to face when making the commitment to her? His own emotional past. And, coupled with this, and even worse, the fact that his collusion in her avoidance and fear might have made her condition worse.

Could he find a way to speak to her differently?

He thought now that he should not have married at all. He was too guilty, too ashamed, too bruised by his own losses. He had diverted his own emotional need for connection into the position of therapist and carer. But he knew now that this idealisation was about to break apart. He could no longer hold it all.

In front of the Buddha, he allowed these thoughts to race in and out, with their connections and continual sickening feeling of falling, leavened every now and then by his concentration on in-breath and out-breath and the moment of stillness enjoyed. After an hour's sitting within the gaze of the stone Buddha he knew that he must have time alone.

He cleared his thoughts well enough to have the energy for those important last sessions with patients before the Christmas break. For some patients Christmas brought excitement and a welcome gathering with friends and family. For others it highlighted what was missing.

Saxon Pierce seemed resigned about her impending travel to Florida. He wished that she did not have to go. Their work was in such an early stage. There was so much emotion that remained split off which had already resulted in impulsive action. He thought that she might find meeting her parents more overwhelming than she imagined. It was her highly defended, efficient, "I've started so I'll finish" self that had arranged for this visit, trailing behind it the unmet need.

Vera had said, "You're looking a bit peaky. Will you have a good Christmas. Am I allowed to ask?'

Her red clothes were now replaced by black, and she had taken off her make-up. Her loss of weight and haunted appearance was startling.

"My boys are back," she had said. "I love them so much." She looked at him with watery eyes, trying to be brave. *Maxie, Maxie, I love you so much, don't leave me now, please don't...*

"Luke's with his friend Jason now so I could come for my session. But he hates this new school. It's not right. He hates what's happened." She paused. "Dominic is cool, of course, as older boys feel they have to be. I've tried my best with the house, getting everything ready. Then my mother comes. Christmas sort of takes over, doesn't it?'

*Life, life takes over, it's taken us over, Maxie, and I don't want it, not like this, I just can't...*

Max breathed steadily. "How are you getting on with the breathing exercises, and the yoga. Are they helping you to steady yourself when you find your mind scattering?"

"I do try. And I forget. There's a dreadful emptiness and a sense of 'What's the point?' But there is a point for the boys," she looked at him. "I still can't go in the bedroom. Not sure what I'll do when my mother comes. I just hope she won't notice where I sleep."

He was aware that she wasn't really answering him and saddened that over Christmas she would have so little support. "But Mother's not very aware, unless it's got something to do with her."

*No one cares for us now, Maxie, they only think of themselves and how it looks. We're all on our own...*

"Will you miss coming?"

She was thoughtful. "Do you know I will. I will miss your concern. And your stillness." She withdrew slightly. Then, "Sometimes I think about your stillness when I'm on my own. It's better than the stones because you are a living, breathing person. You have been kind to me and you believe in me. I don't want to let you down." There was a good silence between them.

"I won't have a session here now for two weeks, will I?"

"That's right. We begin again in early January."

" I do feel weird some of the time. My most difficult time will be when they've all gone skiing. I just don't know what

I will do."

"Let us think together now, what you might do then."

\* \* \* \*

He then cancelled his Friday meetings and went to Suffolk, leaving Emily to her lace making and to fret. He threw off his London clothes and dressed quickly in whatever clothes he could find by the back door, for the cold and wet, the animal nature of his body leading the way, oblivious of the elements. After waiting about on the cliff top, he stumbled down the old wooden steps that led directly onto the beach. The steps were badly worn by the weathering blast of salt and wind. The rough edges of perished wood caught the pitted soles of his walking boots, and he kicked out, his rage starting to come to life from inside. It added to the weight of his fear. As he neared the last step, he wrapped his old black anorak around him more securely and pulled down his felt hat against the wind in his ears.

The beach, that familiar threshold between earth and water, waited for his tread, for his curiosity about the stones with their myriad colours and patterns. But today he saw no invitations. He stood still, holding himself against the December wind. He stared at the sea as if it were alien, no longer his friend. He felt disconnected, heavy in his body and in his heart. Somewhere he remembered that rage, like justice, was blind.

The grey swell of the North Sea filled his entire view. It rebuked him for his neglect and its salty wet embrace met his inside tears as it seemed to wash into his body. He had been walking here for months without seeing or feeling its presence.

Then he began walking again, with the sea on his right. He let the salt wash of tears emerge and swim down his unshaven face and lie in the dark stubble. The tears misted his gaze. His throat ached. The voice inside him that he now felt compelled to follow, that had said "It is time", wanted to yell and for his body to follow the yell and lash out. But his body, despite its weight, felt liquefied and without bone. He might as well have been a creature beneath the sea.

When he could no longer bear to walk, he stopped and crouched down, took his sailing knife from his pocket and plunged it into the sand. He made deliberate forceful stabs into the sand, disturbing stones. Then turning toward the sea, he took onto his face the force of the white spray as the waves pounded in.

"If only they would come for me," he thought. "If only they could wash their wet and salty way into the grit made sore inside my heart."

He gave in to thoughts, in whatever form they appeared. 'Wallowing,' he heard his grandmother say. He knew that 'thoughts are just thoughts.' But this new stirring energy wanted to let them have their course and see them through.

He had to face his old idealism and his illusions. He had imagined, with the hope of the new initiate, that suffering would get less with time. But time had not softened the visceral link with his awful past, and he felt now as if something new had awakened it all to be met again, full on. What happened when he was ten years old and his response, was the hand he had been dealt and it had formed the foundation for the way he was. He believed that with the right attitude one could have a meaningful relationship with suffering. And because he had experienced his own suffering, he believed he could sit with others in theirs.

But right now, on this beach, once again the wind blew hard. Had he got it wrong? Had this search for meaning been just a distraction from his emotional pain, the pain he was acutely aware of right now?

But in this place, on this beach, he could not be distracted.

He had been digging his knife more deeply into the sand, extracting stones, as he kept watch on the grey horizon line, in the ritual of pain defence, as if trying to rock away the diamond grit. The toe of his walking boot hit hard against brick. It was brick left by World War Two debris, and before this the debris of a deserted medieval town. He was at the actual place on the stony shore where the remains of All Saints Church had fallen from the Dunwich cliff, littering the beach with brick and flint, the last brave post of a lost city now under water. Folklore said the sound of bells from the drowned church still tolled under the sea. They had tolled for Max's parents and for Margaret from near enough this very spot. Somehow his poor tormented body had found itself again in this place. This was the place where his godfather had told him when he was just ten years old that both his parents were dead.

He fell, into the gritted hole he had been unconsciously digging and put his head onto the wet stones and stabbed into the stone cavern that had opened up.

He and Margaret had been building all morning, on the tiny sand strip that was revealed only at low tide. It was early September, they had had a charmed summer of walks and swimming, picnicking in the sand dunes of Walberswick. As they dug and shaped, flocks of sand martins made caves in the red cliffs, digging out the thin red sand from in between gorse and scrub-filled patches, contributors to the eternal pattern of erosion.

Nothing here would stay for time.

"Devil birds are back," Margaret would say, confusing all swifts, swallows, and martins with signs of the Devil. They were the two 'M's. Twins, born within fifteen minutes of each other. Max first, then Margaret. They were an unexpected, overwhelming gift for two devout Christians who married too late, they thought, for children. They were special, seen as a direct gift from God. And they loved each other so much.

The black of Uncle Gareth's formal suit and polished leather shoes were out of place on the wet beach. He had come straight from his office in Norwich to tell them about the accident. Max's father had swerved to avoid collision with a car overtaking on a bend, too fast, the driver too young, too drunk, out of control. And on that bend nature supported the hundred-year-old evergreen oak tree, strong enough to stand firm against the east coast winds or the impact of a Rover car. These were the days before seat belt laws, and his parents' skulls were shattered by the impact.

He had never been able to touch his rage about it and now he felt he could kill with his own hands. As he dug about furiously and kicked into the stones he wondered about his own violence. He would like to kill that youth full of cheap booze, who had jumped a car he found in Bessel Street and destroyed his beloved parents. The youth was given a fine and community service, he had probably done it all again, several times. Max and Margaret in their shock and in the numbness of grief, had been helpless, the paths of their lives changing direction in that moment of impact.

His whole body reached out to kick, bite, lunge, stab, some harmless fragile little thing, to beat the living daylights out of anything that reminded him of that mindless act, of his own tragic vulnerability.

He stared angrily out to sea, onto that grey blue stretch of water that had so often saved his life. He understood then how the tight fist of hate operated and why people killed. It was no intellectual thing. All those years of lying on a couch or talking could not meet the demand of this visceral hate, the seeds of which had been sewn into his body tissue all those years ago. Now they had germinated, and they wanted action – revenge even – in the form for which they were programmed.

Margaret, always smaller than he, in her pale blue shorts and T shirt, whimpering like a wounded puppy, her thick dark hair trembling over her wet face and shoulders: "Tell him to go away, Maxie. Tell me it's not true."

Gareth's embarrassment, not used to children.

"You'll be a man now, Max. And you'll look after your sister."

There it was. His fate. His destiny. Decided at ten years old..

Only he had failed. He had failed to keep Margaret alive. And now Emily, he had failed to bring her to life too. And most recently that patient who reminded him so much of Margaret, and yet in some vital way he hoped, was so different, Vera.

From the back of his throat came the growl of a long-held scream.

They had clung together in their freshly orphaned state, swaying in the wind, the high peep of the martins screaming in their ears, the smell of salt and sand forever identified with this day, alongside the crash of the North Sea washing into them as they began their journey into the grey ocean of grief.

Max lost his childhood skin overnight. He moved from the one who made up the games to the one who made up being a grown up. But Margaret never made it.

He picked stones at random, hurling them out to sea, oblivious of the stares of walkers and the curious dogs that stood on the edge of his excavation wagging their tails.

Those images of Margaret with her wild and pleading

brown eyes, forever stuck in childhood and precocious teens, failing to mature and thrive! His long-held mantra: "What would Pa have done? How would Ma have spoken to her? What could/should I have done."

After the funeral they began sleeping in the same bed, clinging together like babes fending off the terrors of the wood. He would watch her, curled up as she must have inside the shared womb, sucking her thumb, her little face swollen with crying the way he imagined his heart would cry if given the water of kind permission instead of grit. He would keep a night vigil, unable to sleep himself, realising that she, and his shocked elderly grandparents, were all he had left. Friends were marginalised. "Thank heaven they are twins," the adults said to each other, "at least they've got each other," as if this meant they would be OK. They dismissed any sign of unusual behaviour as belonging to twinship they did not understand. Their mother had never dressed them alike because she believed a matched pair to be a mother's show-off thing and twins could never benefit from such fancies. But after their parents' deaths they wore the same red shirts and blue jeans with notes written to each other in their pockets. They shared wrist bangles and songs by Bob Dylan, and a sign language of their own.

Their godparents were appointed guardians. Gareth lived in Norwich and godmother Rose in Sussex. Both were in their sixties and thinking of retiring. It was difficult for them to relate to children. They appointed a live-in housekeeper to oversee their needs in London during the week, a kind, but old-fashioned woman who had had a series of these jobs throughout her life. Each weekend the twins returned to their grandparents in Suffolk, to be warmed by their care and to run along the beach in the wind. As they became more and more inseparable their future schooling became a concern. They were due to go to different boarding schools, Max first, paid for in advance by their traditional parents who had imagined they would be ready to make their separate journeys by then. One thoughtful teacher suggested they continue at the same London day school, or a boarding school which would take them both in order that they were kept together in their orphaned state. But Gareth and Rose, keen to be seen to deliver the parents' wishes to the letter, and to get on with their retirements, were afraid of change and the uncertainty of its management. So things were left as the parents had decreed and the fatal separation began. Max became serious-minded and hardworking, throwing himself into scholastic achievements. Those looking on took it as a sign that he was over his grief. Margaret was often disorientated, unable to concentrate at school. Teachers would sometimes find her small body curled up under a table or in a cupboard. She would wake from nightmares to a wet bed, and wander about wearing Max's pyjamas. She clung to him at every opportunity. He was the only person able to interpret her inner world and make her feel safe. He wrenched himself away to go to boarding school as decreed and resigned himself to further bereavement. Margaret would go off on her own and the harassed housekeeper would telephone around trying to locate her; Max would be called into his master's study to help. She would be at Liverpool Street Station, trying to return to the cottage, or at Kings Cross trying to get to Max. When she too was sent to boarding school she would run away only to be brought back, tearful and angry. There was a slight reprieve during her adolescence, when she started cravings for young teachers with whom she would be sexually precocious in her attempt to attach. Max knew that this was a distraction from her unhappiness, but she was less demanding during these crushes and a part of him felt guilty relief.

He thought now of those troubled years and the way he had disappeared into academic achievement and Margaret into other people as a way to cope with the pain of unbearable loss. He could see it all so clearly and he wondered: "Had no one else seen it so?" Where were all the grown-ups at that time? It seemed as if there had been no one who could soften the blow of death at such a tender age, and in the absence of any wise or parental care time had driven each of them into their survival corners and each other. Psychotherapy was still in its infancy and Margaret saw countless professionals but was never able to complete the course of suggested treatment. She remained inconsolable, and wild. And for himself, Max could see that his way was to avoid the risk of emotional intimacy and its consequent pain of loss.

He dug some more in the cave he was creating with his

knife and raged at fate. His grandmother's stroke and death; his grandfather's demented frailty trying to keep the cottage as a home for them whilst it deteriorated around him. Gareth had come out as a gay man and moved to Australia with a long-term lover; Rose moved into non-communicative retirement.

He had gone to his new school feeling slightly in awe of the tradition of his ancestors, father, grandfather and great-grandfather, and in part excited by a new life. But the wrench from his twin was a constant pull. He too suffered from the void left by her absence. There was no one for him to look out for and feel the warmth of being needed. He was also in constant fear of what would happen to her, and guilt for not being there. The efforts he made to keep in contact whilst stoically continuing with his studies and having little social life and friends of his own!

And one night in the holidays, here in Suffolk, after both his grandparents had died and left them everything, she had pledged herself to him, begging him to love her, to make them a proper couple to fend off the harshness of the outside world. That look in her dark brown eyes he had seen recently in Vera's. The look of a hunted trapped animal who knows there is no escape, who cannot see any other way to live other than a fantasised return to a Garden of Eden. He had seized her, trying to make her stop, to see sense. He had felt angry with her and pitied her. He felt trapped by his own inadequacy and his own guilt, she demanded the impossible and he could not meet it. He saw now so clearly the starting place for his idealism. His false belief that he should manage heroically even when up against an impossible task, or the bottomless pit of inconsolable loss.

He felt that shivering of her shoulders, his fear that she would not be able to grow up, to have a life of her own, find someone to love, even have children of her own. If only he had known, then what he knew now! If only he had been able to ...

Yes, to save her. He had been unable to save her, and now he had to face that he was unable to save Emily. He saw the pattern so clearly, here in the grit and harshness of the beach, that so many of his actions since the deaths of his parents had been that of believing he had to save. An impossible task and an act of hubris. Looking after and taking responsibility and trying to make things better was what he knew, what he was good at. And he had never questioned it. Until now. His parents' Christianity taunted him "to give and not to count the cost". Through Buddhist philosophy he understood that life included suffering but that once the roots of suffering and the forms of attachment to suffering were recognised and accepted, could be transformed. His Screwtape self lunged at him: "Well Mr so bloody clever Mr Psychotherapist, what are you going to do now?".

He sat up and found his mind clearing, so many understandings rising, things falling into place. This discovery, that inside the calm compassionate exterior was this desperate wild man who stabbed at the wind and kicked at stones whilst tasting the salt of his own tears. He understood the trap of his thinking, that unless he tried to 'save' others and make it all OK his life would be crushed by guilt, a non-life. He could see now that he had not been living fully anyway. He had never learned to receive. He was blaming Emily for not being able to put herself in his shoes but he had never allowed it. He caught the shadow of his idealism that did not dirty its hands with the stuff of ordinary feeling – longing, need, sadness and pure vulnerability. He had been able to work with others' vulnerability, but not his own.

He was about to recognise his shame and then he laughed. No, he would not go there. He did not need shame, or pride, or guilt any more to fire him into action. He could, right now, on this beach say goodbye. Goodbye to many, many things.

He lay on the stones laughing and crying. He laughed and laughed, loud and long. And kept on laughing as he picked himself up and brushed off the sand and bits of stone that had gathered in his old jeans and in his shoes. He kicked the stones and pebbles to fill the cave he had made and strode along the shore, the wet pebbles softened in colour by the lick of the sea. Nothing was ever all sorted. The sea rolled in, it rolled out, patterns of waves and beach stones never the same. The heaviness in his body was lifting, he could see what he needed to do. New realisations were just beginning.

He needed to say a proper goodbye.

\* \* \* \*

In the Suffolk cottage, now his alone, he split logs and lit a fire and warmed himself before moving into his usual formal meditation practice. The Guardians came back into his awareness with their constant forgiving grace and acceptance.

After, he walked around the cottage, seeing its contents and its history with fresh eyes. He reached into the old cupboard and poured himself a local beer and then went up the old cottage staircase and into the spare bedroom, the room he had once shared with Margaret. There was an old chest in the corner covered by a cloth. Inside it were old photograph albums of his early life. Black and white photographs of his parents, of his mother holding the twins as babies, one in each arm, an impossible pride on her face. There were photos of the twins at different ages. He saw that the distant starry gaze of Margaret and his own serious look were qualities always there. Max remained the more serious, Margaret always the one playing to the camera, with a funny hat, a clown mask, a box of sweets held high.

There was a long gap, marking the time from ten to seventeen. Then one last black and white photograph taken just near to where he had been today. They had lit a fire there often in an attempt to heal its memory, to claim the beach back for their children's freedoms. He and Margaret had placed the old camera on a tripod and dashed to get in view, laughing, with arms around each other. Max tall and athletic, Margaret small and thin, each with the dark thick hair. He remembered it as a wonderful moment and present there on the page forever.

During the early part of that summer, which was to be his last before university, he thought he and Margaret had been close – decorating the cottage, walking along the sea wall, cooking the local samphire to go with the fish they caught on their moonlight fishing trips. But there was unease in her sullen moods. She would disappear with, he presumed, local boys, returning to look at him reproachfully. Then one night she did not come back.

He brought the album from the cold of the upstairs room and returned to the fire and warmed his hands, the last photograph on his lap. He stared at the flames licking around the ash logs, the woody fragrance scenting the room. He thought suddenly about choice. What is it in us that chooses and what influences choice?

He knew where she went when she was unhappy and what he had to offer no longer consoled her. And he had found her, behind the beach where they had grown up together, near the small marsh where archaeologists had found what they thought was a Viking ship. She had said of the Vikings - *Oh to be a conqueror, where you think the world is yours!* She must have been taking the pale blue sodium amytal tablets all day for the pathologists found the lethal dose had shut down her robin's heart. Max had wept over her in anguish as he carried her back to the cottage, stumbling and stopping, the sound of the sea in his ears. At the fence on the edge of the car park he had fallen awkwardly, tearing his Achilles tendon so badly that it needed later surgery. It had never healed, as he had never healed, causing him to limp.

"I am so sorry," he whispered to Margaret in the photograph. "My dearest sister, I loved you so much. I am so sorry for all that happened to us. I wish with all my heart that it had been different, that you were now here with me, enjoying this place, bringing your children here even. The life we might have had but didn't. I know that you found life unbearable, that you never found a way to be in this life. Please forgive me if I let you down." Tears ran down his face. "I never wanted to let you go; I've not been able to let you go. But I have to let you go now in the old way. You will always be in my heart and I will carry you with me, so that you too can see the stars and the waves on the beach, you too can feel the wind on your face and hear laughter. I let go now of all the old wishful thinking, all the old thinking I should have done it all differently. It was not my fault. I know and I believe that you also know, I did what I could at the time with what I had. I believe that you forgive me for not making it different, for not being able to give you better choices for how to live. And I want you to help me to forgive myself. What life I may have now I want to live it fully, not a half-life on the edge."

He turned over the album and noticed some loose photographs tucked into the cover. He had not seen them for years. He and Emily together in Oxford, wheeling bicycles across the Magdalen Bridge. Emily looked so young, but so happy, and serene. She did have that serenity. Then another photo some years later, of their summer honeymoon in Switzerland when wildflowers covered the hills and cow bells rang out. This was where, in the same place as Thomas Mann wrote The Magic Mountain, Emily had been happiest and was at her most stable. She had milked the goats and learned to sing and make lace. This is where she had retreated during the time he was in the Order in the valley below, where she had waited for him.

He had shut her out. Too much psychology, worry, and his own preoccupation with failure. Too much in thrall to the old guilt that he should have done better, that he should have saved his sister from a premature death. He was more of a stranger to life than a stranger to death. He had shut himself down and had closed the avenues of true compassion between Emily and himself.

He wondered whether he and Emily might be able to rekindle something of that serenity again. He had stopped asking her for anything and resented that she gave so little. Perhaps she did not know what to do around him anymore.

He remembered how she used to cook for him. She had learned to make rosti in Switzerland. He would ask her to cook rosti again.

*The Pale Green Room*

## 12

MYRA watched her daughter over her teacup. Her dark brown eyes fastened intently upon Vera's in the way a baby fastens on the mother's when sucking from a breast or bottle. That same fixation, that same gulping in of the other's essence.

"Well, Vera, where are my grandsons then?"

Vera shook slightly. She went to the sink to fill up the kettle again. She held it under the tap and watched it fill, then turned the switch to red. Tea in vast quantities was her mother's 'calling' and a useful distraction. With her back to her mother, she said: "You know where they are, Mum. They will be back later." She knew, of old, that her mother expected her grandsons to be on parade to greet her. But today, Christmas Eve, the last shopping day before the day itself, Alistair had chosen to take his sons to buy their ski-gear. Vera could not stop her voice from trembling and tears started to fall. She remained with her back to her mother, her body slightly shaking.

If Myra noticed she said nothing. Then she gave an impatient sigh. "All the same, damn men. I knew this would happen sooner or later. I knew no good would come of this marriage. The upper-class bastard." Her voice was winding up.

Vera remained at the sink, knowing some of what was to come at the same time as realising that her mother really hadn't a clue. Alistair had never been 'posh'. His background had been just as humble as theirs. She had suspected during these last few years that he had married her out of spite to his parents as well as their sexual bond and this latest indiscretion was now a way to notch himself up the social ladder. Alistair was feasting on the new shift in power, that now, in Britain money spoke louder than class. And Alistair had lots of 'new' money.

Vera's silence encouraged her mother. "You've got to be stronger, my girl. You're in the right. He's in the wrong. You've got to put your back into fighting him every inch of the way."

Vera stayed by the now stirring kettle, its water just beginning to turn over inside. Where's the healthy island, she thought. She looked up at the postcard she had stuck on the wall over the cooker. It had arrived yesterday, from Leo in Tanzania and showed a setting sun over a red earth path. "Take care Mum.

You are the best and always will be". "My sun is definitely setting," she thought. The newly developed resolve to take charge of her own life that she was learning in Dr Max's green room was being drained away. The familiarity of her mother's voice and habits was sucking her back to the terms on which her mother lived, those terms she had tried to get away from. Myra was gunning for a fight, a slanging match about Alistair. Now that the marriage was over, had failed, Vera was in impasse. She could not resort to old ways, and it was hard for her to speak from the new voice she was beginning to develop in the green room.

There was a shift in her mood when she remembered the power of the house rules about smoking, introduced some years ago. Her mother had sulked and pouted but had had to adhere. She was longing for a fag right know, Vera knew, and she felt some control which set her apart from her mother. She had done something good of her own volition.

She looked at the red and white tiles of her kitchen wall. Laura Ashley of the 1990s. The red and white oak leaf frieze, red and white polka dot curtains, red kitchen china. She had been so pleased to get it right. But these small successes had not held her man and her sons were gone. The flash of raised mood and control disappeared. Her past achievements felt shallow. And in the great emptiness of now she felt small and frightened. The hopes of therapy and self-help that she could in time sort herself out and move on seemed an impossibility. She was not even at a solid first base for accepting that her marriage was over. She felt for the scratches and cuts under the sleeves of her sweater. She could always do a little bloodletting when things got really bad. A slight guilt then, she did have the breathing homework and sometimes it did work for a small release of feeling. But the reality of the vast empty space required super strength. She did not know if she had it in her.

She took the tea she had made and sat down at the kitchen table, opposite her mother and faced her.

Seeing her there now through the eyes of her own grief she realised her mother could give her nothing, had probably never been able to give her much except for food and a roof, and there were times when that was thin. In between the slating of her appearance, Myra was oddly contrite. "I know I should have come earlier, Vera, but I just couldn't." She paused, "You understand, don't you, love... I know it's a mother's duty to stand by her only daughter, but there was the shop and Uncle Frank, and. Well, Vera, you know I've not been well..."

She trailed off, unnerved by Vera's silence, by the fact that she had not held her eye contact, by the fact that her daughter might actually be in difficulty. But not unnerved for long, she was soon irritated by her own daughter making her feel uncomfortable, in her cold, big, fancy house down in London.

"Haven't you got anything to say for yourself?"

Vera shrugged. "There's not much to say, Mum. I feel so tired, and so, helpless." These were words she had not used before, especially with her mother, but she found herself speaking in this way and felt a quiet pleasure. She would not tell Myra of Dr Max.

Myra looked blank. "Well, that's no good. You've got to go after the bastard. Go round there, cause a fuss, break a few windows, cut up his clothes."

Vera remained quite still. "And what would that do? I would be behaving in the way he might expect. Dare I say it, Mum, but it's what you used to do, and we all know how that—"

Myra held up her hand and Vera thought for one moment that this hand might slap her. "Don't you dare! Don't you dare bring me into this ..."

Vera continued, refusing to be bullied. "But it's true, isn't it? And think about it, about how he would crow wouldn't he, and say "She's just like her cheap Northern mother." Myra looked aghast and Vera worried she had gone too far. "Yes, he would put it like that. It would justify why he had to go, can't you see? I would be giving him what he wanted. Justifying shacking up with this posh ..."

Myra's eyes glinted. "That's more like it! A bit of spirit. Who is she then, this bitch?" Vera stood up and walked around the table. "I don't know, Mum. I don't want to know. He's always had affairs."

Vera's mother started to speak but it was Vera's turn to hold up her hand.

"No, don't. I never told you because I knew how you

would be. You always told me that it was what men did."

Myra's mouth set in a pout.

"And as long as he always came back to me and was ever more generous, I let it go."

But now. She did not want to tell her mother about the therapy, but she wanted the therapy to help her with what she needed to say to keep her end up. She had practised with Max speaking to the bullying other, in whatever form he or she might arrive. She had thought it weird and contrived at first, talking to a chair, but now it was coming in handy and she would try it out for herself. Perhaps she had more of the mountaineer in her than she realised.

"Now I've had some time to think I realise that I've been living a lie. It stopped being a proper relationship ages ago I. In fact, I rushed off to Harrods to try and get back something I'd known as normal. To make this Christmas work when it can't. Not in the old way," she laughed a little laugh. "As if Harrods could give one normality!" She looked at her mother keenly, wondering whether she was following her or wondering when she get outside for a cigarette. "I had a lot of thoughts about how things have been, and how I just desperately wanted things to work. So I was blind. I blinded myself," tears were welling. Her mother was silent, looking down, she had no idea what to say; this was not the Vera she knew, this was not what she had expected. She didn't really understand what Vera was saying. Oh God, was this going to be an awful Christmas!

"I was there as an object" –Vera used a word she had latched onto in the self-help books, but not a word used by Max – "an object for his pleasure and a mother for his sons. But what I haven't got is class or distinction or contacts. He's got money and this Arabella's got the first three." She paused, hoping for dramatic effect. "He wants to go into politics."

"Bloody man," said Myra. "He's got to see you decent then."

"Yes, he has."

"So, what are you doing about it?"

Vera felt the extent of her fatigue. "I've got a solicitor, Mum. A good one. Michaela got her for me."

"Huh, that bitch," said Myra. "I'll bet she was here

sniffing round as soon as he'd gone. I saw her eyeing him."

Vera frowned. "Did you?"

"Yes, several Christmases. She's a chancer, a real mover I reckon, and out on the hunt all the time."

Vera sighed. The gulf between her mother's thinking and the way she was trying to develop her own was widening.

"She's been helpful. More importantly, Mum, if you must know, I'm trying to get my head sorted out. I've got someone to talk to about things and it's helping. I'm not quite there yet but I think I want to get used to the idea of Alistair not being here and actually I'd like to not want him back." Vera smiled a weak smile. "There, I've said it. I've not said that before." She looked pleased. "I'd like to not want him back," she repeated.

"But", said Myra, "what will you do for money, love. He's got to provide, he can't have this house ..."

"I'm not there yet."

"And what about Christmas?" Myra was about to say, but on sensing the new fragility in her daughter she said: "Let me sort out those bulbs for you that have been hanging about outside. They'll make a nice show in Spring." Vera felt the heat of tears, and gratitude that her mother had stepped aside from her usual responses.

"Better have a gin before I start," said Myra, looking cheeky. Vera smiled, opening the cupboard where the Bombay was kept.

\* \* \* \*

They were in her father's Cadillac, passing the place where Route 95 moves through Fort Myers. Her father in the driver's seat right next to her seemed a long way away. Without looking, she was aware of the distinguished profile of neatly curved nose and smooth jaw, indicating German ancestry, his full head of hair greying evenly. After three days in her parent's house the glass was well established and thick around her, the pale green room far away. She looked out from the smooth gliding air-conditioned cave that accentuated her separation from anything living. Shoppers wearing shirts decorated with palm trees and sunsets were buying from watermelon stands, or lifting huge sacks of oranges into the trunks of their cars, the heat of the Florida sun warming their arms and backs. She felt cut off and anaemic, forced to join the white skinned folk driving to the shopping malls or take away food outlets, for whom sweat was abhorrent.

    The visit had been mainly spent in the permanently air-conditioned apartment. They had eaten out at formal fashionable restaurants in the evenings, twice joined by friends, and the conversation evolved around the failures of the Golf Club committee to keep out poor players. It was as if the violence and loss of lives in the illegal war in Iraq, so present and vivid in the UK news and in Saxon's life, so protested about, did not exist. They had sat on her parents' covered verandah and watched the golf course; they had exchanged Christmas gifts. She had slept in the blue and yellow guest suite with its laundered sheets, matching monogrammed towels and shell soaps. There were no signs of the childhood she was now reliving in the green room in South London and no natural reference to it. Saxon realised that her parents had never spoken to her about what she was like as a child or about what they had done as a family, the three of them, in Europe. Had she ever had toys or created things? If so they must have been discarded at each of their many moves. The only photographs were of her father's business awards and handshakes with famous people, no sign of the dark carved Spanish furniture whose doors were too solid for her child's hands to open; or the exquisitely painted chests of Italy and exotic German china. Some of her mother's beautiful needlework decorated the white and silver rooms, but only those in muted beige and soft peach colours that would not jar. Where had the hot shades of Europe and the creative mess of painting gone? Saxon wondered whether she had ever brought a splash of colour into their lives or ever been allowed to make a mess.

    They moved to Germany after Spain and Saxon's mother retreated further, and the myth of her being someone who needed looking after grew. "Tell your father to look after me," she would whisper from the white sheets of her bed before Saxon walked the mile to school by herself each morning. She never told her mother about the boys who waited to pee on her from between the cracks in the wooden fence, or about the large man who always watched her as she came along and whispered something in German she did not understand. One day he showed her what he grew between his legs. She thought there was something wrong with him and felt sorry.

These memories were more alive in her as she made this journey to the airport than at any other time. She had never made friends in Germany, but that was where she had learned her scholastic discipline and developed a desire for the control of excellence. In her isolation in the car she watched the warm-blooded life of the people outside, and wondered if they minded mess, if they were happy, if they had arrived at a state of acceptance as to their lot, even peace. She agreed with Walden that most people lived in a state of quiet desperation. Now that she had put together the flesh and blood parents with the ones she had spoken about in the green room in South London she realised the depth and intransigence of the glass. That procedure Max had outlined for her: either perfect control or perfect mess. Well, yes, this is where she had learned it, at her parents' side and for their sake, and it had probably started after her brother's death when she was three years old. The point was, could she unlearn it and lean into the 'third position'? Would it stop weird things happening? At least here, in Florida, she had not seen her dark stalker.

The digging about in her inner world had exposed a sense of herself that was built upon her skill at governing order over all that was irrational, never showing need of any kind, never letting go, or getting close. But the idea of change, of finding this third position where she developed more tolerance of those things she had banished, such as feelings, and got to know them more safely so they did not leak out and do damage – this she understood intellectually, but oh how to do it? How to practise it in her present world she and the glass had created? She breathed deeply in the soft leather seat. It wasn't as if she hadn't tried! She had tried to let go a little! And each time it had ended in disaster. The pain of failure at relationships because of her terror of closeness and of not being able to control her body or tolerate feeling. Whilst the glass was cold and unyielding and shut her out from others and others from her, it offered protection and was a comfort. It was what she understood best. In accepting it she would never have to look again at the painful things she now knew were there, nor would she have to work at change. She just could not run the risk of humiliation and mess, it would destroy her forever. And if those voices were right, if she was a potential murderer, then was it not better that she held on to the glass and never let that potential out? The glass must win! And she had her work. She knew she had always been good at that, and soon she would be back to it properly she felt sure.

The face of Lewis appeared, and she was reminded, as they passed the manicured lawns of Pine Ridge, of his exasperation during the summer months after they had agreed to remain in their separate apartments. It was not what he wanted. He wanted to help her trust and let go; he would be there for her, he would hold her as she learned surrender. Because he considered it important for their relationship and he had seen her ability to be warm and spontaneous. He believed it was in her, and he wanted to shake her. She saw it in his tight face, the way his jaw had receded, and mouth formed a thin line. She had experienced all this as if it were happening to someone else. She saw herself resisting him, knowing at the same time that it would most probably lead to the end. But she could not, after Hong Kong, take any more risks. Their living together would have meant being exposed in her entirety, and there would be nowhere to hide.

"You're the tin woman and the cowardly lion all in one. You have no heart! The nearest you get is everyone else's hearts through your doctor's gloved hands..." He had never spoken to her so aggressively and she had recoiled. If she felt hurt, it was far away. If she allowed herself to get close to that hurt, it would break her in two. Perhaps Lewis was right. The doctor's gloved hand she had perfected was the nearest she would get to touching the heart, and it would be someone else's, not her own.

But even that was taken away from her for now.

The glass was thick around her, distorting and exaggerating her thoughts. The fantasy that so strongly possessed her was that everyone else was living and she was dead or living completely alone on another planet.

In the house in Sarasota everything was white, silver and glass, and the plants were made of silk or plastic. Nothing was ever out of place, or spilled, fallen or messed up. The manufactured air created static and dried all moisture whilst those able to release their bodies to the rays of sunshine relaxed around the pool, diving in to keep cool. Saxon knew from her mother's tight suck on peppermint sweets and huge, watery eyes that she was drinking, and she wondered where she kept the bottles, or where she could throw up in a house with no unstructured corners.

Three days was the limit of her parents' tolerance for the disturbance visitors brought. She knew that her mother went around with the vacuum cleaner as soon as she was out of sight, swallowing up any trace of her daughter's visit. Saxon had once returned to the apartment having got part of the way to the airport in her hire car and realised she had forgotten her parents' gift. It was not a gift she liked nor was it anything she might wear. A pink T-shirt embossed with a sparkling unicorn. But she felt guilty and rude. She had rung the bell and her mother had answered. "I realised I left your lovely present behind." she had said. And her mother had shrugged, looking off guard, pulling off the purple gloves used for cleaning. She could see, just from the entrance to the room where she had slept, that her mother had stuffed the T-shirt into the bin that had been brought out of the bathroom. The bin that Saxon made sure she always emptied into a plastic bag and took away with her lest her mother be aware of any intimate details.

That scene, prompted by her unexpected return, of the guest room where she had slept being scoured for traces of her presence, when Saxon knew the maid was due the next day, made her feel she could just be poisonous.

This visit they had asked her formally about her work, and she had had to tell them that there was no promotion to clinical director. But she could not tell them why, letting them presume it was something to do with the bureaucracy of nationalised medical services they never understood.

Her father had frowned. "I never did understand why you insisted on staying in the British Health Service," he said. "You must come out here. You could make bundles of dough out here." Her father, once so European, had caught Americanisms from his wife of all these years, and from living in Florida for so long. Saxon just shrugged. She could not tell them anything.

There had been one day alone with her mother, when her

father had gone to a directors' meeting in Tampa. Mother had taken her to the Country Club for lunch. Saxon looked at this mother and was startled to realise that she was thinking "This is the body out of which I emerged, whose breast I once suckled". Had holding a newborn baby made her think about these things? She wondered what she might say to her mother now that she had started thinking about her childhood. Would she be able to ask her about her brother? Or tell her about Hong Kong?

The Country Club was filling up with smartly dressed older couples in designer golf wear and perfect coiffures. The table was covered in a perfect white cloth and the waiter brought sea shrimps and clams on a bed of iceberg lettuce. They drank cold Californian Chardonnay.

"Are you happy, Mother?" she asked.

"Happy dear, of course, I have everything I need."

"But, happy. I've been thinking about it recently."

Her mother's eyes glinted, the lids shutting over them like a Brazilian lizard. Her lips pursed. "Don't spoil this lunch."

"Can't I ask you, Mother? I've noticed that…"

Her mother cut her in mid-sentence. "Don't! Just don't, Saxon, don't you dare prod me with your medical ways. I'm not getting into this again. You know how it upsets me."

She had once tried to get her mother into rehab, and it had ended in disaster.

"I'm in therapy," she said suddenly, not anticipating she would confide this to her mother, but wanting to break the glass suddenly, to see if she could. To find that third position.

Her mother shrugged. "So is half the world," she said. It was like a slap. This is new, thought Saxon, I would not have felt that before.

She blinked, "So, you're not curious?" She was trying to keep in this new third position, not total control but not messy, just experimenting with being playful, but it was very painful.

"It's nothing to do with me." Her mother put a forkful of shrimp between her lipsticked lips. "You're grown up now with your own life all those miles away in London." Her mother did not like London. It was disorganised and full of strange people from Eastern Europe not unlike the gypsies from her own childhood that she preferred to forget. It was also full of English gentlefolk, like her mother-in law, whose eyes and complexion Saxon had inherited, who had made her feel small.

Saxon kept going although her heart was racing and her lips dry. "I've found myself talking about Begonia, and Spain."

Her mother's eyes looked steely.

"I've been remembering Spain and being a little girl in Spain. How it was when you were painting, Mother, and playful then, and learning the flamenco—"

Her mother cut her off again. "I don't want to talk about it," she said in a choked voice. "You know all too well what happened there and it's unfair of you to bring it up when I've brought you to a nice lunch here."

"But", Saxon persisted, "when is the time to speak to you, daughter to mother? I wondered whether you would tell me yourself. You have never talked about it, about that time when Tom …" she tailed off for her mother's face had closed down completely. "Surely it's something we should talk about, isn't it?"

"You have no idea what you are talking about. The matter was a long time ago and it is closed. I won't be upset! What are you trying to do to me, Saskia?" Her mother's eyes swam with the water of self-pity.

"I'm sorry. I was hoping that it might not be still so raw after all this time. I am sorry. But that time affected me too, the way things closed down after that time," she could not say it properly, "and I am reliving some of it in my …" She saw again her mother's closed off face and knew that she would get no further. But she felt a surge of what must be pride at asking for something for herself, that she had tried to open the door. She was starting to get a feel for what it meant. She felt exhausted suddenly.

They sat in silence, eating awkwardly and in some discomfort, the waiters hovering with five different kinds of bread rolls, iced water and more wine, the flick of their white napkins distracting. Her mother waved to friends on the other side of the room.

"Do you ever wonder what my life is like?" asked Saxon.

Her mother answered immediately, "Of course dear, you are always on my mind, my concern. A mother is always a mother."

"No, about my being a doctor. And about not being married."

"Well, it's what you always wanted, dear, to be a doctor. And, well, I don't like to pry into your private life."

"Is it what you wanted for me, Mother?"

Her mother said nothing.

They continued their meal mostly in silence, exchanging superficial remarks about people in the room, her mother brightening a little at returning to her comfort zone. Outside in the Florida sunshine they walked toward the parking lot where her mother's silver Lincoln was parked in the shade. Saxon could sense that her mother was trying to work something out when she paused, and walked toward a hibiscus bush, their vivid red blooms wide open in the full force of the sun. Saxon followed her and watched as her mother paused, touching one of the red flowers lightly with her now soft artist's hands, and in a gentler voice said: "This reminds me of Spain. So much red there, the blooms, the dresses, the red sun too."

She looked up and Saxon saw a glimpse of the happy, dreamy, playful mother. "I had hopes then you see, high hopes, of being an artist like my great aunt. You liked to paint too, did you know that?" Saxon had no idea. She was enthralled at her mother's offering. She held her breath, never wanting it to stop. This is how it all might have been, she and her mum having a little chat about the past and feeling nostalgic …

"I haven't been much of a mother to you I know that." Her hand dropped away from the red bloom and the hanging down of her head and droop of her shoulders signified utter defeat. She began putting on the cotton gloves she always carried. Her mouth became set. Saxon was too overwhelmed to speak.

"Nothing can be done about it now." Her mother walked toward the car ahead of her, continuing to look defeated and closed.

She could not tell her parents about Hong Kong. She could not tell them how odd she felt about her life suddenly. She could not ask them questions about her early life. She'd written a list of things to ask them, in the small notebook she had bought as a nod to Max. She wanted to know about the places they had travelled, about Spain and Begonia, and most of all about Tomas, the child mother had lost, about their marriage. But in the white apartment where everything was safely sealed in, she could not open her mind or her mouth.

So, the glass world her parents had taken forty-five years to perfect had somehow won. Her mother's drinking, her father's infidelities and of course the death of their son had threatened to shatter it many times. But the glass world had become the container for the way to be for both of them. A way to be without shock or challenge, where life continued smoothly with no feeling.

Saxon was outside it, in a glass world of her own.

And it was suddenly over. When she got out of this smooth Cadillac, checked her bags, went through security, she would be on a plane on her way to – where now? Home? To Lewis, would he want her, could she change the pattern, could she break the glass? She remembered with a lurch of the heart how tenderly he could hold her, despite all their difficulties. Could they start again? Could she try to be close, to recruit Max's help with the problems she had with intimacy? Lewis! She realised how little they had seen each other recently and when they did meet how sad his face looked, as if he knew he had lost her. She had felt guilty and brushed it away with impatience, blaming him for being emotional and demanding. And yet he was neither of these. Max was right: she could not bear feeling, her own or other people's. She could not bear it when she thought she should feel but could not. She was no longer top of the class and in charge but in the mess of feeling bad and guilty. Guilt again! When people wanted something of her, she felt under demand and often, as if being used. But a small voice said inside, what if Lewis really cares about you, Saskia? He called her by her proper name. He thought her a woman whilst she thought of herself as an automaton.

She felt homeless and pointless. She belonged nowhere, she was no one.

She leaned back into the soft leather seat of the Cadillac and looked away from the window and down at her hands lying still on her green dress. Green silk, lustrous, and beautiful, like the moss when she was a child in Spain. A dress she had chosen in Hong Kong before the boat trip. How could she wear it now, with all its associations? The thought struck her forcibly. Again, she realised there was so much wrong with her, with the way she was. She was like a person with lots of pieces of a jigsaw, but all mixed up. Nothing fitted.

She felt deeply and unbearably sad. As she sat with this sadness the leaden quality with which she had become so familiar pulled her down, not into the green chair in the pale green room, but into the deep viscera of her own body.

She was inside a red cavern. It was wet and pulsating. She had to hold on to what looked like hanging gristle or she would have been swept away. Ridges packed with crystals lined the ceiling and small creatures on podgy infant legs with no heads, but huge beaks picked away at them. The ribbed ceiling seemed to brace itself, as if trying to hold firm. The creatures worked their way along on automatic and she recognised them as the pickaxe people who had been living inside her chest. She watched with a horrified interest, and with disgust. She felt sick as she hung onto the gristle, a sinewy stalactite reminding her of the old hanging straps of the London Underground she had travelled daily as an undergraduate. She kept trying to swallow. It was very dark, and she was utterly alone. Dense patches of white flesh, like butcher's suet, patched the ribcage ceiling which gave out no light. But the parts that were skinned remained alive, steadily bleeding in tiny rivulets. She could see the swellings of bruises on the softer sides of the rib room. There was the pounding of a great pump which surged with a great roar and caused the creatures to be folded back against the sides. She wanted to reach out to the places of softness because they felt so innocent. She was still hanging on, wondering "What is this place?" An answer came: "This is the Heavy Heart."

The creatures inside were hammering with their little pickaxes and in the hurt and bruising, there was resignation. "It doesn't matter what it feels like, pretend you don't feel anything, you don't want anything ... harden yourself to it". Her heart was racing. There was a moment when she feared that the little androgynes might turn on her, pinning her down like Gulliver with their pickaxe heads and threads. She drew back, came out of the image, felt her head swimming, her eyes staring, her mind confused.

Am I mad? Is this psychosis? She kept resting back in the seat, grateful for its support, shaken by what her mind and imagination could produce.

But there was another sensation, not rational, but quite compelling, that she had visited something wounded that had been there inside her own heart for a very long time. It had drawn her into itself, she could not have contrived it. It was quite different from the sharp-edged glass with its distortions, and unlike the lead which corseted her chest. She was curious, and horrified.

"You're not with us are you?" said the voice of her father. "Not slipping into your dream world, are you?"

Saxon was startled by his voice and by what he said.

"My dream world," she asked. "What dream world?"

"Oh, you were always going there as a little girl."

Saxon was interested. "You've never mentioned it before."

"Didn't need to, it was as much as we could do to keep you out of it, keep you on the straight and narrow. You couldn't have become a doctor if we'd let you dream your life away."

She felt cold. "These dreams, what were they?"

"Damned if I know. Your own little world. Made up things all the time. Drove your mother and I to distraction."

"I never knew about this."

"We managed to get you out of it, thank God. You see kids all the time, think they can live in a dream world, you see them now, ageing hippies on the street without bricks and mortar, without any skills under their belts. Hopeless."

"But where do you think it comes from?"

"What comes from?"

"The dreams, the dream world."

"It doesn't matter where it comes from Saxon, it's a parent's job to get a child out of it." Her father's grip on the wheel had tightened, his mouth was set. She had seen this a million times. The hardening of oneself for life.

"But why shouldn't children have dreams, don't they mean something?"

"They mean that a child isn't paying enough attention to

reality. You soon gave it all up when you saw sense. Never was anyone who became so dedicated to her books than you once you got the right idea." Her father looked at her curiously, not without concern. "You're not having some sort of mid-life crisis, are you?"

Saxon was silent. "Was that in Germany?"

"I don't remember. Sax, you've not been yourself this time I have to say it. I mentioned it to your mother who thought you'd probably been working too hard because of all these changes in that wretched health system you insist on working for. You could make a mint out here with your qualifications, your British accent and all that. I've told you."

Saxon was silent, thinking. After Spain, Germany, trading in dreams and playfulness for work and achievement.

"What did I dream about, Father?"

"Oh, you insist, don't you." he shrugged. "Don't rightly remember, although I do know you imagined yourself as some sort of dancer. Prancing and dancing all over the place dressed up in the maid's skirts. Your mother's high heels, doing one of those flamenco dances".

Saxon stilled at his tone. Disapproval. Gone wild. Bad for you like the shoes. Never know where it will all end.

Then she said, "Flamenco." She loved, loved the sound of that word.

"It was that Spanish woman that got you into that". Her father brooded moodily over the steering wheel.

"So much happened in Spain, Father. Mother burned my dancing shoes." He looked at her sharply.

"I suppose all this questioning and digging about in the past is to do with therapy. Your mother told me."

Saxon was in it now and wanted to continue, at least she had to try.

"Father, please tell me, what happened when my brother was born."

"You don't mention that."

"Surely you can tell me about it. I tried asking Mother and I could see it still upsets her. Was Tom a stillbirth or did he live a few hours?"

Her father was silent.

"Even if you cannot answer this, please tell me something really important, and yes this has come out of the therapy investigation. Was Tom's death my fault?" Her heart was beating furiously, her mouth dry but something in her was stirring itself alive.

Her father was startled. They had arrived at Southwest Florida Regional Airport. He breathed a big sigh and turned off the ignition.

"Of course not, Saxon, what a ridiculous idea. Is this shrink putting those ideas into your head?"

"It was never explained. And it seems that so much started to go wrong after that. For you and Mother I mean." She could not say, and I've got this glass that gets in the way of getting close to other people. That's why I've no husband and you have no grandchildren. She could not ask "Am I a murderer?" The very words seemed ridiculous in the Florida heat and travellers waiting to check their travel bags.

"We've done alright," her father said quietly.

"I'm not sure I have," was all Saxon could bring herself to say.

"Look at you, a fine doctor, a cardiologist. I'm very proud."

At least that's something she thought. "But I'm not a whole person, am I?"

Her father looked at her, not understanding.

"Don't start getting introspective, Sax." He looked at her, suddenly concerned. "It's the menopause I suppose. Your mother, well you know, she had an awful time."

She gathered her things from the car. Her father watched her, suddenly unnerved and wanting to make up for all the things unsaid and unasked.

"What about your fella, what's his name, something very English?"

She was surprised he had remembered Lewis.

"Lewis."

"Yes, Lewis. I always think of Alice in Wonderland."

They were both, at the end, reluctant to part. Right there, at the end of her visit and about to fly to England for Christmas she was nearer to making some contact with the feel of her past.

She so wanted to find out the child she had been and who she could be now. She knew that it was probably far too late, but she felt child-like suddenly, and afraid, wanting her father to give her a shape and identity and most of all approval, or even, love.

But the people in uniforms who move on cars at airports were approaching, which made her father ready to be off, back to the certainty of the white and silver apartment where everything stayed the same.

"I'd better be going."

She watched him get back into those warm leather seats, tuck in his seatbelt and look round before leaving the curb, not to see her or to wave, but to check the traffic.

She stayed at the kerbside until long after the Cadillac was out of sight. She wondered whether she would ever be back here.

\* \* \* \*

On her flight to London, she fell into a reflective interlude. The load was light, and she had no companions either side. She ate sparingly, for once curious rather than impatient about what was happening to her. Her briefcase, filled to overflowing with notes and papers that would normally occupy her attention, remained in the overhead locker unopened. She leant back into the seat and realised how little she had done this in her lifetime, a lifetime of sitting on the edge of seats, leaning forward, or running, hurrying, headfirst. She thought again of what she had learned in the pale green room. "I've lived on automatic, without dreams. Because dreams are irrational, pointless, and I've just had that confirmed." Her mother's voice, "You used to like painting"; her father's, "You were always in the dream world". But what if that little girl had been expressing a playful and creative self that could feel real and did not need the glass? Might she have been able to grow if Tomas had lived and she had been free to also live fully? She felt suddenly overwhelmed, and deeply depressed. So, if I've banished some aspect of myself, have I been trying to kill something off all this time that actually belongs to me but has become projected onto someone else, onto a vulnerable tiny baby? Was that a bit of me I banished to the filthy waters of life?

Had she been alright before Hong Kong? The permanent exhaustion, and tension, never relieved, that iron grip always on the back of her neck and down her spine, the heavy chest and sense of impending doom. She had been taking a mixture of amphetamine to keep alert and benzodiazepine to go to sleep. Then, some mysterious inner force had propelled her into holding the baby on the Hong Kong junk and it had ended up in the harbour water. An unconscious act that would determine the rest of her life. Had she thrown the child over the edge, or had the wake of the ferry caused her to stumble and the baby to leave her arms? She just did not know.

The image of Lewis returned and an unwelcome feeling of dread. His was the face of the man who, for the last six years, had always been there, who she had taken for granted because he never asked for anything. He waited for her, he was patient, loving, accepting. His love unstated, definite. He loved her in a way she had not been able to fully recognise. He loved her despite how she had been. And she had let him down; she had rejected his love because she had rejected herself.

Could she become Saskia, rather than Saxon? Could she connect with this original name chosen for her by her mother because of Rembrandt's wife, because Rembrandt had been able to create his dream, to bring light into darkness.

She realised as she leant back in the aircraft seat that the mysterious sensations she contacted in the green chair in the green room had come to her before, in different forms. The sight of the beating heart and thinking it brave; witnessing the love between families of patients; the little boy's posy; the painting of Torcello in Venice where she had been first with Lewis. And probably earliest of all, in Spain with its hibiscus bushes and the colours of paint. All of them involved some dialogue within her body where physical symptoms took the place of sentences with feelings.

These remembrances took her to Lewis, to her very first image of him pruning the rose bushes in his garden in Sussex when Virginia was alive. A man of medium height looking very ordinary with a serious face and blue eyes like hers. "Hello" he had said "you must be Virginia's friend named after Rembrandt's wife. She's told me about you, all good stuff!", and smiled, showing neat white teeth. Virginia, her dear friend from medical school died a year later from complications after routine surgery. Too awful, too young, and before decisions on children. Lewis was inconsolable as the bereaved husband, and they had drifted together into an easy companionship where Saxon felt relaxed because there were no demands. She was good at practical care and support. But after they had become lovers, she became nervous, withdrawn, sometimes angry for no reason. She watched her weight obsessively and imagined he was looking at her. She became on alert, vigilant like a startled horse.

Lewis was the same with people as he was with roses. Firm and tender, appreciating new blooms. He probably knew her better than anyone and probably understood what she was trying to face in the pale green room. He had once asked her about children and she said that she had made up her mind about it all a long time ago, it was out of the question. She thought then that he looked sad, and a little afraid. He had tried again, twice, to engage her, quietly insistent, she the stubborn prickly rose. She had buried these interactions deep, not wanting the thought that she might have let him down to disturb her further. Her heart ached. It was too awful to consider that he might have wanted children and now it was too late.

How could she have got it all so wrong?

## 13

MAX and Emily sat either side of the wood fire in the cottage. The village carol singers had made their Christmas Eve visit and sung for them under the star-lit sky before being welcomed to warm themselves by the fire and enjoy Emily's mince pies and mulled wine. Silent Night. Holy Night.

Emily had been brought to life by Christmas activities. Her eyes sparkled as she and Max went out to the edge of the garden to dig up the tree they had had for every Christmas at the cottage since they were first married. She had decorated it with stars, moons and angels she had made, and with tiny plain white lights. Max noticed with fresh eyes her gaze upon the tree and her enchantment took him back to the innocent rapture he and Margaret had enjoyed at Christmas until they were ten years old. In that instant some deep part of him recognised why he had chosen her for his wife. She would, forever, link him with the innocent past he had lost so abruptly and to the possibility of playful enchantment. Emily loved the pagan celebration of solstice and the theme of new life in the Christmas story. These simple treats, together with the Christmas trappings such as chocolate bells and stolen, encouraged her child self to blossom in a positive way.

Max felt more relaxed than for a long time. He was allowing something of her aliveness, her positive and creative child-like energy, to move in to him. The tensions created by her sullen silence and his bitterness were gone.

On his return to London from the cottage after reliving the time of Margaret's death he had viewed Emily with more genuine compassion. There was more space between them and his fondness, even love for her was able to come nearer to the front. She had not asked him about his time away but when they had arrived together at the cottage in preparation for Christmas she noticed immediately the change in atmosphere, as well as the clearing of books and magazines and the packs of old papers. She had looked at him curiously.

"It feels different in here." Then, mysteriously, "Have you been clearing out some old cobwebs?" and touched his arm.

She set to almost at once to make the cottage warm and

glowing with Christmas life and spirit.

She had looked happy as they did things together, simple things such as making food and gathering kindling on their walk for their evening fire. He wanted soon to find a way to speak to her of his experiences on the beach just a week ago and he needed to find a way to speak to her about his changing needs.

"You look happy," he said, smiling.

"Just now, I think I am, just in this moment.'

"Is it Christmas that warms you?'

"You are warmer," she said.

"Yes, I guess I am. So, how are you these days?" He had not asked her this question for a very long time. She looked startled, then cornered and frightened.

"What is it?" she asked suspiciously.

Max smiled. "Well, we haven't had much of a heart to heart lately have we?"

"I know that you've been moving away from me," she said, looking at him keenly.

Max breathed in deeply. Then he said, "Yes, I've felt that too."

Her eyes darted from side to side.

"Let's not let our fear get in the way," he said.

"Have you stopped caring for me?" she asked, in a trembling voice.

"No, I haven't stopped caring for you. But I have become aware that I am very tired. And—

"Yes, you are tired of looking after me. I know."

He paused. "I want us to be honest together. It's true that I have found your illness demanding at times. And recently I have had some difficult experiences of my own that have taken a lot of my energy. I've spread myself too thinly and have had very little left to give," he said. "That's why I decided to come down here for that weekend on my own. I felt very unhappy, very disturbed." He paused.

"It's that patient, I know it is!" she cried.

Max held up his hand.

"No, the work is OK, Emily. It is true that the person you saw with the black aura is in a very troubled state and she is a worry. But it was me, I was troubled by images of Margaret, and all the memories suddenly came back to haunt me. It was probably triggered by another of my patients who is uncannily like her, she even says the same things and has the similar expressions after suffering a personal loss." He speaks slowly, trying to express himself to him wife in a way that is new and unpractised. He realised how afraid he was of revealing his own feelings.

"I have also had the feeling of falling into something unknown. And there was also an intuition that it is time," he added.

He felt Emily listening more actively than before and decided to continue telling her about himself.

"I have always known that I felt troubled about Margaret and the way she died. Those years leading up to it…. Of course, I've always known intellectually that in making a burden of guilt I was sort of keeping her alive. But I realise now that I haven't been able to actually touch the feeling, and so it remained entrenched. I've been like the Ancient Mariner, and it's influenced me very powerfully, and unconsciously."

"Always that, the unconscious," said Emily unexpectedly.

Max was concentrating on what he needed to say next.

"It's hard to grasp something like guilt, particularly guilt for something you cannot possibly be guilty for, because it blinds you. You can only see its corrosive results. The way it can sabotage happiness, the way it can be the driver to helping anyone else but yourself, the way it can get in the way of allowing other people to get close or understand you because guilt closes off true feeling, it makes vulnerability impossible."

"You are hard to give things to these days."

"Am I?"

"Well, you have been shut off and so I just hide."

"But we've not been shut off to each other these last two days."

"No, that's right. It's been nice. Like the old days," she paused. "I do really want to try and make you happy."

His heart was touched. He breathed out a long breath. The Guardians were close by, smiling.

"I want to tell you more. This patient who reminds me of Margaret. She is not a psychologically minded person like many people who come into psychotherapy. In fact, if it were not for her husband abandoning her, I doubt she would consider it. And she was pushed into it by the errant husband. So, she's had a serious life event, and a pretty abusive background. She has fantastic common sense and a sort of animal instinct. You know that I'm always drawn to that question about what is it that helps people to become self-reflective, what helps people change from destructive habits into helpful ones? This woman is using me as a safe sounding board to work out a new way. I can see that she has it inside her, this means to survive. But I think now that Margaret never did have it inside her."

He paused, his hands together around the mulled wine. Emily was listening intently, her pale face flushed with the wine and the fire.

"What happened could never have been your fault," she said and the honesty and simplicity of her tone moved directly into the sore place in Max's heart like an unexpected gift.

"I am beginning to accept that now. Thank you." He went on. "When I came here that time, I felt angry, really, really angry. I had never known such a visceral feeling. Rage, true rage."

Emily looked frightened suddenly.

"I think you have been cross with me too."

Max did not answer straight away.

"I have never known anger like it. I can analyse it of course, find meaning in it, but I realised after a day on the beach wrestling with these feelings that I had never allowed myself to be truly angry at the senseless, random death of my parents. That drunken kid, it was just mindless…

And then having to grow up so soon… I'm not sorry for myself, it's just that I can see how I plunged into a grown-up world taking responsibilities way beyond my years…"

"And then you got me," she said.

"Yes, I got you."

Emily looked down, unsure what was coming and afraid. But here they were talking at last and warmly and in the best of places. And at least she had him to herself for a while, no patients for him to become distracted into.

"When I went to Bhutan, after Oxford, you and I were

meeting but unsure about a future together, I was still clearly troubled and wanting something deep, wanting to get right down to fundamentals... I had a series of profound experiences. Walking up the mountain..." He broke off, remembering.

"I remember how you spoke to me about that, Max. And then you went into the Order. Does that phrase "The door is always open for you" still carry the same meaning?"

Max eyes filled. He had forgotten how they could communicate, how she had listened, how patient she could be in her often-silent world. "Yes," he said simply, "yes it does, completely. And I am so touched that you should remember it."

"I have never forgotten it," said Emily quietly. "But I have wondered whether you had."

She had known him through all these experiences. On the other side of her illness there was something very clear. She was really trying to be with him. He felt some excitement stir.

"Emily, I have loved you so much."

Emily was silent, noticing the past tense.

"Is your love in the past? Have I not been a good wife..."

Silence. Then she nodded. "It's sex then, isn't it? You've met someone. It's that blonde patient. I knew she would take you away from me!"

"No, no, no!"

Max stood up taking deep breaths and put another log on the fire. It was part of a dead branch off the old ash tree he had cut during the summer. Only a few months ago when things seemed so OK, so much the same. Now everything had changed.

For a moment Max felt like a spectre of Alistair. Was he just as callous, challenging his poorly wife, even thinking of casting her off because he could no longer look after her?

"I feel freer than I have done for a long time. And I can see that I have neglected you."

"No," she broke in.

"Yes, I've done all the 'right' things, but I haven't tried to stay with our areas of difficulty. I have just moved away from it, and let your illness take the blame. I think that I've fallen into a martyr's response and colluded into making you a depriving brute. I have shut myself away from allowing you to give to me."

"All this psychobabble! 'Brute', 'martyr'. But it is true you've not been receptive to me." She paused. "And it's true that I have turned away from sex."

Max looked at her fully and moved forward to take her hands.

## 14

THE day after Boxing Day dawned with a peculiar menace. Vera felt increasingly detached from her own body without the cutting to bring her back into focus. She often felt as if she were watching herself from high up on the ceiling. She had tried her best for Christmas, but it had been dismal. No one had had the heart or energy for it. They had just gone through the motions to get through a day, because it was there.

Vera's mother was preparing to go out for the day. She was excited because new Manchester friends were visiting relatives in London, and she was to join them. There had been moments of warmth between her and Vera. She came down the stairs dressed up, a cream-coloured skirt that creased angrily around her thighs, and a tense angora sweater knitted to resemble the skin of a leopard. A tiger-print scarf was fastened in a brass ring around her neck. The white stilettos were scuffed at the back. The image of these shoes, incongruously large on the end of her mother's stick legs, and the double click as she walked, were part of Vera's childhood memory. Myra's face was painted in bright colours, the edges of brown foundation not quite meeting the beginning of the dyed hair line. She had a habit of fiddling with bits of dark hair that hung over her face and giving Vera a twisted grin, her pearl nail varnish matching the lipstick (you must wear lighter things as you get older, she advised). Vera was distracted by the pain of her situation, and by the failure of her Christmas. She did not notice the slightly guilty look on her mother's face as she was eager to be off, to enjoy a day out, to leave the house she would describe to friends as a morgue. And to leave her daughter to her own devices.

Signs of Christmas lay in the two boys' empty rooms. Games had been begun and not put away. Rubbish bins were full of discarded tinsel and shiny wrapping, Sellotape ends, cards and gift tags that had been barely looked at. Gifts from elderly northern relatives lay on the floor under the tree where they had been opened. The debris brought a kind of sickness with it, Vera's usual methodical tidiness as scorned as was she herself.

There was too much food now left in the fridge and unopened treats lay inert on larder shelves: tinned pate, peaches, stuffed almonds. Any hope that Christmas might have revived her was dashed, as was the hope that because of 'her most secret knowledge' Alistair would come back. It was based upon the illusion that Alistair still cared deep down, and all Vera had to do was find a way to trigger this part of him. But it hadn't worked that way. She had not been able to sit round the table with her two sons chatting naturally or eating supper by candlelight so that they became a unit. Luke would have just one more night here before returning for the Lent term, then it would be Easter and who knew what then. Alistair might have succeeded in getting her out of the house. They might all be crammed in some flat, she might be...

Neither of the boys knew what to say to her about the new arrangements. They saw how thin and distracted their mother was becoming but they felt helpless. Dominic covered his fear with a secret contempt. He was embarrassed. He thought Mum should just get over it and get on. After all, so many people got divorced, it was what to expect these days, and he liked the new woman in his father's life, she was bright and fun – and rich. But he felt he had to show a display of concern. "I'm so sorry, Mum" he said, with what sounded like sincerity. "It must be awful for you."

Vera smiled, said she would be OK, told him not to worry about her. She did not want it affecting his travel plans. At the end of the summer term in May he was to join Leo in Tanzania. Dominic was relieved. Mum was being a good sport, although he was not entirely convinced. He looked at her from all of his nineteen years and realised that he did not really know her. She had always been something of a cipher for other people. He had no idea what she really liked or might do with herself without her children and husband. He didn't want to think about it. He could see his father's need for elevation and admired it. Arabella was very well connected.

Vera and Leo had had awkward telephone conversations from Tanzania, where the lines were always bad and their conversations echoed, like this large, silent house, and Vera found she had little to say to her son. She had read all about Tanzania and the building schools project and had questions prepared, but on hearing his voice she lost the words. "Poor

Leo," she muttered, whatever would he think now of his home life. But Dominic knew that Leo was OK with it. The boys had known about some of their father's earlier conquests and half expected this all to happen. They knew it was what a lot of men did at a mid-life point, especially if their wives had not kept up. And Mum was, after all, the best mum in the world and still very pretty, but a simple soul and not, no she was not, cool.

Vera had no way of knowing what Alistair had said to his sons about their mother. His flight into his new life had unleashed a fresh unscrupulousness. Vera knew that staff at the school looked at her with unease. She thought that Alistair might even have indicated to the staff that his soon to be ex-wife was unstable and to be handled carefully. She imagined him telling them that he had seen to it that she was receiving professional help, that he was to be informed if anything untoward were going on. Her heart sank at the realisation she was thinking in this way, the way that Michaela thought, always suspicious about men and their motives, always seeing the worst.

Since he had been the prime instigator of the boys' education and had been at the school himself, he wove a certain authority around him. Vera had always felt out of her depth, and left everything, bar the summer picnics and looking right to her husband.

Leo and Dominic had several friends whose parents were in the mess of divorce, two of the fathers having found other women. The boys could easily think that if this was one of the norms for a man then it was in their interests to be flip about it all, and they should just grit teeth and get on with it, as they had done when sent away to school at nine years old, some even younger. To be wrenched from home and not mind because it was part of being male had already taken an inner heroic slant and it did not do to have feelings about it.

Over supper on Christmas night Dominic had said Mark Holland's parents had split up. "It was all in the papers. His mother had a go at Mark's dad with a candlestick. One of the family heirlooms!"

Luke just looked sad.

"He had to have stitches."

"What did Mark think then?" asked Vera dully.

Dominic shrugged. "Dunno."

"How many stitches," asked Luke.

He shrugged again, and with his mouth full said, "Lots."

"I expect he felt stupid," said Luke darkly.

"Are many parents split up then?" asked Vera, in her choked voice.

Dominic was looking down and wishing he hadn't started it. That look in Mum's eyes, like the rabbit he had once found with its leg caught in the barbed wire fence at his Gran's. He hated it. It scared him and he hated to be scared. But he was the eldest. He should do something. Granny Myra was out in the back garden having a smoke.

"Never mind, Mum," he said trying to be bold, "it'll all be alright." He poured the water out of the glass jug very carefully.

"But it won't, Dom. It isn't. It's not what I want, not what I want at all. It's …" she couldn't finish because she was choked up and her boys had never seen her out of control, emotional. She saw the closed off looks come over their faces. She couldn't do this to them, she had to be strong, she had to show them she could cope, she mustn't make their home an unstable place, as hers had been.

Luke got off his chair and came round and put an arm around her as she was shaking.

A terrible silence descended with nothing to mediate it.

Dominic got away as soon as he could and went upstairs.

"What will happen to Mum?" said Luke, coming in to his brother's room looking worried.

"Oh nothing," said Dominic airily. "She'll soon get over it. It happens. I've heard of it. She'll find someone else too."

"And then there'll be another," said Luke glumly.

"At least we've got the skiing," they said to each other.

\* \* \* \*

Luke clung to his mother at every opportunity and crept down to the sofa where she was still sleeping at night. All the suggestions in books she had read, the conversations with Max about speaking to the boys, died on her lips. She had collected stones and positioned a line of them on a small table near where she slept. As often as she could she touched them, reminding herself that strength could come from within, that she had the potential for such strength, and she had to keep on believing in it. "Can I touch the stones?" Luke had asked.

She wanted to hold back the tide of events that were now racing out of control. She could not speak to her favourite child about her failure to hold on to his father and to keep them all together in cosy domesticity. She no longer knew what she could offer them. She had no power.

The failure of her Christmas hit her hard. And now, this day, her mother was out and her boys were on the flight to Geneva on route for Gstaad, their bags full of brightly coloured new skiing gear, woolly hats, gloves and snow boots.

Vera was yet again alone in the house, desolate, saddened to despair by the boys going, aware somewhere that the unit she had until so recently considered her family had plans from which she was completely excluded. She suspected that Dominic might, trained by his father to set himself after the main chance, be only too glad to be away from her in her current miserable state. She feared that the hunted looking creature she had become could only make her sons feel bad, and guilty. At least Leo was spared the sight of her. But for Luke, her special boy, it was all so unfair. He was too young for the burden of guilt.

There was the impossible knowledge that her own sons she had gestated inside her own body, nursed, loved, worried over, were right at this moment being seduced by a complete stranger who could only be interested because she wanted their father. They were being incorporated into another family unit from which she was actively barred.

The observer in her continued to feel quite separate from her body so these realisations did not take the form of active thinking, but hovered around her in what spiritualists call ether, within the quiet tomb of the empty house, in the faint fog which swam in front of her eyes, in the lead stomach that had become her permanent companion. She wandered about from room to room, as she had on so many days, the mocking gaiety of her Harrods-decorated Christmas tree glinting on the stairs. The expensive wrapping paper now discarded into black plastic bags had not helped to make her Christmas a happy one, nor brought back any of the substance from the past. The card with the stone circle placed so carefully by the front door had been knocked aside again and was lying somewhere and she had not looked to find it.

She wandered in and out of the boy's rooms picking up clothes and shoes, tidying playing cards, dominoes, emptying half-empty drink cans.

Coral had said, "It's all greed. Take what you can get, steal, grab, lust after anything you want until you get it and when it's lost its edge, dump it. Like the government with all the different services. Say anything to get what you want, and then do something completely different if it suits."

The thought that it was now all too late for Alistair to come back brought impossible feelings. If she allowed that thought to settle, her body would be filled with panic and her brain would splinter. Much better the position on the ceiling, out of it all.

She sat on the Ninja Turtle duvet cover on Luke's bed and looked at Donatello. A copy of *The Wind in the Willows* was on the floor. The homey comfort of the friends on the river, the lure of happy endings. She shook her head, trying to get control over herself. She must not panic, she must try and do something. She kept shaking her head to try to relieve it of its cotton wool substance. She had believed that the drive to get away from the narrow life of her mother and improve herself would mean that she would not have to look back. But a terrifying thought came into the cotton wool, what if she had been wrong? What if Amy Beckett, despite her abortions and being a single parent and living on welfare, was actually better off?

They had all said, when Vera announced she was to marry Alistair, the boss's son, "Take your chance, luvvie, go for what you want, you've got the looks, the figure. You're not without a brain in your head, take it, and more fool you if you don't." The voices that had urged her to move out of the estate had not done so themselves. She could not go back. But she could not imagine the movement forward either. She must stop these ruminations, but how?

Back in the kitchen she remembered that she must eat. She was too strict about her figure to have ever allowed herself to let go and enjoy eating. But she had to get strong, she had to get out of all this. Food might help. She fumbled with an opened packet of cream crackers. The pieces of cold turkey slid off the hard baked surface on to the floor. In the fridge was an untouched home-made trifle covered with little silver balls. The boys now chose brie, and Ben and Jerry's. Trifle's too naff, Mum. Had she not kept up?

As she closed the door on the trifle she wondered if there was a way she could save Luke for herself. Not let him go back to a school that taught boys to emulate the grasping ways of their fathers and to make strangers of their mothers. She might even think about going to live somewhere else, somewhere no one knew about, where no one would find her. The thoughts shocked and revived her a little. But she was unable to hold onto them.

She tried watching television to get her mind out of dwelling on things. An old black and white film of *Jane Eyre* with the wild image of Mr Rochester's mad wife in chains was too much, her black tangled hair on end. "See, see, that's what you're like now, good for nothing, mad, crazy," sneered the croaky voice that had got inside her as she switched channels. "Nothing left for you, dearie." The voice was winning. With a muted sob she collapsed onto the plumped-up sofa in the sitting room, decorated in blue peacocks, and closed her sore, dry eyes.

When she opened them, it was some time later and she remained transfixed, not moving, gazing out through the net curtains to the far-away world outside. She was becoming embalmed by the silence of the street upon which she lived, and its alien quality. The street was ghostly in its stillness. No trees bending or leaves whispering with the wind, no bird calling, no walkers, cars or children's bicycles, no chat. In the silence was an eerie emptiness as if everyone had gone away leaving their houses intact, and she were the only person remaining. Perhaps she was the only person remaining on the face of the earth, a person completely alone, barely alive, at the mercy of the ether and those unbidden voices. Despite the embalming process she shuddered. Can no one come and save me? Please.

Her whole mind was fibrillating like a quivering heart, her brain accelerating in sudden jerks, trying out half-completed sentences, odd voices and tones. Her pulse was racing, and her hands and feet ice cold. Her chest, now thin and fragile like the ribcage of a sparrow, was pressed with a great weight, so very tight, sucking in and swallowing air. How could she go on like this? She tried to think who she might be able to talk to. She knew Coral was at her mother's in Scotland; Michaela was skiing in France with a new lover; the mother of Luke's friend Jake was away with her family and after that there were only acquaintances, people she knew merely by sight. Even if she had had friends she wouldn't call anyway. She couldn't remember any numbers. She wouldn't know what to say.

Could she ring Dr Max? It was a weekend, he wouldn't be on call. And then a chilling thought she had not considered since she had come to feel Max to be her friend and on her side, and he had promised that all they shared was confidential: Max had known Alistair. Alistair might persuade Max to get her locked up.

She remained sitting on the blue peacock sofa, her hands by her side, taken over by this accelerating panic, her mind coping by splitting itself into fragments. Into bite-sized pieces like the dry turkey that slid onto the floor. Everything had become too much, she could no longer hold it all together.

She became a body, just sitting, with no one in charge. A body staring at the white nets shielding the street, the pretty veil she had chosen to screen the window so that people outside could not see in, becoming the veil now being drawn over the person she had been so far. And as it drew its filmy mask more tightly over her it began dividing, like an amoeba, into quite separate compartments, which arranged themselves in whatever space they could to shield each fragment. The body was hardly breathing, it had become merely a shell with its substance drained away. Then, as the light began to change outside, from white grey to blue grey, the body housing Vera found itself putting on the red cape coat which hung near the front door.

It seemed to be getting very dark as the body left the house. The row of trees in the square looked like the sharp-edged silhouettes Vera used to cut out from her grandmother's felt as a child, black, sinister and one-dimensional, not the living things that swayed and flowered green in summer. The body was wearing denim jeans and small flat shoes, which it had had on since the boys left at six that morning; it had been up since four. Under the red cape was a red cashmere sweater, a much-loved prize bargain from Barrymore, but the familiar feel of soft, cosy comfort on the body's skin had lost its attachment.

The body started walking, in the direction of the river, and sat in one of the small gardens opposite the darkened Board of Trade building, watching the lights on the Thames cruisers and boats as they motored each way up and down. It was a cold, grey and unforgiving evening, not much brightened by the lighting up of ropes of light beads strung between beacons that celebrate the embankment edge between Westminster and Waterloo. Not many people were about, and the body was still alone, not joined by any of the voices. Even Amy Beckett seemed to have gone away for Christmas.

The body began to smell something. First the ether, its silvery, mercurial tang, then the water surfaces of the river and the oily exhaust from cruisers, and something else, in the wind, an animal fragrance, earthy, primitive. As the smell persisted Vera became conscious of a small black poodle dog that had run towards her and was sniffing around her shoes and ankles.

She came back into her body and was alarmed and stunned to find herself sitting on a bench by the river, in the dark, alone, in old clothes, and being sniffed by a dog. She had no idea how she had arrived here. Now surely this meant that she was going mad, losing her mind completely. She remained numb. The dog was watching her and placed its paw gently on her knee, its eyes imploring, and made a little whining noise. Does he know I'm going mad, said a voice inside her?

"It's all right all right, luvvie, he won't hurt you, will you, Jim?"

Jim's owner, an elderly local resident, probably from one of the flats nearby in Dolphin Square, approached her, taking off his soft hat in his large, gloved hands and saying again, "Don't mind Jim, he just wants to be friends."

Vera could hardly see the man through the haze of remaining ether. She blinked and shrugged her shoulders, to try to clear her way, to try to get back into something resembling normality.

The man seemed kindly enough. The first person this

day to show her some friendliness. His face crinkled as he gave his crooked little smile between lips like a flat envelope. He had no visible teeth, and he coughed nervously as if unused to speaking. She could barely make him out in the odd light and in her current confusion, but his eyes were like small dark buttons, watery and bright, in his large bony face, its skin stretched tightly across the old skull. Although he had little hair under the hat he had thick bushy eyebrows, which met in the middle and made him look both curious and cross at the same time. He wore a loose mac without a belt that looked very old and worn and swamped his large bony frame. His shoes were polished well, and their round tips shone in the weak embankment lights. Once he must have been large and imposing, but now she was aware only of his frailty. He was probably a pensioner, alone at Christmas with his best friend, the dog. He probably hadn't spoken to a living soul all day. He could well be like me, she thought.

She was slowly getting back in her body again and thoughts began to jerk her brain into action. She gave a little weak smile to the man because he was there and had approached her, his dog was panting with its head on one side and looking at her with concern, and because she did not know what else to do.

Encouraged, the man sat down on the bench beside her and began asking about her Christmas, twiddling his felt hat in his hands; and because of her continued silence he began telling her about his. That he had a tin of salmon he'd saved, and he and Jim had watched the Queen. They had waited for Flo from the Day Centre to come in for tea but she had never turned up because her sister had been taken queer in Brixton and she'd had to go to her and hadn't been able to leave word until later. And he and Jim hadn't known what to do with the sandwiches he'd made and the Christmas cake, but that would keep he felt sure.

"You got family?" he asked, after a long silence.

Despite what was left of herself, her pride, her red cashmere sweater, Vera felt moisture on her face and realised that tears were spilling out of her dry, tired eyes. A water spring rising from an earth parched and cracked too long.

"My husband has left me" she said in a strained little voice, her empty stomach heaving with effort.

It sounded so simple, and so awful, so final, now, now that she had said it for the first time. There it was, the stuff of people's lives the world over. Husbands, wives, girlfriends, partners, lovers, all leaving each other, an everyday happening. And she could say it to a stranger on a grim evening just after Christmas.

"My wife left me years ago" said the stranger from Dolphin Square, his large feet in their polished shoes gripping the embankment gravel, his hat on his thin macintosh-covered knees, his woolly gloved hands folding over each other like the closing of a page, or perhaps a marriage.

The waters of the Thames continued their quiet passage in front of them, and Vera longed for them to swallow her up. For a time neither spoke.

Then the man grunted. "I tried to top myself. But it didn't do any good."

Another long pause followed, during which the throttle opening on one of the Thames boats sounded a crude note. Vera's frail body was shaking slightly, her face still wet from tears which she did not wipe away. Again, that wanting the Thames to wash her right away.

The stranger turned to her. "Just fresh is it?" he asked, with a strange tenderness. She said nothing, weeping fully now, shaking, wet through.

"People don't realise," he began, more gruffly now. "Things will never be the same. Another woman, is it?" Again, Vera did not answer, and the man took her silence for acquiescence and therefore permission to go on.

"That's what does it," he went on, bitterness now in his voice. "It's those who are *unscrupulous*," he spat it out, "who take other people's property. It's not right. They should be strung up, should be a law against it." His voice was rising. "In olden times adulterers were stoned or fed to the lions."

He was getting an edge to him, winding up for more, that might go on and on with Vera powerless to stop it, she was getting frightened and mute, lost in the water, and it was starting to be cold. Jim began yapping, wanting to be off. Perhaps he knew if his master got into one of his tirades, they would be there all night.

"All right, all right, young man," he said to Jim, "I'll not go on. At least dog'll always put me first," he said as he got to his feet.

"I hope you'll go on all right, love, pretty little thing like you, you'll be alright." He paused, peering at her but not looking. He raised his gloved hand and pointed a grey woolly finger. "Before you finish it, make sure you get even."

Then he was gone, disappearing back into the cold grey night, into the anonymity of London's Victoria, Jim hurrying on his little black feet, leaving Vera in her watery womb of silence and tears and the metallic ring of the man's words.

"They used to be stoned, or fed to the lions."

She continued to sit on the bench, the chill of the Thames now well and truly in her bones, any fire of fight there might have been inside her dampened by the happenings of the evening, the wateriness everywhere, by the man's comments. Time passed and once more she again lost her ordinary consciousness. When she came to, she was no longer sitting on the Thames bench but walking in St James Park. The vibrating tones of Big Ben and an urgent desire to pee had brought her to herself. She couldn't count the strokes but there were a lot of them, maybe ten or eleven, and she realised it must be late, maybe even midnight.

The urgency to pee had her staggering into the darker recesses of the park to find a suitable place to relieve herself. A bush or tree. "You can't do that! Unheard of, unseemly behaviour," said a matronly voice waking up inside her, whilst another voice giggled and thought it a lark. A good non-ladylike lark. She was shaking and unsteady as she pulled at the button and struggled with the zip, finding it hard to undo as she kept crossing and uncrossing her legs. Pee was already warming her thighs. When at last her pants were down, she felt the hot relief flood out of her body, its smell familiar and moist, the stream making an unexpectedly loud noise for the quiet of the night. Its heat caused a slight steam to rise amongst the tickle of the long grass, the tickle she could feel touching her fanny. The gentle points of the grass aroused her, and she remained crouched in their caress, moving around slightly to get the most benefit, a curious lone figure in a scarlet cape coat made dull brown by the midnight park and their dim lights.

After she had finished, she began stroking herself in the fur and moisture, enjoying the feel and the smell of the grassy wet urine-soaked glade she had created. She felt like a child, happy for once, absorbed in her private experience with her body, knowing how to let it receive pleasure and oblivion. So simple. When she had finished, she leant against the tree and allowed her naked bum to squirm about on the wet grass, making it more, coming again. Perhaps she could be like this forever. Just her and the tree and the grass and in this way, she would be no longer stranded and dried up but wet and flowing and alive. Big Ben struck two o'clock.

She felt among the grass for her jeans and finding them wet, discarded them under the tree together with her flimsy black underpants, and got up to walk and dance about, enjoying her naked fanny and bum, the way they rubbed along together in the night air concealed by the red cape, wiggling from time to time with remembered pleasure. She decided to undo her bra and let her breasts also live freely, amongst the red cashmere, playing, as she was doing at last, and when she began walking, she could feel the rub of her nipples on the red softness, and the night air reaching deep unto into her. Every now and then she would stop and make a cartwheel.

She thought she would walk on to Buckingham Palace and gaze a bit like a tourist at this solid mansion of British privilege. Pay her respects to the late Princess Diana. Did she ever play like this in her own back garden?

"You need something solid," said a new voice inside. But the Amy Beckett voice urged her to stand in front of the gold-edged gates, knowing that underneath her cape she wore nothing but a red cashmere sweater and that she had discarded her underclothes in the Queen's back garden, having peed on her lawn.

She was fired up now, no longer frozen then melting, no longer the timid sparrow who did not know what to say or do. She also convinced herself that something about the Royal Family would help, they as a family, also torn with betrayal, adultery, and scandal, but holding firm to something, keeping going with dignity.

She danced and cartwheeled on, across the grass where

the bright blue deckchairs are rented for a pound in summer, towards where the fountains play until midnight, where so many people have happy walks, watch the black swans and feed the ducks. There was excitement as she approached the Mall, with its pink road and pretty lights and the respectable glow of Buckingham Palace. She stood for a moment her arms swinging like a pretend soldier, wondering which way to go, and a thickly dressed man came towards her suddenly from out of the shadows. He mouthed some words and she giggled, putting her head on one side like a budgerigar, her red cape opening slightly as she moved her arms.

"Well, aren't you just a sweetie" said the man, in a foreign accent. And then he was closer at her side, grabbing her by the elbow and running her back into the dark recesses of the park where she had had her private pleasure. He was heavy and brutal, a smelly lump of a man, with his tongue hanging out, hardly able to believe his luck, eager to be inside her with his short, thick penis and she gasped at the sudden thrust of him. She had become so thin that the man might have broken her in two had not some animal yielding, held in one of the veiled-off compartments, woken to the smell of sex and the urgency of his rutting grunt. And in rutting and grunting she could be at home. She did not protest, something at last was alive inside her, bringing her life, making her alive.

"*This is what you need, you silly bitch,*" said the crone, and she began to ride the man as he rode into her. And Nag the Destroyer came from behind the tree and whipped his great whip in the air above her. "*Yes, yes, at last you know where you are, where you belong.*" Nag had come to claim her, to save her, and she rode on until the man collapsed on top of her, slithering out, coughing, panting. And then he was running off, looking quickly from side to side in case anyone had seen them, in case Vera might cry rape. Running more swiftly than she imagined would be possible for someone with his bulk. She lay once more in the wet grass, made warm and moist by the pressure of the two bodies. She touched the stickiness of the body fluids and smeared it onto her face then turned over onto her belly, trembling, breathless, feeling a desperate triumph. "*You might as well sink into the gutter from where you came,*" said the matron voice.

Then, as she lay in the long grass enjoying the delirium of her body, she became aware of noises, the rustling of chains, some panting. She lay still, smelling a strange animal smell, hearing the ground thumping against her pressed ear. She was watching something through the stems of the grass, something moving, large, moving towards her. An animal of some kind.

And through the grass she saw her. She saw that her protector had at last come for her, drawn as animals are like to, by the smell of urgency and body fluids, by the calling card of pee she had left under the tree. Now here in this outside place where she had got down to basics, where she had met her animal, base self, here was her animal come to save her. Her vindicator. "He should be stoned or fed to the lions."

Here in this least expected place, in Central London's most manicured park, a young lioness, in the exact form of the animal of her dream, had come for her. Her eyes glowed amber, fierce yellow round the black centre, on fire. Torchlight lit her coat of many golden colours.

Vera stretched out to meet her.

*The Pale Green Room*

## 15

WHITE frost and white clouds of breath illustrated early January. The blackbirds feasted on old apples as they lay on hardened earth in tiny London gardens.

Saxon left a message cancelling her first session after the Christmas break. She left no reason, but Max noted the flatness of her tone and contacted her, waiting until she answered the phone herself. He invited her to come at another time in the week and she said only that she would think about it. Daniel had called him late on Sunday evening, speaking hurriedly before Max could stop him. "I know you won't discuss a patient, Max, but I'm worried about her. She might not tell you herself, I know what she's like, but she's had a bust up with Lewis. Poor guy, he's really upset, but, well, he'll be OK, but I can't say the same for her."

Max detected real concern in Daniel's voice and whilst he never welcomed unsolicited information about a patient, he respected the man's goodwill.

"I note your concern and thank you for this. It's good she has you for a friend."

"I just thought I'd add my pennyworth..."

When she did come later in the week Max was relieved to see her, for this meant there might be some hope for connection. She looked pale and tense and more obviously depressed. He wondered whether she was sleeping and eating, and if the gloomy thinking had accelerated during her time away. The glass that surrounded her seemed more brittle. Max found his breathing shallow.

"Well, I got here."

"What has been happening?"

She shrugs. "I never knew things could get as low as this."

"What is it that you are feeling now?" He looks at her intently.

"I really did not want to come today," she says, remaining rigid on the edge of the chair.

"I can see," he pauses. "It looks as if you have had another shock," he speaks with feeling, noting dread in his heart.

She breathes out a heavy sigh. "You must get so sick of hearing other people's problems. So pathetic." Her glassy harshness was as sharp as the frost.

She continues impatiently. "I am just a disaster for everyone, there's no way round that. The visit to my parents was pretty awful. It just confirmed what I know, and what we've been talking about here. I tried to find your middle ground, but my try fell on stony ground."

"Your parents?"

"Yes. I saw them more clearly and I saw how the glass was made."

"What was it like being there?"

"As if I was surplus to their requirements." The blue eyes seem made of glass, like the Murano beads. Max's heart feels heavy, so much sadness.

He takes a risk. "I was concerned about how it would be for you at this stage of our work."

She looked surprised. "Really. Wouldn't have thought it would make any difference to that!"

Max chooses not to respond directly but to try to tease out anything that might have been positive, however slight. "What happened whilst you were there, anything new or different?"

She sits back in the chair.

"Actually, yes. But that is the really painful thing. My mother told me that I had once loved painting, as she had. And my father told me that I once had a dream world, an imagination. And they also told me that they had to get me out of these things because that was a road to ruin."

Max has to steady his breathing.

"So you see, the glass world wins in the end."

There is a long, cold silence.

"Say more about the really painful thing."

Unexpectedly, she laughs. "Do you know, on the plane I got quite excited, quite hopeful." Max is listening. "Coming to this room and talking to you has made me think about things in a more analytic way I suppose. And seeing my parents I could see that they had honed the glass world to perfection. My brother's death finished them off and because of that the little girl that I was – and might have become—" there is a pause and a slight break in her voice, "had to become part of it as well." She continues to sit back, and Max can see that she is gathering her memories of that time and how she has made sense of it.

"In that apartment is no sign of creative life, of anything living, even the air has been through a filter. There are no photographs of Europe and my growing up years, no colour or mess. How could a child, or feeling, grow in that?" Her insight is clear.

"So you see, all I can be is a cold, hard bitch."

Max feels a flame of anger on her behalf. He feels that this could be a turning point in their work, that they might be becoming allies. He feels warm toward her and toward her desperate loneliness.

"I do not believe you are fated to be a cold, hard bitch and your life has shown the seeds of warmth and care."

She appeared not to hear.

"When I was in my father's car, I had a very strange experience. I hope it wasn't a psychosis, but I was definitely not in ordinary consciousness." Max notes how much she has picked up from the sessions and integrated into her language. "It was as if I visited a kind of wound, and it told me, in response to "What is this?", that its name was Heavy Heart. It was red, pulsating, bloody and there were tiny little men, homunculi with pickaxes, picking and picking at the most tender bits."

She looks at him directly. "That's what I do to myself, isn't it?"

"Yes, I think that is right."

They are silent together.

"I am really impressed by the way you are speaking," says Max. "It's as if, whilst this time in Florida was difficult, a lot has come out of it for you in terms of understanding of your learned way of being. The men with pickaxes do not have to stay picking away at your heart and your feelings. Now that the little men have made their presence known you can choose to face them, find out what they want and ask them to leave. Then those tender parts might have a chance to heal."

"That's a novel idea. Very creative."

He does not know whether she was being sarcastic or real. But the communication between them is more real than at any other time.

"On the plane I realised how much Lewis had been there for me throughout all the years we've known each other and how I had taken him for granted. How I'd been unable to think of what he wanted. I've been so immersed in myself and in keeping control. As if I could have a relationship like painting by numbers." She is silent. Then continues, "I got off that plane feeling quite excited. I even entertained the thought that maybe we could try again, try to live together like he wanted and that maybe, if I stay in therapy, I might even be able to tolerate being close without feeling I would shatter into shards. And it was silly I know, but I half hoped that he would be there to meet me. Bit like a little girl, even though I know now that I've never known how to be a little girl."

Max is touched again by her insight. He smiles. "Yes, but the fact that you were feeling something like a little girl indicates that she's in there somewhere, waiting for an opportunity to express herself and be seen."

"Waiting in there somewhere. You mean like the stalker who could murder at any moment?" Always the challenge, the brittle fixed thinking.

There is a shocked silence.

"The stalker?"

"There's been someone stalking me for the last six months, since Hong Kong in fact. He's a dark man in a crumpled suit. He's always on thresholds, stairs, passages and doors and behind trees, waiting, looking out at me. He looks a bit like you."

The shock slows Max right down. He tries to keep on with the direction he had started in.

"The image of the potential murderer in yourself is fuelled by fear and guilt, it's a distortion around feelings of badness you have carried since your brother's death which was never explained to you. Any one of us is a potential murderer. I am, my friends, colleagues are, that capacity is in everyone. What is important is in recognising the potential and what fuels it. Being able to stop and reflect helps us not to act out of it."

She is silent. "I see," she says, "I see, or I think I do." There is a pause and the green room seems to hold its breath. "But it's all too late," she says, suddenly defeated.

"It's never too late to rethink distortions in thinking and perception. It's never too late to ask for the courage to change old patterns. And, its never too late to be a little girl," he smiles, hoping to encourage her, to breathe some warmth into this stone-like coldness.

She continues as if he has not spoken.

"Silly, I know, because we've never done that kind of thing. Only after Hong Kong he came to pick me up. He was so thoughtful, so caring."

She had not before expressed to him any real connection or intimacy or feeling for Lewis, and he had felt that this was a closed area. He wondered what had happened at her parents to make her so reflective. He felt some relief, maybe his misgivings about her going were unfounded but to do with some anxiety of his own. But now, a stalker? Imagined or real? The baby in the water, pushed or dropped?

She continues. "But he wasn't there, and I felt disappointed. There was no message either, and in the flat, nothing, no welcome. And, well, it was the early morning of Christmas Eve."

\* \* \* \*

*She had got a cab back to her apartment and freshened up with a shower and some coffee. Then she had telephoned and got his answering machine, which threw her, she was so used to his being there and waiting for her. By the time he phoned back later on she had worked up a good deal of anxiety, something new to her which was hard to suppress. She feared that something had happened to him, or was about to happen to her. They had planned to have Christmas Eve together, with him staying over so they could walk Alma together on Christmas Day round the Serpentine.*

*When he arrived, she knew immediately that something had changed. Something around his eyes, his slight detachment, despite the warmth of his greeting. She felt as if some invisible thread that had joined them for all these years had been cut. She felt afraid, again new, and pestered him to know what was wrong, what had changed.*

*He held her at arm's length with his strong arms.*

*"Sax, you're just back from your parents and it must*

have been hard for you. Don't let's rush into a discussion now. We have Christmas Eve and Christmas Day. Let's enjoy it."
"So, it's to be the last is it?"
He looked at her, searchingly.
"You've met someone haven't you?"
He dropped his arms and sighed, turning away from her.
"No don't turn away. I have to face you. I have to be brave."
"You've always been brave. I am so, so sorry. I am so sorry for what has not been able to happen between us. I have wanted it so much. I've seen that softness in you" and ....
"Please, Lewis, this is not us, hedging around. Please, just spit it out. I know I've been hell, especially this year. I know. I deserve what's coming."
He had been silent, hating her self-attack.
"Yes, it is true. I have met someone. But nothing has happened yet."
She felt the newly discovered, tiny opening of her frozen heart shut tight, and sat down.
"I know that it's my fault."
He sat close to her and put his arm around her.
"There is so much inside you that never gets out. In all our six years, Sax, I've waited and hoped that you would be able to allow the softer side of yourself emerge."
She cannot cry.
"On the plane. I've been thinking. Perhaps we can try again, Lewis? I'm in therapy now..."
"But you hate it!" He sounded surprised.
"Yes, I know. But going home, being with my parents, seeing things objectively. I can see how much I've got to learn about being a simple human being that I was not able to learn before."
Lewis got up and walked toward the fireplace, looking up toward the Picasso print. Phoenix arising from the ashes. His heart felt heavy.
"Our timing, Sax. Our timing. I would not choose this for the world. But it has happened."
"What has happened! I thought you said nothing had

happened yet! Please, please let it not be too late for us, Lewis!" She instantly hated herself for turning into the needy, pleading woman she despised. She would surely lose him now.

Lewis took a deep breath. "I think that I might be, quite unexpectedly, falling in love."

The air was electric. Her heart stood still. Then, clipped and glassy, she said, "Oh, I thought you and I didn't do that."

"Yes, I thought so too. But now I believe that is what's happening. I was wrong to close my heart after Virginia died and because it was the pact we made not to become more emotionally involved. It's not me."

"Does she – I presume it's a she – know?"

"Yes, it's a she, despite my closest friend being gay!"

"Go on then, you'd better tell me." Her voice was clipped, and she was trying to stay in control. But inside she was quivering.

"I honestly did not want to be saying this to you on Christmas Eve and after what you've been through. But let's get it over with. She is an ex-student, she's now got her PhD and is working at the archaeological museum. We met up again over the exhibition. All since you and I decided to live in separate apartments."

"I see. I do know that it's my fault. You don't have to tell me that. It's only what I deserve."

Lewis' agony showed in his face. A naturally kind and sympathetic man who had nursed and lost his first wife after medical blunders, so patient, he hated hurting anyone.

"After we agreed to separate apartments, I was glad that we could still be friends and even stay together some of the time, and we had Alma, our child. But I was lonely. I found myself longing for closeness, the closeness I had known with Virginia. And I also have realised that I do want children, Saskia."

Her heart continued to freeze over.

"And this woman, girl – she's young, she can have, and wants children?"

"Yes."

He remained standing next to the Picasso whilst Saxon stayed on the sofa, looking increasingly small and marooned.

"When were you going to tell me?"

*"I don't know. Probably in the new year."*

\* \* \* \*

The pale green room listens, closing its arms around the deep sadness. Hope for the tenderness of the recently opened heart frozen over.

Max is sad and troubled. Another blow and rejection, another piece of evidence to prick at her guilt and her feeling that she turned everything into bad.

"I am so sorry that this has happened now, just as you are starting to look at the possibility of change within yourself. How do you feel?"

They look at each other directly.

"Shit." She has not used that word before.

"How bad does it get?" asks Max.

"Pretty bad." She looks up. "You know don't you, you know this place?"

Max is surprised and does not answer, but the shared connection with desperate feelings is intense and the room's strong arms hold firm.

"When it gets pretty bad, do you think of harming yourself?"

"I had that thought for the first time last week, after Lewis left. Suicidal ideation the books call it don't they?"

"When you had that thought, of killing yourself, what did you do?"

"I thought that it might be good to get it all over with."

"Did you make a plan?"

"God this is awful. This is so awful. Here I am. I'm right at the bottom, aren't I?"

"You are in a dark place, yes," says Max. "And this room and our conversation within it is aimed at helping you to name the ingredients of the dark place and find the best understanding and light you can so that you make the best and well-informed choice you can."

"You cannot stop me."

"That's right. I cannot stop you taking your own life, but I can help you see what your choices are."

"Not many choices right now, are there?"

"Well, let's look."

"What is there left to live for?"

"What did you live for before?"

"I never thought about it, I just got on with being a useful doctor. Now I can't even be that. Nor a girlfriend."

They are both thoughtful and the green room waits patiently.

Max asks, "I wondered whether you would agree to something with me. Your world has been turned upside down and your emotional muscles are in the process of being rediscovered and strengthened. This is the work we are to do together, and I intend to be with you all the way. Will you come here, to this room, twice a week so that we can give you the best chances and choices for the future? These won't be found overnight. We don't know what there will be, but we will share the journey."

Somewhere behind the glass she is touched by his care, his determination and firmness, and his professionalism. He is not going to abandon her nor is he going to have her carried off to the asylum because she has admitted she felt suicidal.

"I am very grateful," she says. "I will think about what you have said, and I will come next Monday."

"And if you feel suicidal in between the sessions …."

She interrupted, "Yes, I know, I know where I can call. I've called them before."

Max is surprised, and pleased, there was a lot more in her than she had been able to show him.

"So, you have a safety net for when thinking becomes too much?"

"A year ago, it would never have occurred to me to telephone someone like them!" God, have I come to this, she finds herself thinking.

He continues, "If you telephone me and get my answer machine just ask me to call you back when I am free and I will. During that time what will you do to postpone acting on the thoughts?"

She thinks and realises his suggestions are practical and helpful. "I guess I will play music. Music that does not remind me of Lewis. Bach most probably, and Philip Glass."

They smile at each other at the irony of the name and Max feels they have something of a pact he hopes will hold.

"Are there other people to whom you might speak. How about Alan Mayers, I know he's a friend, and Daniel?"

"Alan, well I suppose I could. I'll have to think about it. And Daniel, well he's away for a few days...but I know he is concerned for me ... I'm sure that it won't get that bad." She feels ashamed for being a nuisance. This really was a mess now.

"Are you still taking fluoxetine?"

"Of course. Do what the doctor orders. Alan was quite clear about that: antidepressants and mood stabilisers just in case I try any other form of involuntary weird behaviour and it's a grown up rather than a baby I try to knock off."

"Ouch," says Max. "That's a really cutting remark about yourself, designed to make you feel bad inside."

"True though, isn't it?" Her challenge was back, her earlier use of insight to communicate with him, to share, to show softness and openness, now closed down. The tender heart now completely frosted.

## 16

SHE wore a fitted black padded anorak and sensible boots, simple makeup, none of the pillar box red. Underneath were tailored trousers and a sweater. She looked fresh, and very much alive.

She no longer looked like Margaret. The realisation made him breathe a deep satisfying breath.

She sat down in the green chair and took out a small notebook with plain pages full of her writing. She was holding a small round stone in her left hand.

"I'll come straight out with it," she says. "Over the Christmas break I did something very stupid." The green room held its breath. Max wondered what he was about to be told. She still looked thin, but he saw life in her, and resolve.

"I allowed myself to get into an extremely dangerous situation. I feel I should try to tell it to you although I am shocked and I feel sure you will be, by what I have to tell."

*Here again, the image of the lioness.*

"On the day after Boxing Day, after my boys had gone skiing, I allowed myself to have sex with a strange man in Green Park, in the middle of the night."

Silence.

"I wasn't raped, I wanted it and he was there. It was pretty awful and disgusting actually and if I'm lucky I won't get any disease. I've taken all precautions since."

His eyes are full of interest and true deep listening. He has said nothing. He and the pale green room are waiting for the story to unfold and for this new energy to continue to reveal itself.

"You don't need to be nice to me, but then again I don't think I should be punishing myself anymore."

She smiles. "It's a lot to take in, isn't it? A bit like since I last saw you, I've died and been resurrected!"

"I can feel a new energy in you."

"Yes. I'll tell you the rest. Christmas was awful. Although there were some good moments with my mother, real responses when I didn't play into her game, she just didn't try to understand what I was going through. And she complained a lot.

Then the boys went away." She pauses, remembering the awful day. "I sat in the house with the Christmas litter and I didn't know how to go on. It really did feel like the end. I tried working with the stones and the safe circle, I practised the breathing, I thought about the idea of transformation. I tried TV. But I kept coming back to this awful crone like cackling voice telling me I was done for." She pauses, deep in her account.

"I felt as if I really had lost everything, that I had lost my mind, and had no will to keep going. I think that I must have split off, like I've told you about before, like when I ended up at the zoo and in The Boltons. I came to on a bench near the Thames –rivers are wonderful, aren't they?" She swishes her black mane of hair. *The proud lioness.* There was this lonely man with his little dog called Jim and I found myself telling him what had happened, about Alistair going off. His wife had gone left him as well and he said that people who betray their spouses should be stoned or fed to the lions." She looks up. "Lions and lionesses, they seem to be everywhere. They've have had a role to play in all of this, and I'll come to that...

"I must have walked and walked and then I needed a pee – excuse me – and after I peed on the grass, in St James Park, because I heard the strikes of Big Ben, I got sort of, well you know, excited. And I pranced around quite a bit there in the dark on my own. And it was then that this bloke came out of the bushes and grabbed me." The green room was still holding its breath.

"I didn't fight. I had this voice in my head saying, *"You're just a slut and now you've come to this. There's no hope for you."* And when it was over, I lay in the grass hearing those words and realising that they were words used about my mother and by her. They're the words she uses when someone has failed, and I think she probably used them throughout my childhood. When she saw the uncles looking at me she would call me a slut as if I were to blame. It was what she said to herself when she tried to take her life. And she'd started talking like that over Christmas. I was glad the boys didn't have to hear any more of it. But there, in the grass, I realised how much this voice, inside of me had been influencing my self-esteem. I've been thinking of it since, and I can see now how basically deep down I still thought of myself as a slut made good because of sex and luck. And when the sex and luck ran out what was left was this worthless slut."

Max's heart is on fire. Tears run down her face. "I'm sorry I didn't want to cry here because actually although there's been a lot lost there has been so much... gained..."

"It sounds as if you have gained a sense of yourself and this self is no slut."

"It was a rock bottom moment, the kind I imagine that drunks have to get to before they realise how self-destructive they are being. Only while I was lying there, I started to think that it wasn't true. And as if to confirm this, my champion turned up."

She looks at Max expectantly.

"Your champion?"

\* \* \* \*

*The grass in Green Park had been wet with heavy dew and cold. When the effects of lying with so few clothes on began to have an impact upon Vera's awareness, she got to her feet and looked around for her jeans before walking slowly to the path, stuffing them into her pocket as she went. The soft lights of Buckingham Palace were nearby. There was a slight hum of cars on Hyde Park Corner and in Birdcage Walk there was one solitary white van, parked. She stood unsteadily from the physical efforts of the evening and watched as two police officers emerged from the darkness of the park, the lioness leaping playfully alongside them, on a long linked chain.*

*So, she had not been dreaming.*

*She watched the officers open the back doors of the van for the young animal to leap in obediently with one magnificent leap. Soon the engine started, and the vehicle made a U turn, coming toward where she was rooted to the spot, staring. As the van reached alongside her, she froze in fear. What if they had seen her and her activities with the unknown man, they might accuse her of soliciting in Her Majesty's Garden and making a lewd spectacle in a public place. She wrapped her coat around her, grateful for its capacity to hide all underneath. Of course, if they asked her to open her coat and to search her...*

*But the van window rolled down smoothly and a young Indian policewoman with a lovely face leant out smiling and* said, "I do hope that we didn't alarm you," she said in beautifully modulated English. Vera opened her mouth to speak, but no sound came. "You see, we have to exercise her at night, as during the day she causes too much publicity." Vera still could not speak. "But she is very sweet. Just a kitten really"

The engine of the white van was running and the young woman's partner, a Sikh wearing a turban, was also smiling and looking toward Vera. He said, "You see, she lives in one of the embassies in Belgrave Square."

Vera's eyes were settling and getting used to the semi-darkness. She was also gaining ground at taking in the oddness of this sight and that she was not dreaming. Through the bars between the back and the front seats she recognised an golden animal head and realised that the two lights were the eyes of her champion.

She stammered... "I thought, well I thought, I was dreaming."

"Yes, like you had one too many," said the man, as if it were a great joke.

"Well, I've not been drinking," said Vera, suddenly so happy to be having a surreal conversation about a lioness whose midnight walks were supervised by two officers from the Metropolitan Police. A lioness that lived in Belgrave Square no less. If she was mad, she did not mind.

"I just think... I just think... well, she's wonderful isn't she. Wonderful." Should she tell them about her champion?

They both smiled. "We think so. We love taking her out. There's quite a queue for this job!"

"We'd best be off," they said.

\* \* \* \*

Max smiles at her story and at the happy resonance in her energy.

"It all sounds quite bonkers doesn't it?"

"It does a bit," says Max, smiling, "but it feels only too true! You've been in real danger and here you are just off the edge. What are you feeling right now?"

"I feel a bit weird, but I do feel very alive. And amazed how things have since then fallen into place. In my mind. I feel sad too, for what went on all those years ago."

She pauses breathing deeply and suddenly nervous.

"There is something more, and I find it's harder to speak of it than I realised."

\* \* \* \*

*She had stood on the pavement and watched the van go on its way, carrying her champion to the top of Birdcage walk and around Hyde Park Corner. The growl of London was getting stronger and Big Ben struck five o'clock. She pulled on her jeans and wrapped her coat once again more firmly around her and slowly walked past Buckingham Palace, giving a little nod of apology in its direction. She would not be Diana, she would not throw herself into landmines or disappear with a forbidden man. She was aware of being very tired but did not want to stop. She felt more alive and in her body than she had ever done. The realisation excited her. She noticed her nose quivering as she imagined an animal's nose might quiver. She felt her hands, those strong hands that Max had commented on, start throbbing. They wanted to do something, to get their hands on something. Am I hysterical she wondered? Am I losing it again? But the feeling itself was enough to propel her onwards, following her quivering nose and the feel of the air through her hands and the sensations of control, so that she walked on until she got to the river once more.*

*She stood watching the river, lit by the embankment lights. The river she had sat next to only a few hours earlier in an out of body state. She watched the movements of the currents as they marked an pattern underneath the water. This tide comes in and goes out she thought. This is what one of the books referred to, the rhythms of a life, the phases of ebb and flow and the process of the ever-changing seasons. Nothing ever stayed the same but had its own rhythm.*

*"What would be your natural response," Max had asked her in one of her sessions. She had not known what he meant. But now, sitting by the companionship of the river, she understood how when she was a teenager, she had resolved to create her own interests and her own life. She wanted independence from having to be what others wanted. She had her own simple dreams of getting out of the limited gossip culture where men, although despised were courted, used and even sometimes outwitted. She did not want that anymore. The healthy island. Was this it?*

Max had asked about the 'uncles' and she had not been able to tell him. Tonight, the man in the park had brought back the memory of one of the uncles, older men who came after her when her mother was drunk or out. Who tried to get her to trust them, who tried to put their hands up her skirt. How many of them had abused her? Her stomach turned over at the thought. Would she know one day for sure and if she ever found out what good would it do? She needed to see things as they were right now. Perhaps what had happened tonight was a replay of something that had already happened, and that she had allowed it, courted it even, because it was what she had known when she was very young. And, without the protection of her marriage, her social standing and good fortune she had returned to almost expecting it.

Max had always been very careful about asking her about abuse and she felt that it had been an unspoken fact between them. She had been grateful for this. He had asked if she had been bullied. The uncles and her mother were bullies all right and she had wanted to protect her mother because it always ended up in trouble. But now, this night, she realised that she was the one who needed protection. What else had she known from men? Until she met Max, a decent, honest, safe man, men were either there to outwit and seduce to get what you want, or to be run away from in fear and disgust.

The realisation that she had probably been sexually abused hit her hard, but also made sense, and here by this river, she was able to think it and be strong with it for the first time. If she could face this, she could face anything.

*  *  *  *

"What's hard to say, and I am grateful to you that you've not pushed me at all on this, is that I do think that the "uncles" who came to the house, I do think they … did what they shouldn't do," she avoids eye contact.

Max breathes deeply. "I am so sorry," he says with deep feeling.

Vera weeps.

"Do you think that your mother knew?"

Vera is scornful. "She certainly did."

"So you feel your mother used you too?"

"Yes. And she did. And we've had words." She looks very fierce.

\* \* \* \*

*She was writing a note to her mother to say that she had been up all night, was going to have a long sleep, and would she please get herself a taxi to the station and go back to Manchester, when Myra shuffled down the stairs in her velour dressing gown and mule slippers.*

*Vera took a long look at her mother.*

*"Where were you when I needed you?"*

*Her mother was startled. Her mouth opened but no words came.*

*"So, it doesn't bother you if your daughter was raped?"*

*Her mother went white.*

*"No," she faltered. "No, you haven't..."*

*Vera stood up "I want you to go now. I want you to pack and go. I've got things I must get on with."*

*Her mother seemed dazed, shocked. "But..."*

*"Please, just do it. I'll phone for a taxi."*

*"But my ticket..."*

*Vera snorted, furious, she wanted to slap and kick her, to frighten her, to make her feel as helpless as she had felt. She wanted power over her for the first time. Why had she never done this before?*

*"Yes, I thought so. More worried about the cut price ticket than finding out what has happened to me and how I feel."*

*"You may have money, but I've got to be careful."*

*"But I paid for your ticket, didn't I."*

*Myra looked sly. "What is it? What's got into you suddenly? Miss nice as pie one minute and a screaming witch the next."*

*Yes, thought Vera, you have bitchiness on the tip of your tongue and are far better at it than me. I'm not getting into this one, I've not had enough practice and I don't want to start now.*

*"You weren't serious, were you, about being raped?"*

*"All those "uncles" at home as I was growing up. What they did was rape wasn't it? How old was I? You knew? Did you encourage it? To get me out of the way or to pay for your debts?"*

"*I never let them lay a hand on you, you little...*"

"*You are a lying bitch, Mother. A lying bitch.*" She had never before said those words. They felt good. She felt the rise of the hair on the back of her neck. Lioness not far away. "*What about when you were out, or asleep, or drunk? What about the time you got George to take me to Grandma's and he stopped his truck on the way and demanded a blow job? You set it up, didn't you. I even gave you the ten quid.*"

Vera was standing with her hands by her sides, her feet firmly on the ground. "*Ten lousy quid for your only child's innocence. You disgust me.*"

Her mother went pale. Her voice changed. "*Do we have to go back to this now. You've done well for yourself.*"

"*Yes, temporarily, and who made sure that I continued to prostitute myself for a man? My marriage to Alistair was one of several years of prostitution. We were never equal. I was sold, bought and kept on certain conditions,*" she swept her hands around the large house. "*I remember that I wanted my own life, my own business, to be in charge, not to be at the beck and call of some man who could take my very soul away. It was you who stopped me doing that. I did not want your life, to be like you. I gave in because of your emotional blackmail.*"

"*I can't believe you are talking to me like this.*" Her mother folded her arms across her dressing gown. "*I'm your mother, you're a mother, you should know not to speak like this. How would you like your boys to speak to ...*"

"*I hope I haven't given them any reason to!*"

Her mother's hands went limp, and Vera wondered if she might try fainting. But she just stood there, the stuffing suddenly knocked out of her. In that moment Vera knew that her mother too was the result of the ebb and flow of the tides of influences and opportunities. She wondered if her mother had ever been shown kindness or decency, if she had ever tried to be different, to move away from the depressed and angry foundations. At least Vera had had the opportunity, even through the false life she had been living. And now she had the chance to read, to think and to discover, with Max, that she could change her attitude.

"*We are all the product of our influences, aren't we? I've had a really exhausting and painful night and there's a lot for me to think about. I'm just discovering how much my past has influenced me and the choices I make. I'm learning to live with the consequences of that. I'm learning that I have to make clearer choices, to be independent. Right now, I need you to pack your things and leave. I need to shower and to sleep."*

*The two women stood facing each other. Vera said, "Right now I would like the house to myself. There may be a time in the future when we can have a different conversation, but not now."*

*"So that's it?"*

*"Yes," said Vera firmly.*

\* \* \* \*

"I don't want to see her for a while. I know that she too is the product of her environment, her childhood. But I haven't got space for that right now. It's all I can do to sort myself out."

"I am so impressed with all that you have been thinking and sorting since before Christmas." Max is genuinely moved. In the pale green room he is feeling into the huge changes in his own inner world and in Vera's, since the last session.

"I don't suppose I'll make of sense of it for a while. But I feel that I had to sink to rock bottom to really see the most raw state I could be in, and to come alive to myself."

Max is so happy.

She is thoughtful. "I've always seen my body as the enemy, trying to control it to be what a man wanted. Dieting, exercising, make up, the lot. In the park I realised that I had probably not owned it properly because it was invaded so young. It had become the enemy. And because of that I attacked it, didn't I?"

Max is in awe at her understanding.

When you first pointed out that I had strong hands I was embarrassed because I thought they were ugly. But they've had a sort of energy of their own. I think that my body has been trying to tell me something all along. I had been trying to control the emotional pain by the cutting and then you taught me the breathing through. This helped to begin with but it didn't touch the feeling of rage. And the way ... it's weird, but I sort of wanted to use my body to attack, and it was all upside down because I only knew how to attack myself. I didn't want to die, I just wanted to be hit and hit again ... something like that. That's what I've worked out."

"It's as if you had internalised all the anger and rage you possibly felt as a small girl who was used by the adults for their gratification. There was nowhere else for these strong feelings to go. Your rage at Alistair's callous behaviour was hidden because you so wanted him to come back, and its only avenue of expression was through cutting yourself."

"Yes, that makes sense, I can see that."

"And the lioness?"

"Yes, the image, and seeing her in the park that night, so amazing, isn't it?"

"Jung calls it synchronicity."

"Yes, I've read that. When outside events mirror internal happenings and help the internal to have more ground for life."

"You have been busy," says Max warmly.

Vera is delighted. "I had the image of the lioness and it sort of captivated me. Then I lost it. My mother came and dominated when I felt weak, and I fell into a sort of hole." She pauses. "People say that about drunks, don't they? That you have to sink low and on your own before you can get up properly on your own behalf. Then you can start to look at yourself properly."

"That's right. I am thinking about what happened in the park. It's as if you discovered something childlike and playful and spontaneous. This is what I think got used as an object for others" gratification. The experience with the man in the park, highly dangerous, brought you right into your early experiences. Rather than being crushed by it as you might have been you were able to reclaim something of your own free self, who could be in charge, be the champion and not the victim."

She looks down and feels relieved that she has someone who understands what she has been through and does not judge her or, worse, take advantage of her.

"And Alistair, how do you feel about him at this time?"

"I wanted him back at any cost and I would have done anything to get him. But not now, eh?"

She did not need to bend and twist herself into something she was not in order to try to keep him. She could let him go and not be less than herself, in fact perhaps she could ever be more.

So what she had lost might be a gain.

\* \* \* \*

*The dawn was rising as she left the bench.* "Sweet Thames run softly" *– words she remembered from a poem.*

*She went home, and as she came into the house, she knew what she must do straight away, before dealing with her mother. She went into the bedroom she had shared with Alistair and stripped the bed, placing all the linen into plastic bin liners. Then she emptied Alistair's drawers, pulled from the wardrobe the clothes he hadn't yet taken, cleared his dressing table and the bathroom of everything that had been his. She filled bag after bag and put them outside. Then she moved the bed around to a different position. She saw the videos they had made, felt the rise of disgust, and dumped them into something she could burn.*

\* \* \* \*

"I've been going over what my life had come to and all that I pushed aside. I got out my books and started reading them just for myself, not to improve myself for him. I've been trying to get fit, eating properly. Oh and yes, I've decided that I'd like Luke to go to the local school. I know I shall have to fight Alistair over it, in court if I have to, but he's staying with me."

"You have been really busy," said Max, happily impressed.

"I thought you'd be pleased…" then she stopped. "No – that's it isn't it. I'm not doing it for you. It's quite freeing really, I suppose, but scary. I don't know if I can keep it up, But I want to try. I want to be in charge. There is a life without Alistair after all."

*The Pale Green Room*

## 17

SHE was spending the day sorting research papers in her room at the hospital. They did not need sorting, but she had to do something. She could not stay in her flat, she could not walk the streets. She wished, too late, she had cultivated women friends, someone with whom she might have coffee or chat. But Saxon did not know how to chat.

She had tried reading and listening to Philip Glass; and she had tried to hold onto the image of the beating heart and to the feeling she had when she first described it to Max. She had seen so many beating hearts and had never tired of them. But the image, and any feeling connection was too far away. She felt cold. She could not look in the mirror. She tried going over the last conversation with Lewis. He had been so patient and now he had met someone else. Of course he had! A proper flesh and blood woman who could warm him at night. Laugh, drink wine and go on holiday. Not her, the Ice Queen, whose splinter in the heart could not melt. And, perhaps most piercing of all, a woman who would like to, and could, give Lewis a child.

But then she had her work; Or had had her work.

She sat down at her desk and stared out of the window at the garden life going on outside. One of the nurses had brought in a bird table for the pleasure of the patients, and small garden birds – greenfinches, wrens, coal tits – were eagerly enjoying bits of toast and bun. She realised she had started to make a habit of looking out through the glass of windows at the untouchable life outside. Even though the earth was undergoing the darkness of winter there were signs of new green, the tips of snowdrops and crocuses were just appearing, spearing upwards through the hard ground.

What was there left for her, now? Was there anything for which it was worth making the effort to live? And the effort to be made in dying if one chose to bring it about oneself, easy for a doctor in the practical sense, but not something to be done lightly. Who would miss her? What was there she still wished to accomplish? She had always felt that she would not mind dying, for it would be a relief from having to make an effort at life. The colossal effort she would now have to make to get her life on some sort of comfortable footing did not bear thinking about. Max had said "I am here with you right through" as if he had a destination in mind, or better still knew that there was something inside her that might flourish.

She continued watching the garden and the movements of the collared doves as they nodded their heads on the bird table, holding her breath in case the force of the out-breath would disturb them, even though the glass was between them. She sat held in some mysterious peacefulness and when the doves flew she remained sitting, and watching. Some part of her was absorbing the detail of each fine blade of grass, the movement of the wind in the laurel bushes, the sound the dark green leaves made as they shook together. She hugged herself, aware that something was trying to soften inside. For once there was no demon command.

Then she was in a high-up place. Golden and, shining. Its warmth softened her more, helped her to lean back into its gentle holding as if she were the smallest petal floating in the centre of a great flower. The flower glowed like still warm embers of a deep-hearted fire that had long burned and still more was to come. As she breathed in, she could feel the softening reach into the familiar tightness of her sternum, her place of great pain.

She knew now that the young man in the crumpled suit would find her here at last. He had been following her all this time, in Hong Kong, near the Thames, in the green room of Dr Max. Always he was on thresholds, by steps, in doorways. The bitter waiting was over, replaced by a stillness that was part of natural law, and peaceful, with its end already there, within the waiting. All her earlier waiting had been to do with the void, a place worse than emptiness, a vacuum primed only to suck at the first available filler. The natural ache for love becomes cruel when it can court only substances like food or substances, sex or money. The sly grins of those great seducers would promise relief only to bring more demand.

She knew that when he was ready he would come. She liked the idea that he would walk along the path where the common wallflowers threw up such heady scent at night, their daily ordinariness transformed by the dark into perfumed enchantment. He would breathe in the fragrance, and she would smile, knowing of his pleasure. She liked the idea that he would walk alone, his light tread bringing him nearer to her. He would carry a gift for her – a flower, or stone from the beach, some wine, or a poem he had written just for her. When he came to the door which she had left open his long hair would be thrown back by the air created by that space between inside and out. And then, all movement would steady as he climbed the golden stairs to meet her.

The darkness and desperation she had felt most of her life was transformed. She could see the deep golden light of the flower, shining and moving, formed by quivering petals opening and closing with the variations of day and night. Each opening brought a little more light for the dark depths. Her heart was being opened in a way that she could never have envisaged and which her rigorous medical training had informed her was impossible.

And when the young man came, they would smile at each other, content in this, knowing that they belonged together, and that something was able to be complete. He would be taking her through the looking glass of this life and all she had gestated or completed, into her place in the future. He would help her to see the face she had before she was born.

She came into the ordinary dull light of her office as the door opened and one of her students came into the room. He apologised for disturbing her and she smiled, not minding, feeling easy going and relaxed. The warm glow of the golden flower was still radiating. She looked out again into the garden, at the empty bird table. Some of the deep relaxation remained around her heart and she was glad of it. What was she dreaming about before the student had knocked? "In your dream world" her father had said. "It was all we could do to keep you out of it." But this waking dream was so lovely. The young man in the crumpled suit that she had first glimpsed on that boat in Hong Kong was here now, coming for her. And she felt so much at ease.

She looked down to the desk and saw her last research paper into cardiomyopathy after habitual cocaine use. It had stimulated interest and debate. Could she design a new study, one that would take a wider sample, maybe the effects on the

... Something nagged her. That time in the regional hospital, the experimenting that she had done. The man in the crumpled suit. Another man who must be worse for wear by now. She had not thought of him for years. But oh how she had loved him, and how passionate they had been under his influence. She had been able to surrender then, with the help of the substances he excelled in providing.

But why did she think of this now?

*"Because I'm desperate,"* she thought. She was so desperate she was thinking of either killing herself or resorting to drugs.

She became more restless and after pacing the room, went out to look for her assistant, intending to engage him with a future study. The cardiac preparation room where she expected to find him was empty. It had an air of expectancy, the flat silver scalpels neatly lined up on the metal trolley; scissors, sutures, needles, swabs, tweezers, all sterilised in their own little packets.

She always looked at the list for the day and she knew that the next patient to be prepped was one of her own, a young boy of just nine. He needed cardiac catheterisation to explore a repaired valve that was now leaking. She had managed his care since he was a baby, born with a heart defect, and transferred to this hospital from the countryside where he lived with his devoted parents. She had always spoken to him directly about what would happen and drawn pictures of the heart that illustrated the work and repair that would be done. "It will make you bionic," she had said. The fact that she could not now even complete this simple procedure for him was yet another rejection of her worth.

The room had an eerie sense of waiting, of things suspended, like on Hammersmith Bridge, like her status in the hospital and in her life. They would be bringing him soon, on the gurney, small for his age, thin and pale under the white sheet, his anxious mother most probably at his side, holding his hand. And she, Saxon, his own doctor and the most thorough of cardiologists, could not place her hands on him. It would be a locum doctor she did not know. Another nail in her coffin of failure.

What had Max said? "It sounds as if you are giving me

reasons why you should not go on living".

She heard a slight sound and, turning, saw that someone had entered the room behind her and shut the door. She faced him, and she knew in that moment that he was the one who had been following her. He had come for her at last. *Would he release her from her prison?* He was the man in the crumpled suit she had seen on the boat in Hong Kong and the man who had been following her; he was Dr Max when she first saw him, unshaven and shabbily dressed. He crouched in the corner and was both sinister, and familiar. They looked at each other. Her light blue eyes and his dark brown eyes, the eyes that had introduced her to drugs and to passion. Kim Reynolds was older, had gained weight. Thirteen years ago – how lonely she had been then, just thirty-three, in her first consultant job in the northwest, the glass well-formed and in place. She had never sought the lonely-hearts columns before, despising those who did. But she had placed her own cryptic note in the personal column of a respectable paper because she was lonely and she thought it would be easy; it would be arm's length, and neither of them would get involved in emotion.

How wrong she had been. How foolish she had been courting such danger, and she had only just managed to escape. Or had she escaped? And into what? More severe distancing of herself from others; always the refusal of intimacy. She shuddered now when she thought of the things they did together. Somehow, he became the only person to get between her and the glass.

But what was he doing here? He said nothing but started moving toward her. His eyes were pinned on her, menacing. *What was he doing here?*

"What do you want?" she asked.

When he spoke, it was with the rough voice she had once thrilled at and melted into. "I want what you took away from me."

At first, she thought it must be drugs speaking. He looked as if he had been sleeping rough, as if he had become an addict despite his declaration of mastery over it. What had he said? "Come on, you need to let go, girl, have a good time. Relax, chill out. Try a bit, no harm. You and me, we're scientists, we can be on top of it."

And she had. And it had worked, at first. She had let go and let him play with her and tease her. She had let herself become undone with him. She felt sick as she remembered the consequences of that abandon.

Did he know? How could he have known? She had been so careful. So very careful.

"I took nothing from you." Her voice was dry, unconvincing.

"A life for a life, Saskia."

So, he knew. He knew that she had gone into a public lavatory and aborted their child, even when she had never told him that she had been pregnant, and she had moved away shortly afterwards. There was no point now in protesting. Here it was, her judgement, the price she must pay. Here was her last call.

"How do you know?"

He laughed. "Huh, clever cold fish you consider yourself, don't you? I followed you. I followed you when you kept creeping about, after you had decided to avoid me."

So, it had all started so long ago. There was to be no release from it, no escape. And he had been following her all these months. She remembered that windy, wet summer night thirteen years ago. She had been grateful that no one was around. The car was parked in a small public car park, and she had crossed the muddy compound as the light was fading and was quite sure she had not seen anyone.

"And I saw – I saw him." He had started wailing, his voice rising. "You killed him."

"He was dead."

"No! He was not dead. His little chest was moving. You bitch. You murdering bitch!"

Saxon was rooted to the spot. Could this be true? He was twenty-five weeks' gestation. The horror at discovering how far the pregnancy had advanced without her knowing! She'd been too high on amphetamine and work to feel into her body. That old nausea threatened to return now, the same sickness she had recognised that first day in the pale green room.

She had delivered him and cut the cord with surgical scissors. She could not look at him but she was sure there was no breath. She had put him in several plastic bags, rammed them to the bottom of the bin. But had she? Or had she just run out of there? She was flooded with relief that the procedure had worked, that she was rid of it, and anyway it would never have been able to survive as normal, deformed by the ...

"No, no, it's not true. You're making it up ..." she said.

He snorted. "Got you. Got you, your high and mighty." He came closer. His pupils were dilated, his breath sour. Drugs, always the drugs. He edged toward her unsteadily.

"What do you want?"

"I want to get you."

"Is it drugs you're after?"

"Easy that would be," he said. "Morphine – do you keep it here? You can get me some. That would be good." He edged further and suddenly gripped her arm, pulling her toward him. She looked toward the emergency button that was on the other side of the room. He pinned her arm behind her back.

"A life for a life," he said.

There was a sudden burst of noise and a porter pushed through the double doors with his back, pulling the trolley into the room whilst remaining completely unaware of the drama unfolding behind him. As he swung the trolley around there was barely time for recognition before the dark stalker sprang with more dexterity than he seemed capable of, and threw the porter back into the passage, wedging the trolley in place across the doors as they closed behind him. In his next movement he turned and seized the sleepy Martin from off the white sheet and clutched him against his chest. He had managed, in all this movement, to reach a silver scalpel from the table and was holding it at Martin's throat. Saxon noted that the blade was turned outward, and the blunter side was at Martin's throat.

"Him... I get him... or..."

"What do you want?" screamed Saxon.

"I want you to apologise. I want you to suffer, as I have. I want you to die. You took the most important thing away from me. I can't have any more children."

"Neither can I," said Saxon steadily, calming herself, hoping to calm him.

"But you could have. You could have. You could have

kept that one. The next month I contracted mumps and that was goodbye to any of my seeds finding fertile ground. No inheritance. Nothing of me to be passed on."

Reynolds' hand holding the scalpel shook. The boy was white and shivering, his eyes huge. Saxon looked directly at the frightened boy. "It's OK, Martin. I will get you out of here."

Why wasn't the porter getting help? Where was Martin's mother – she was usually so vigilant, just when they really needed her she wasn't there. Saxon knew she needed to play for time.

"How did you know I was here?"

Reynolds smirked. "Don't try that."

Martin was still and scared. "Help me, please," he whimpered. "You always help me…" She worried for the state of his heart with the shock.

"It's alright," she said. "Just breathe slowly. This man needs a doctor …"

*I'm supposed to be a doctor for God's sake!*

She saw his mother's face appear in the porthole window. Her only child, come here to be rescued by the knife and now about to die under it. Her face became the face of all mothers when faced with a threat to their child. Horror at what might happen, tortured by helplessness, unable to protect her young. Martin's mother, Saxon's mother, the mother of the child in Hong Kong, Saxon as mother. All mothers.

It was not a considered decision. It was just a quick movement. But the boy and his mother would remember this movement in this moment and its consequences. They saw it all as if in slow motion, as if it had been prepared, just like the room and the trolley, with the actors waiting to perform. The moment when the eternal dance of the heart in Saxon's body finally came to rest.

With a seemingly unrehearsed gesture, not unlike the moment that precipitated the child into the Hong Kong waters, Saxon swung her body against Reynolds and onto the outward-facing blade of the knife. It caught her carotid artery and made a perfect incision. Reynolds was too shocked by her unexpected action to react. He remained staring, stunned, having let go of Martin who fainted onto the trolley. Saxon slid onto the floor to lie in her own blood. The face of Martin's mother, contorted in a scream, was pressed against the porthole. There was silence in the room.

Saxon bled out in three minutes. She exsanguinated.

In those three minutes Saxon was Saskia once more. She felt the embrace of the golden petals together with the light touch of butterfly wings and knew that she could now embrace her fate. For so long she had lived behind glass and now it was gone. She was free. The freedom for feeling to arise by itself rather than struggling to make it happen. This heart, my heart, has waited until now, listening with an intelligent and poetic ear for the right time to come in with the right response, trying to find its moment of connection. This, now, is the very best thing I can offer and it will not be rejected. The terrible waiting is over.

She was no longer suspended. At last, the young man had come for her.

\* \* \* \*

Vera and her two sons tidied the small garden, sweeping all the debris of the winter into a bonfire. Vera watched the flames light inside the rusty old burner and with purpose threw a collection of old letters and scraps of newspaper cuttings. Magazines and old clothes she had bundled up into neat packages for the recycling bins.

"We need to move on," she had told them. "I am not sure when or where, but we need to move from this place now. Your father has a new life, and you will be part of that, and I must make a new life for myself and for you too."

Her throat constricted as she spoke, and her sons clenched their fists in their pockets. Dominic realised that despite the excitement offered by his father's new life he would miss his mother's homely domesticity. Luke had stopped biting his nails and started reading again. Vera had told him she wanted to discuss his education with his father.

"We will make it as good and as fun as we can," she said. "We will all plan where we go next."

Dominic went back to Bristol, relieved to be returning to the rough and tumble of college life but with a nagging uncertainty about his parents' divided lives. He had had a good time in Gstaad. There was a new life opening up for him here and he welcomed it. But he was not sure what would happen to his mum. He was afraid she could do something weird.

Vera and Luke went to Tachbrook Street market for fruit and vegetables, and she collected cardboard boxes. Later she took Luke to the cinema, and they laughed and skipped home, hand in hand. When he was asleep she took the boxes and packed away the remainder of Alistair's things, slowly and with satisfaction. There were things from his life that she knew now she had never liked. Silver photograph frames that always needed polishing. The fussy Royal Doulton porcelain – so pretty and so impossible. The life she would be building would not be one that included figurines. As she packed these things away, she sensed the new space inside her that was thinking forward instead of back. She would buy interesting china from market stalls and a few old pieces of furniture that were colourful and interesting.

When she was ready, she telephoned Alistair. The first time she had pressed his new mobile number into her phone. Her voice was strong. She had packed the last of his things, they needed collecting and she also wanted to see him for there was something she needed to speak to him about.

Relieved at his wife's shift into reasonableness and communication Alistair responded quickly. He was surprised she had taken the initiative. He didn't care about the things Vera had decided she would send back, and wondered what they would be. He wondered awkwardly where he would put them in The Boltons.

\* \* \* \*

They had not met alone since the time he had waited for her outside in the car and discovered she had changed the locks. She was wearing a neat dark blue trouser suit and white shirt, and she looked fit, as if she were on a regular exercise routine. She had less make-up and looked young and fresh. The cream pearls at her throat reflected her fine white teeth in contrast to her mane of black hair. The pearls had become her constant companion, her stone circle. He thought she looked different and wondered if she had met someone. She made fresh coffee and indicated for him to sit at the kitchen table. The kitchen had been cleared of its old clutter: the photographs, cards, candles, and catalogues.

He thought, *Poor Vera has had nothing better to do that to keep on tidying and clearing.*

She poured the coffee. "I've made some decisions," she said.

"Good," said Alistair. "I knew you'd come to your senses sooner or later."

She looked at him coldly. That smug look on his face, the slack wet lips and the way his mouth went down at the corners. The hair she had once loved now slicked back with expensive pomade. She did not like the new fragrance his woman had probably chosen for him. She saw clearly the results of their years of growing apart and how far they had come. She had been kidding herself that she could cling on to what they had had.

"So, what are these decisions?"

"I've packed the personal things that were still here. Books, photograph frames, rackets, wine stoppers etc. We need to decide on the furniture. Until I know what my next place will be like I don't know what I will need. But there are several things that I know I won't want. The grandfather clock, the decorated chests. They were your grandparents and it's right you should have them."

Again, Alistair wondered where they would go in Arabella's house. "They might have to be sold."

"OK. Perhaps you can arrange for that. The house is being valued tomorrow and then I hope we can agree on the asking price and get it on the market straight away."

Alistair was startled. "But I will take charge of that!"

"No need," she said. "I can manage, and I want to be in control. It is still my house too."

"But I've been waiting for you to get your act together. I've got Jeffrey Bates from Savills all lined up."

"I have already been thinking about where I should like to live. We should get over a million, about 1.7, I think. I have started looking for places and I'd like to stay in this area as I would like Luke to go to day school. The local school in fact, where his friend Jordon is. But I don't need a very big place and I will need you to help pay the mortgage for a while. Luke is still very young, and you are legally obliged to support him until he is 18. The lawyers will of course be arranging all the details. I do not expect you to be difficult over money." She looked at him clearly and expectantly.

This was not the Vera he knew. He noticed that she wore no rings on her strong fingers.

"I do have some places in mind and I'm also going to do some professional training so I can get a job. I would like to continue in psychotherapy and thank you for making those arrangements for me. It has been really useful. Once I've got a job, I should like to pay for it myself, but in the meantime, I should be obliged if you would continue what you started."

Alistair's coffee was getting cold. He looked around his once familiar kitchen with its red and white oak leaves, and outside at the small garden with its winter shrubs and berries. It looked different. She had gone minimalist. He, like Dominic and the other two, had enjoyed the homely warmth she created. She had been a wife who had made him feel so much bigger, so wanted in the way she had stood by him. But that was over. Suddenly he felt sorry for himself. He had nothing to say.

* * * *

The coroner recorded a verdict of accidental death. Alan Mayers and Max were called to speak of Saxon's state of mind. Her clinical depression was noted but her death was not clearly a suicide. Hospital security was tightened in response to the publicity about an addict being able to enter the hospital and take hold of a vulnerable patient and threaten a member of staff.

There had been several newspaper headlines: "Depressed doctor saves boy in knife attack in hospital room." Some headline-seeking papers had researched further afield: "Did well respected cardiologist throw herself onto intruder's knife to escape consequences of baby in water in Hong Kong?" There were photographs of her. From her graduation, receiving an achievement medal, with her parents in Florida. The most recent was a newspaper photograph from Hong Kong when she had attended the accident hearing. She was looking pale and sad, but closed. She was wearing a green silk dress.

Also in the newspapers were details of her American parents, her distinguished medical record, her research into cardiomyopathy and cocaine use. The reporter also added that she had been receiving psychological treatment for stress after the accident in Hong Kong and during her suspension. Commentators in some papers speculated. Were doctors under intolerable pressure due to the changes in the NHS? Was it suicide? Was it due to an unhappy love affair?

What no one knew was the story of her life as a whole and of her struggle with feeling bad, with impossible guilt, and with loneliness and intimacy. This was carried and held safely forever within the walls of the pale green room. This room had witnessed and sat alongside a human soul whose heart had been broken and was unable to be mended.

Despite trying to keep her funeral quiet and modest, many patients, as well as colleagues, grateful for Saxon's care and guidance over the years, attended her burial next to the nature reserve in south east London. Several of them brought red balloons in the shape of hearts. One by one the winter woods were touched by hearts of red that hung in mid-air between twigs and branches, before freeing themselves into the February sky. Others brought cards and teddy bears and, being unable to give them to her stony-faced parents, left them on the unmarked plot where her ashes had been placed. Lewis and Daniel had made the arrangements according to her precise instructions. She had prepared for her own death as thoroughly as she prepared for her daily routines and work. There was to be no religious service and she had already organised the plot at Nunhead cemetery. This helped them resist the request of her wealthy parents to have her body flown to Florida, which she disliked and where no one knew her. They stood, a couple in Florida pastels covered by the hasty purchase of winter coats, their skin bronzed and polished among the bare trees, their breath white, their limbs cold, and they shook Lewis' hand, uncomprehending. They had not mentioned the inquest, even between themselves. They had tried to have an investigation. They believed their daughter had suffered an injustice and had been a victim of some scheme of the NHS to be removed from her post. They thought the lax security was part of it. They did not know what had happened in Hong Kong and neither Lewis nor Daniel wished to tell them of the turmoil in which Saxon lived for her last months.

Reynolds had had a right to be inside the hospital that day for he had a genuine appointment at dermatology outpatients, for a chronic skin condition connected with long-term drug use. He had moved from the North a few years earlier and had known for some time where Saxon was working. His offence, of holding a patient hostage, was presumed to be connected with drugs. Martin was either too shocked or too loyal to reveal what he had heard of the conversation between them. Saxon had saved him, again. His mother had seen it all and was the star witness to exactly what had happened, to how Saxon had deftly moved herself onto the knife and caused Reynolds to release Martin.

After leaving the woodland ceremony, Max took one of the white roses from the mass of flowers and went across London to a house in Ealing Broadway. He stood outside the front garden and looked over the wall. A child's red buggy was by the front door and a swing was in the process of being created under an old apple tree. He rang the bell for the ground floor flat.

"You must be Dr Max. Come in."

Max had tried to imagine what he would feel when he saw the child, the child who might have drowned in the waters of Hong Kong. The child it was impossible for Saskia to hold in her arms without igniting unimaginable fear and rejection of something so small and helpless. He noticed a sense of anticipation, a little fear.

The mother took Max into a light, bright room, where the small boy, now eight months old, was crawling. He was blonde and bonny and on seeing Max he stopped and sat on his plump behind and looked, before flashing a toothless smile.

"This is Gabriel."

Max bent down to be level with the boy, and held out his hand. The boy looked up at his mother, who nodded encouragingly, "It's all fine, Gabriel" And the boy reached out his small podgy hand and placed it near to Max's large bony one.

Max thought of Saxon in that moment and consciously brought her into the room so she too could hold this child's hand that it had been impossible for her to hold in life.

"So, you are Gabriel. Hello, Gabriel," he said, to which the boy smiled again.

"He looks well," said Max, thinking, Gabriel, the Angel, the Messenger. And the name of Begonia's boyfriend who brought colour to her childhood.

"He must have a lucky star," said his mother.

Max smiled, unsure how much to say. The mother continued, "He could so easily have drowned. He was picked out by the nets of the cleaning junks and rescued by a Chinese family. They were so proud, so happy to be rescuers. We are still in touch with them. They think Gabriel has luck, lucky karma."

They were quiet for a moment. Those images of Hong Kong he had shared in the pale green room coming into focus.

"You must have been so happy to have him safe," said Max quietly.

"Yes. I understand that you cannot say much because I know from the inquest that Dr Pierce was your patient. I've had some therapy myself since the accident. I was so furious with her, so angry. I couldn't sleep, I had nightmares, panic attacks. I couldn't leave him for a minute, couldn't trust anyone." She stopped, "You know, I really understand now why people kill. I could have killed her for what she nearly took away from me!"

Max looked at her. He had felt that way himself just a few months ago.

The mother noticed the long-stemmed white rose Max was holding. "It looks like a peace offering."

"Perhaps it is, in some way. I think that I bring it for Dr Pierce also, something she was unable to do herself."

"I asked you to come because I needed to settle something, and also speak to someone who knew her, who perhaps knew about Hong Kong. I am grateful that you said you would, many therapists wouldn't. But I've a feeling that perhaps you wanted to come too?"

Max smiled. "Actually, it's good to be here, for myself, and for Dr Pierce."

The mother went to her desk and took out a letter. "I thought that she didn't care. She seemed so cold, so indifferent. My husband and I, we were so upset. Gabriel did nearly drown, his poor lungs were damaged and we had to have him watched for some time. We never knew what it was that actually happened. Whether she threw him or was just careless." Silence in the room, except for the sound of Gabriel's humming as he pressed a plastic brick into a space in a cube.

"She never followed it up. She never apologised or

asked after him." The mother looked down. "I read about what happened at the hospital. I'm sorry, of course. Rather an accident-prone woman," she sniffed.

Max looked at her.

"Do you think she wanted to die?"

Max was silent for a long time.

"She was obviously very unhappy," said the mother. "Anyway," she handed Max the letter, he saw a solicitor's headed notepaper, "she made a will in December last year leaving everything she had to Gabriel."

Max felt his heart become full. The date on the letter was a month ago.

"Stunning, isn't it? If I were to be sarcastic, I'd say it was well and good that Gabriel should benefit from her guilty conscience. But I've learnt from my therapy not to be bitter, or to seek revenge, because that only harms more people. I've got to look at both sides, to try to stand in her shoes. That's why, when I read that you had been treating her for depression, I asked if you would come. I guess that what happened was part of that serious depression. I wanted, I don't know, I wanted to find some sort of peace with her memory."

Max nodded and held out the white rose.

"Thank you," he said. "Compassion can be an important part in healing, and we can only offer it genuinely when we go through really deep feelings and own them and are able to see both sides, as you say. Feeling is the living water we all share, and which unites us."

\* \* \* \*

A few weeks later Max returned to the woodland where Saxon's ashes lay in the earth and walked among the trees and shrubs, enjoying the feel of the soft wind as it played around the emerging daffodils. Daniel and Lewis had planted an English oak. He felt its bark knowing of the strength to come. He and Emily were closer, something inside her had relaxed its hold and he had found a new warmth in himself toward her. They had started looking out at the birds again together. He thought about her words "she will take you away from me." Did she sense then that he too was moving behind some glass like substance and was at risk of joining Saxon Peirce? The black aura, the hopelessness, perhaps it was that?

He thought about why people sought him out, what they wanted from therapy. Sometimes to be relieved of disabling symptoms, emotional suffering, unhelpful habits; sometimes to develop self-reflection. Sometimes they needed permission to have an inner life. And sometimes, he thought, they come because they need to find a way to choose to die consciously.

A family of green woodpeckers slid their way in and out of the Scots pine and willow. To his left he felt the strong presence of the Guardians, as he had on the steep climb up the hill outside Thimpu. He thought about what it really meant to be touched in the heart, and to be able to bear it and find space around it. When something or someone touches us in the heart there is an opening. And then we have the key.

*The Pale Green Room*

# Also available in the series

# The Ruthless Furness

The Ruthless Furnace is the second of three works of fiction featuring psychotherapist Dr Max Maxwell and his work with patients. Badly wounded in Afghanistan, Corporal Frank Bright finds it impossible to return to everyday life; his marriage suffers and after discharge from the army he has been living rough in London.

Two cousins take him in after he stumbles into their church after being inspired by the sound of singing. They encourage him to visit a clinic run for soldiers suffering PTSD by Dr Maxwell. He and Max embark on a complex and ultimately transforming therapeutic journey together. Frank carries the shame of his attack upon his wife. Max carries a secret shame as his own private life is falling apart.

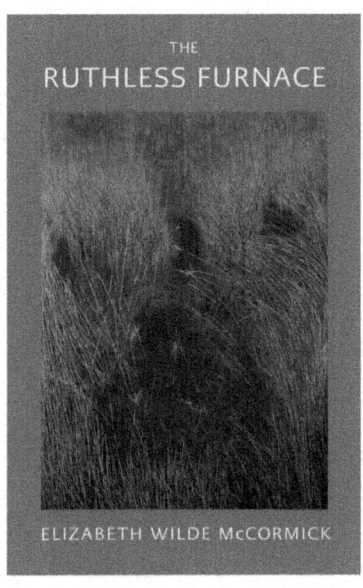

*The Pale Green Room*

# Also available in the series

# Wordless Threads

Wordless Threads is the third novel of the trilogy featuring Dr Max Maxwell and his psychotherapeutic work with patients. Max is now in his sixties. He lives alone, nourished mainly by music and nature.

He is still enjoying work and takes on a patient called Agnes, who has suffered a cryptic pregnancy. She didn't know she was pregnant until her child was born dead. Working with Agnes therapeutically awakens Max to his own repressed senses due to a painful past. Both he and Agnes find new life awakened within the wordless threads of sound, movement, touch, taste and smell.

Elizabeth Wilde McCormick worked as a psychotherapist in different NHS and private settings for forty years. She is the author of several bestselling psychological self-help books.

*The Pale Green Room*

*The Pale Green Room*

# The Pale Green Room

*The Pale Green Room*

*The Pale Green Room*

*The Pale Green Room*